A Glossary of
Jewish Life

A Glossary of
Jewish Life

Kerry M. Olitzky
and
Ronald H. Isaacs

Jason Aronson Inc.
Northvale, New Jersey
London

Production editors: *Leslie Block* and *Gloria Jordan*
Editorial director: *Muriel Jorgensen*

This book was set in 10 point Garamond
by Lind Graphics of Upper Saddle River, New Jersey,
and printed and bound by Haddon Craftsmen of Scranton, Pennsylvania

Library of Congress Cataloging-in-Publication Data

Olitzky, Kerry M.
    A glossary of Jewish life / Kerry M. Olitzky and Ronald H. Isaacs.
        p.   cm.
    Includes index.
    ISBN 0-87668-547-5
    1. Judaism—Dictionaries. 2. Bible. O.T.—Dictionaries.
3. Jews—History—Dictionaries. 4. Jews—United States—
Dictionaries. 5. Israel—History—Dictionaries.   I. Isaacs, Ron.
II. Title.
BM50.045   1991
269′.03—dc20   91-12399

Manufactured in the United States of America. Jason Aronson Inc. offers books and cassettes.
For information and catalog write to Jason Aronson Inc., 230 Livingston Street, Northvale,
New Jersey 07647.

Contents

Preface

To be a Jew is to be immersed in a body of knowledge that represents the thoughts and behaviors of Jewish life. Nuanced by time and circumstances, this body of knowledge changes as each generation of Jews experiences and responds to it, according to the needs of its community. Thus, Jewish knowledge continues to evolve, ever since it was revealed to the Jewish people on that fiery mountaintop in Sinai almost 3,500 years ago. Throughout history, Jews have communicated with one another through Jewish texts and contexts. Thus, one needs a Jewish vocabulary: words, concepts, and values that course through the blood and are articulated in a mutually agreed-upon language. Obviously, to suggest that such a wealth of information can be relegated to a list of words, albeit carefully scrutinized and defined, is ludicrous. To suggest that one is able to sift through all the layers of Jewish history and isolate those salient elements necessary for functioning in daily life borders on the absurd.

There are those who will argue that such a manageable list of words can indeed be generated. Still others will suggest that a reading of the great books (understood for our purposes as sacred literature), as well as an immersion in the Hebrew language, will provide the value concepts hidden behind each word. This approach, too, is fraught with problems, for as we all come to each concept with a certain bias—each term is colored by our own approach to Judaism. Ideally one should begin with a study of Hebrew texts (in their original), searching out the primary meaning of the text, the ways in which each temporal community responds to it, and finally its meaning and relevance for the contemporary Jew. Somehow, especially for those of us whose minds are also schooled in the tenets of Western civilization, we have to secure a point of entry into this body of knowledge.

Hence, this glossary of Jewish life was born out of a desire to create a ready reference, a construct of terms that are part of common Jewish discourse in American–Jewish life, providing easy access to Jewish civilization. Although the effort resembles, in part, a one-volume Jewish encyclopedia, the approach of this volume is unique in that it offers concise definitions of terms and value concepts, and brief biographical sketches of relevant thinkers, teachers, and leaders who have shaped the community in which we live.

This project began when we, two rabbis committed to Jewish education, representing two different major religious movements yet sharing a like-minded passion for Talmud Torah, sat down to evaluate some of the educational challenges facing American–Jewish life today. We pondered, "How do we fulfill our obligations as rabbis in Israel transmitting a vast body of knowledge to a disparate Jewish community whose interest in Hebrew and sacred literature may be growing, but whose knowledge is still limited?"

We decided to sift through Jewish life in an attempt to isolate those elements that we believe are essential to an American–Jewish culture code. This code allows for discourse and mutual understanding, a common vocabulary of value concepts, which, when fully explored, provides the individual with a foundation of Jewish knowledge.

Like all projects of this kind, it was not a task completed in isolation, nor is the result of our efforts an idiosyncratic collection of unrelated terms. After the initial lists of terms were compiled, they were reviewed by recognized scholars in individual disciplines, including Eugene B. Borowitz, Naomi Cohen, Edward Greenstein, Leonard Kravitz, Jacob R. Marcus, Philip Miller, Herbert Paper, Abraham J. Peck, Jonathan Sarna, Malcolm Stern, Lance Sussman, and Bernard Zlotowitz.

After the terms were unpacked and placed in context, they were reviewed once again, with helpful comments by some of these same contributors. However, we, of course, take full responsibility for the final results. We also want to thank Paula Feldstein, rabbinic student at Hebrew Union College–Jewish Institute of Religion, New York, for helping to track down elusive dates.

We dedicate this volume to the generation of our children, Avi and Jesse Olitzky and Keren and Zachary Isaacs, whose constant questioning inspired us to place the wisdom of our tradition in a modern idiom, pleasing to their young ears.

A Note on the Use of This Volume

We have divided this book into eight discrete sections. While all of the terms are listed in the index, terms have been placed in the section where we assumed the reader would probably first look for the term. Yet it is clear that some words could easily be found in one or several other sections as well, especially when words are used in different ways. Within each definition, the reader will find words that are in small capital letters. This indicates that main entries can be found for these words (even when found with grammatical variations, e.g., declensions). In a very few cases, the reader is directed to another section for a variant meaning. Hebrew, English, and Yiddish translations for words are cross-referenced in the index. Words have been transliterated according to the preferred spelling, unless the well-known spelling is more readily accepted and recognizable by the reader.

CHAPTER 1

Religious Practice

When the Jewish people affirmed their acceptance of the Divine covenant established on Mount Sinai, they responded by saying *Naaseh V'nishma,* usually translated as "We will do and we will hear." In other words, we will express our acceptance of our covenantal responsibility through our actions.

The performance of mitzvot, Jewish actions, has always preceded Jewish belief. This chapter is an articulation of the psychosocial skills that pattern Jewish behavior in a religious context. Because Jewish religion is the understanding of the Bible through the eyes of the rabbis, many of the items in this chapter find their roots in the rabbinic period. Others are creative attempts to innovate Jewish ritual throughout history and, in particular, in the modern period. All reflect the individual Jew's constant struggle to reach beyond the self, to reach toward God.

Ad Delo Yada. Literally, "until he does not know" . . . the difference between HAMAN and MORDECAI. A frivolous and questionable practice of making merry (and drinking) until we cannot tell the difference between Haman (be cursed) and Mordecai (be blessed), as ordained by the TALMUD, MEGILLAH 7a. Often PURIM parties are referred to as *adloyada,* bringing the three words together. Traditionally, family banquets were held on Purim afternoon, as instructed in the Book of ESTHER (9:22).

Afikomen. At the end of the PASSOVER meal, the SEDER, a piece of previously hidden MATZAH is searched for and found, then shared among the participants. (Usually, a reward is given to the finder.) The word comes from the Greek and is mentioned in the TALMUD, PESACHIM 10, probably referring to dessert or after-dinner songs. It represents the PASCHAL LAMB, and is the last food that may be eaten at the seder. It probably was also introduced or enhanced to maintain the attention of young children.

Akedah. Literally, "binding." Refers to the binding (and intended sacrifice) of ISAAC by ABRAHAM on MOUNT MORIAH (GENESIS 22). It is a common reference and motif throughout Jewish (and Christian) culture. Since the story is read as part of the ROSH HASHANAH liturgy, it is a significant theme on the HIGH HOLIDAYS.

Alenu. Literally, "it is incumbent upon us" . . . to give praise to the Sovereign of Everything. It is part of the liturgy recited toward the end of each service, prior to KADDISH, in which God's universal power and the particularism of the Jewish people, as well as the COVENANT that binds us, is articulated. Originally a poem written by RAV for ROSH HASHANAH, it was later incorporated throughout the year.

Al HaNissim. Literally, "for the miracles" . . . God wrought for us. It was added to the liturgy on CHANUKAH and PURIM, when God's miraculous intervention delivered the Jewish people into safety. It is included in BIRKAT HAMAZON and the daily AMIDAH.

3

Aliyah. Literally, "going up," refers both to going up to the BIMAH in order to be called to the honor of the TORAH (usually to recite blessings before and after its reading, or to raise or dress it following its reading). While the REFORM MOVEMENT has removed the distinction in ancestry, in more traditional synagogues the KOHEN is called first, then followed by a LEVI and YISRAEL. The number of *aliyot* (plural of aliyah) of those called up to the Torah is determined by the day (Monday, Thursday, holiday, or SHABBAT) on which the Torah is read. On immigrating to Israel, one makes *aliyah,* taken from the fact that one literally had to go up to (the mountains of) JERUSALEM to make a pilgrimage during the ancient days when the TEMPLE stood. An individual given the honor of immigrating to Israel is called an *oleh.*

Amen. So be it, a verbal affirmation of that which is articulated in a prayer or blessing, to be said by those listening rather than those reciting.

Amidah. Literally, "the standing prayer," because it is recited while standing. Also known as *HaTefillah,* the (central) prayer, because the liturgy is built around it; also known as the *Shemoneh Esreh,* the eighteen, because the original compilation of the prayer (for the daily service) had eighteen benedictions in it. During the early Christian period, a blessing directed against apostates was added. The Amidah is adjusted with additions and deletions depending on the particular service in which it is recited, generally taking the theme for the changes from that particular service. The Amidah is a set of petitions often introduced by a private meditation (suggested by PSALM 51:17), "Lord, open my lips that my mouth may declare Your praise," and concluded by a silent prayer (directed by the thoughts of Rabbi Yochanan). Because the Amidah represents one of the early structures in liturgy, its original intent was to provide themes for the worshipper that slowly became fixed over time. It contains three sections: (1) contemplation of God, three blessings recited on weekdays and festivals; (2) twelve to thirteen petitions recited on weekdays, and one general thanksgiving blessing recited on Sabbath and holidays, related to the theme of the particular holiday; and (3) thanksgiving and a prayer for peace recited on festivals and holidays. This prayer is either read in silence only, or then repeated by the SHALIACH TZIBBUR. In reform congregations, often the entire prayer is read (even if abbreviated) in unison.

Aninut. Refers to the period of initial grief between death and interment. The mourner is called an *onen.*

Anos. Within the SEFARDI community, the anniversary date of the death to be commemorated; similar to YAHRZEIT within the ASHKENAZI community.

Aravot. Willows of the brook, placed on the LULAV for SUKKOT, opposite the myrtle (HADASSIM) and affixed by a ring made from a palm-leaf.

Arba Minim. Literally, "four species," specific to those four (palm, myrtle, willow, citron) used during the celebration of SUKKOT. They represent a thanksgiving offering for the harvest, each with its own unique quality.

Aron HaKodesh. Holy ark used to store Torah scrolls in the synagogue.

Arvit. Evening worship service, as designated by Sefardi Jews.

Attarah. A neck piece on the tallit to ensure that when the tallit is worn it is neither upside down nor inside out. A vestment-like tallit, worn especially by rabbis over robes when leading worship, is also often referred to as an attarah.

Aufruf. Calling up the groom (and the bride in liberal circles) to the Torah for an aliyah on the Shabbat before the wedding.

Avelut. The mourning period and process following interment, an all-encompassing term.

Avinu Malkenu. Literally, "Our Father, Our King." It is a well-known selection from the High Holiday liturgy that acknowledges God's sovereignty over the world. It is a litany of God's attributes, our nothingness, and a confession of our sins, and is recited daily during the Yamim Nora'im.

Avnet. Belt that keeps the Torah scroll together while it is stored in the aron hakodesh.

Avodah. Literally, "work." Refers to holy service (worship) to God and the (sacrificial) service par excellence performed by the High Priest on Yom Kippur at the ancient Temple in Jerusalem. It had two purposes: to purge the sanctuary and expiate the sins of the people.

Avot. Literally, "fathers" or "ancestors." Refers both to the ancestors of the Jewish people and particularly the patriarchs; it also refers to the first paragraph of the Amidah prayer.

Ba'al Koreh. The person who reads publicly from the Torah during the worship service.

Ba'al Tefillah. The person who reads the liturgy during the worship service, alternative term for the shaliach tzibbur, but technically refers to a chazzan, not a lay person.

Ba'al Tekiah. The one who blows the shofar during High Holiday services, as well as during the preceding month.

Ba'al Teshuvah. While historically this term referred to one who had abandoned Judaism (and perhaps even accepted another faith) and then returned, today it is used as a generalized term for a born Jew who has actively embraced Judaism through positive Jewish religious acts in his adult life.

Bakashot. Petitions, particularly in the form of prayer.

Bar/Bat Mitzvah. A rite of passage moving a child into the responsibility of adulthood regarding the mitzvot, established for the boy at age 13 and

12 and 1 day for girls, although most liberal synagogues do not make a distinction in age between boys and girls. It is an automatic transition and is not dependent on ceremony. Ideally, it is an entry into formal Jewish education, since historically parents provided education in the early years. The ceremony for boys as we know it probably dates back to the Middle Ages, with girls joining boys only in the early part of this century (still limited in some liberal synagogues and often nonexistent in Orthodox congregations). In its early years, Reform Judaism generally discarded Bar Mitzvah in favor of confirmation, but it has been reintroduced over the last generations.

Barukh Dayan HaEmet. Literally, "Praised are You, the True Judge," recited when one learns of another's death.

Barukh HaBa. Literally, "Blessed are those who come" . . . (in the name of the Lord), the traditional form of welcome.

Bedecken. The veiling of the bride, done by the groom, taken from the modesty of Rebecca in Genesis 24:65.

Bedikah. An examination of the animal by the shochet after it has been ritually slaughtered to determine if indeed it is ritually fit for consumption.

Bentschen. From the Yiddish, to bless, referring to blessings before or after meals, or concerning ritual acts.

Berakhah. A blessing, specifically has a technical formula "Baruch ata Adonai . . ."

Besamim. Spices, particularly used during the observance of Havdalah.

Bet Am. An alternative name for the synagogue, literally House of/for the People.

Bet Din. A rabbinic court of three, formed primarily for purposes of decisions in religious (and formerly civil) law, as well as for limited ritual/liturgical purposes. During Temple times, the Sanhedrin was the High Court. Today, the power of the Bet Din is limited to voluntary arbitration and jurisdiction in ritual matters.

Bet HaKnesset. Literally, "a house of assembly," an alternative name for the synagogue.

Bet HaMidrash. Literally, "a house of study," an alternative name for the synagogue, especially when used for study, before the notion of school wings and modern structures.

Bet HaMikdash. Literally, "holy house," or house set aside for a special (consecrated) purpose, a reference to the ancient Temple in Jerusalem.

Bikkur Cholim. Literally, "visiting the sick," a mitzvah to that effect.

Bimah. Literally, "high place," refers to the raised platform (or pulpit) in the front of a synagogue sanctuary.

Birkat HaGomel. In the case of recovery from great illness or rescue from grave danger, the blessing is to be said by men and women (including after childbirth) in front of a MINYAN.

Birkat HaMazon. Grace after meals, emphasizing the sacred character of meals.

Birkat HaMitzvot. Blessing recited for the privilege of performing a MITZVAH.

Birkat Hoda'ah. Blessing of petition, praise or thanksgiving.

Birkot Nehenim. These blessings persuade us to take nothing for granted for they help us to acknowledge, when appropriately recited, the beauty of the world and that which sustains us, such as food and the wonders of nature; it is even recited on hearing of someone's death.

Bitul Chametz. The renouncing of ownership of leavened products gathered in a household just prior to PASSOVER. These products are then burned. The formula itself is called KOL CHAMIRA.

Blood. Literally considered taboo in Judaism, blood is dealt with in various ways, whether it is human (especially concerning a woman's menstrual period) or animal (regarding ritual slaughtering).

Brit Milah. The COVENANT of circumcision usually performed on the male child in his eighth day of life.

Cantor. In Hebrew, *chazzan*. The person who chants the liturgy, often as SHALIACH TZIBBUR during worship services.

Chalitzah. When a childless man dies, his living brother has the responsibility of marrying his sister-in-law to perpetuate the family, as in LEVIRATE MARRIAGE. He can escape this obligation through chalitzah, now mandatory and generally performed in ORTHODOX JUDAISM: A woman goes to the elders of the city and tells them, reciting a special formula, that her brother-in-law refuses to marry. The elders call the man forward. If he says he does not want to marry the woman, she removes a shoe from his foot and spits in his face while reading, "This shall be done to the man who does not build up his brother's house." He is thereby released from his obligation. (For a full explanation see DEUTERONOMY 25:7–10.)

Challah. Hebrew for "dough offering." Egg bread used for ritual purposes as a partitive for SHABBAT. It is in the form of a braid to represent the mystical Sabbath bride's hair or round for ROSH HASHANAH, to represent the cycle of the year. The law of challah involves removing a token amount of dough (the size of an olive) and throwing it into the oven fires while reciting a specific blessing. This may reflect the portion given to PRIESTS in the TEMPLE; since there are no longer priests, the portion is burnt. It may also refer to the ancient requirement of making a gift offering. During Shabbat, the challah loaves are used to remind us of the double portion of MANNAH that the Jews received on Fridays in the desert so they would not have to gather food on the Sabbath. The Sabbath bread has also been called *berches* or *tatscher*. Also, the ninth tractate in the MISHNAH, order *Zeraim,* discusses setting challah aside for the PRIESTS.

Chametz. Foods that contain leaven, prohibited during PESACH.

Chanukah. Often called the Festival of Lights, it begins on the 25th day of KISLEV and lasts eight days. The holiday recognizes the MACCABEAN victory of a small army over the Assyrian–Greek forces in 164 B.C.E. and the manifest conflict between Jewish faith and Greek culture, as well as the rededication of the TEMPLE. The celebration is marked by lighting candles in a CHANUKIYAH, spinning DREIDELS, eating LATKES, and retelling the story of the power of the spirit over might.

Chanukat HaBayit. The dedication of a new home.

Chanukiyah. Eight-branched candelabra used to celebrate the festival of CHANUKAH.

Chattan. Literally, "groom," used also in reference to the reading of the TORAH. When one is given the privilege of reading the final paragraph of Torah on SIMCHAT TORAH, that person is referred to as a chattan Torah, a groom of the Torah. The same honor is accorded the one who reads the opening paragraph of the Torah during the same celebration, called chattan *bereshit,* groom of the beginning.

Chatzi-Kaddish. Literally, "half-kaddish," an abbreviated form used as a transition following various minor forms of the liturgy.

Chazak, Chazak, Venet'chazek. "Be strong, be strong, and may we be strengthened"—a traditional recitation on the conclusion of the public reading of one of the five books of the TORAH.

Chevrah Kadisha. An important fellowship, the Holy (Burial) Society, that serves the dying and the dead; primarily responsible to prepare the deceased for burial according to Jewish law.

Chevrah Kebranim. In prior generations, primarily in Europe, an important fellowship, the Society of the Gravediggers, whose responsibility it was to prepare the grave and fill it after interment.

Chiddur Mitzvah. The act of enhancing and beautifying a MITZVAH.

Chol HaMoed. A "semi-holiday" state referring to the intermediate days of the festivals of SUKKOT and PESACH.

Cholent. Often spelled tsholent, a traditional food associated with SHABBAT. It is a meat, bean, and potato stew that is cooked before Shabbat and sits warming in a low oven all night until Shabbat lunch (because of the restriction on igniting fires on the Sabbath).

Choshen. Breastplate placed over the TORAH, reminiscent of the breastplate worn by the PRIEST during the days of the Temple. Often it is used for a practical reason to identify where the Torah is set for a special reading, especially when there is more than one Torah scroll.

Chuppah. A bridal canopy, used during the wedding ceremony and forming a sacred space in the center of the BIMAH. It may have its origin in the times when weddings were held outside and an effect was made to separate the wedding from the hustle and bustle of street life; it also symbolically represents the bridal chamber, where the couple would go after the wedding to consummate the marriage, fulfilling the obligations of YICHUD.

Confirmation. A ceremony that takes place during SHAVUOT, originally introduced by the REFORM movement to provide an alternative to the BAR/BAT MITZVAH, now usually at the end of the tenth grade after Bar/Bat Mitzvah. Early Reformers believed children were too young to accept the responsibilities of adulthood and wanted an egalitarian ceremony for girls and boys. Confirmation was borrowed from Protestant Christianity.

Consecration. A ceremony introduced by the REFORM movement as the time when the child marks the beginning of his formal Jewish education, usually associated with SUKKOT or SIMCHAT TORAH.

Crown. Usually refers to the KETER TORAH, the crown of Torah, usually placed on the top of the Torah as an adornment. Ancient sources speak of the "crown of Torah" figuratively to refer to the respect that is accrued to a worthy student. Crown may also refer to the tops of adorned letters that may be found in the writing of Torah scrolls.

Cutting Keriah. A reference to the rending of one's garment in mourning. As an alternative, some modern Jews wear a black ribbon and cut it as an obvious symbol of mourning.

Daven. To pray; the traditional Jewish posture of prayer.

Devar Torah. Literally, "a word of TORAH," a teaching of the sacred text either within the context of worship or not.

Divine Service. A worship service of/to God.

Dreidel. In Hebrew, *sivivon,* spinning top, part of CHANUKAH festival celebration. On it is written "A Great Miracle Happened (T)here," referring to the defeat of the Assyrian–Greeks by the MACCABEES.

Duchanen. During a worship service, those of PRIESTLY lineage gather in the front of the congregation, in front of the ARON HAKODESH, to bless the people.

Eliyahu HaNavi. Literally, "ELIJAH the PROPHET," who is to herald in the MESSIAH. Also refers to prayer–song recited during HAVDALAH. Elijah's presence is requested during the PASSOVER SEDER, as well as during BRIT MILAH.

El Malei Rachamim. Literally, "God who is full of mercy," a memorial prayer for eternal rest, said during funerals, as well as during YIZKOR services throughout the year.

Erev Shabbat. The evening of the Sabbath, Friday evening.

Eruv. A symbolic wall, a legal innovation that encircles a city in order for it to be similar to a walled city; thereby the individual is allowed to carry things (generally prohibited) in its confines during SHABBAT.

Eruv Tavshillin. Occasionally, ROSH HASHANAH and other festival days may be backed up to SHABBAT (i.e., the holiday falls on Thursday and Friday). This presents a problem because although one may cook on a holiday, the food must be eaten on that day. In order to be able to cook the Sabbath meal during the holiday (e.g., Friday afternoon), an eruv is created. It is a symbolic meal just as the eruv is a symbolic wall; by hard-boiling an egg and setting it aside with a legal formula, it is as if we have already prepared the meals, and all other cooking is considered insignificant and thereby permitted.

Esnoga. SEFARDI term for SYNAGOGUE.

Ethical Will. A sort of will, normally prepared by a parent for his or her children, in order to leave a legacy of learning or principles to live by for one's descendants.

Etrog. Citron, a lemon-like fruit used to represent part of the harvest during SUKKOT, as part of a festive bouquet created for ritual purposes.

Fast of the Firstborn. Required of firstborn male children prior to PASSOVER in recognition of the saving of their lives in the face of the death of the firstborn Egyptian children, the last Passover plague.

Fasting. An opportunity to self-reflect as mandated during several holiday observances. Not intended as punishment, it was historically connected to mourning customs, which, when engaged in by an entire community, might "move the hand of God" by bringing on, for example, rain for farming.

Fence around the Torah. A legal concept that refers to the layers of regulations that have been placed onto Jewish law in order to prevent the transgression of the original or primary law (as a prison yard may have two fences, one to prevent a prisoner from reaching the other).

Festivals. Although often used interchangeably for those holiday occasions that are celebratory in nature, the term is technically used to refer to the three major pilgrimage festivals of SUKKOT, PESACH, and SHAVUOT, as well as CHANUKAH, PURIM, and several other minor celebrations; sometimes used in contradistinction to the holiday or YOM TOV.

Fleishig. In Hebrew, *besari*. A YIDDISH term used to refer to those foods that are either meat-based or to be eaten with meat, as well as utensils used for that specific purpose. It may also be used to refer to a person's culinary state of being; that is, "I'm fleishig," meaning, "I can't really eat dairy (MILCHIG) foods right now."

Gabbai. A lay person in a synagogue, typically responsible for keeping things in ritual order, particularly during the service itself, making sure there are the requisite number of individuals for ALIYOT, that their Hebrew names have been given to the BA'AL KOREH, and the like.

Gelilah. The honor of dressing the TORAH after it has been read during the worship service.

Gelt. A YIDDISH term for money, usually used in reference to coins, previously given on PURIM and currently given as CHANUKAH presents, especially for use in the DREIDEL game.

Ger. Hebrew. Originally used to refer to a stranger or resident alien, it is currently used to refer to a convert to Judaism.

Get. Divorce document. Traditionally it can be given only by a man to a woman, in the presence of a BET DIN. A get is required for remarriage.

G'mar Chatimah Tovah. "May your stamp of approval (by God) be completed favorably," referring to the mythic Book of Life to be signed and sealed during the HIGH HOLIDAY season; a greeting used after ROSH HASHANAH before YOM KIPPUR (some say longer), often abbreviated to *g'mar tov.*

Gregger. In Hebrew, *ra'ashan.* Noisemaker used during the reading of the MEGILLAH (of Esther) during the celebration of PURIM to drown out HAMAN's name.

Hadassim. Myrtle, used in the festival banquet during SUKKOT because of the boughs of leafy trees. We use three branches, because the TORAH refers to it in plural, placed to the right side of the LULAV.

Hadlakat HaNeirot. Literally, "the lighting of the candles," referring to any holiday celebration in which candles are to be lit.

Haftarah. Weekly reading on SHABBAT and holidays from the PROPHETS, following the TORAH reading. Its theme reflects the weekly Torah reading.

Hagbah. The honor of raising the TORAH and showing it to the congregation after it has been read. Historically, this was done before the reading to show the congregation that the correct scroll was being read from, rather than one from a Gnostic group, for example.

Haggadah. Literally, "the telling (of the story)." A book that contains the story of the EXODUS from Egypt in a ritualized form for use during the PASSOVER SEDER.

Hakafot. The processional throughout the synagogue, led by the one holding the TORAH scroll, generally prior to the reading of the Torah. It takes on a special significance during SIMCHAT TORAH.

Hallel. A series of PSALMS (113–118) of praise recited on special holidays, including CHANUKAH, PESACH, ROSH HODESH, SUKKOT, SIMCHAT TORAH, and SHAVUOT, as well as during the SEDER. Hallel may also be said on Israel Independence Day and Jerusalem Day.

Hamantaschen. Literally, "HAMAN's hat," a triangular pastry for PURIM; called *oznei-Haman* in Hebrew (literally, Haman's ears).

Hatafat Dam Brit. A drop of covenantal blood, referring to the extraction of a drop of blood for the already circumcised convert in place of BRIT MILAH, since the earlier circumcision had no religious significance.

Hatarat Nedarim. A ritual during ROSH HASHANAH that releases the individual from one's vows. In the SYNAGOGUE, following the morning service, men gather in groups of four; three compose a BET DIN and release the fourth from self-imposed religious obligations that he may have forgotten. They take turns in this process until all have had the chance to ask release from individual vows and adjudicate that release.

Havdalah. The ritual (using wine, candle, and spices) marking the end of SHABBAT (and holidays) and the beginning of the rest of the week. It acknowledges the distinction between the holy and normative or the sacred and profane in time.

Heichal. Literally, palace, used by SEFARDI Jews to refer to the holy ark, ARON HAKODESH.

High Holidays. A reference to ROSH HASHANAH and YOM KIPPUR, which have taken on primary significance in the holiday calendar.

Hodu l'Adonai Kee Tov. "It is good to give thanks to God," a formulaic litany, part of the HALLEL PSALMS.

Holegrasch. Probably a corruption of the French *haut la crèche,* raise the crib higher. Rarely observed today, it is a ceremony that stems from Napoleonic times; Jews had to adopt secular names for their children and marked the occasion in a Jewish ceremonial manner; the father raised the child high, asking, "Holegrasch—what shall we name the baby?"

Holidays. From holy day, days that are set aside for special ritual and observance and therefore imply specific categories of Jewish law to be in force.

Holy of Holies. The innermost chamber of the ancient TEMPLE in JERUSALEM where the HIGH PRIEST entered only once a year, on YOM KIPPUR.

Hoshana Rabba. Starting the eve of the seventh day of SUKKOT, still part of CHOL HAMOED Sukkot, it moves us toward the end of the festival. Tradition tells us that the final seal on the Book of Life is made during this time. The observance is marked by all-night study, and the liturgy and ritual reflect YOM KIPPUR themes, including a special processional with chants of "Hosannah, help us."

Irui. A boiling-water process, used to make KOSHER for PESACH vessels and utensils by pouring water over them, if they are too large for immersion.

Isru Chag. Literally, "bind the feast." Since Jews often don't like to let go of their celebrations, a little aftertaste is allowed in the case of SIMCHAT TORAH, held after for one more day (based on PSALMS 118–127).

Kabbalah. Literally, "that which is received" (in Modern Hebrew, a receipt). A reference to the inherited tradition, especially when it is placed with another word such as *shalshelet hakabbalah,* the chain of tradition, or *kabbalat* Shabbat, the traditional ushering in of the Sabbath. Also refers to a particular credential for doing something within the context of a religious community, particularly for the shochet, who ritually slaughters animals for food. This term also refers to the general mystical tradition in Judaism.

Kaddish. A prayer of affirmation of faith. There are five different types of kaddish; the text is determined by when it is recited, why, and by whom; it can be recited up to twelve times in a traditional worship service.

Kaddish DeRabbanan. Literally, "the Rabbis' Kaddish." Used as an epilogue to the study of rabbinic texts, containing a prayer for the welfare of all students of the Torah.

Kaddish D'itchadata. Literally, "burial Kaddish." Said only at the grave-site, immediately after interment. It includes a paragraph that refers to resurrection of the dead and a restoration of the Temple.

Kaddish Shalem. Literally, "whole or complete Kaddish." Includes the prayer requesting God to accept all of the reciter's heartfelt prayers.

Kaddish Yatom. Literally, "orphan's or mourner's Kaddish." Recited for the first year after interment, making it the primary prayer of the bereaved throughout the generations; does not mention death at all. The Reform movement introduced a variation of the Kaddish that includes an extra paragraph mentioning death, but it fell to disuse and was eventually excluded. In some non-Germanic orthodox synagogues, everyone rises for Kaddish Yatom. In German-based orthodox synagogues and in many conservative synagogues, the congregation sits. The reform movement instituted a movement-wide policy of standing. Often, parents will refer to a child as *kaddishel*—the one designated by Jewish law to say kaddish for them after their death; it has become a somewhat endearing term of affection.

Kadosh. Hebrew for holy or separate.

Kallah. Hebrew for bride.

Kapparah. This Yom Kippur custom is based on the idea of ransom, one life for another. It rests on the same ritual as the scapegoat ritual from the Temple period. After reciting from the Book of Job (33:23–24), a rooster (for men) or a hen (for women) is swung three times over the heads of the penitent and the following is said: "This is in exchange for me (us, you), this is instead of me (us, you), this is ransom *(kapparah)* for me (us, you). This rooster will go to its death, but I (we, you) will go forward to a good life and into peace." Money or other living things are used as well; alternatively this is called among Ashkenazi Jews *shluggen kapparos.*

Kavanah. One's heartfelt direction (literally, intention) in prayer, used to refer to the immediate feelings or response, in contradistinction to keva.

Kedushah. The sanctification, in the liturgy, "Holy, Holy, Holy is the Lord of Hosts, the whole earth is full of God's glory . . ." In the prayer, God is hallowed in the assembly of people.

Keriah. The act of tearing the garment either at graveside or at the beginning of the funeral service, depending on the custom of the congregation; this act is referred to as "cutting keriah." In some non-ORTHODOX communities, ribbons are attached to the garment and cut instead of clothing.

Kes. The religious officiant or priest among Ethiopian Jews, often called a *chakham.*

Keter Torah. Crown-like ornament for the TORAH.

Ketivah VeChatimah Tovah. An alternative greeting during the HIGH HOLIDAY period; literally, "May you be inscribed with a good seal."

Ketubah. The traditional marriage contract, which spells out the contractual responsibilities of the groom to the bride.

Keva. Literally, "fixed," referring to those prayers that are fixed in word or time by Jewish law or custom.

Kiddush. Sanctification prayer over wine for specific Jewish holidays. For example, the SHABBAT kiddush tells how God completed creation on the sixth day and then rested; we thank God for giving us Shabbat by which to remember creation and the EXODUS and for choosing the Jewish people to be a special people.

Kiddush HaChamah. Alternatively *Birkat HaChamah.* A special prayer giving thanks to God for the sun; recited when the cycle of the heavenly bodies completes itself, at spring equinox, every twenty-eight years.

Kiddush Lavanah. The moon's renewal is associated with the restoration of Israel; this forms the guiding principle behind ROSH CHODESH; the prayer is said several days after the crescent of the moon has reemerged.

Kinyan Sudder. "The acquisition through a cloth," a ritualistic ceremony by which the wedding contract is legalized through a transaction and exchange of goods, namely the handkerchief.

Kippah. Hebrew for headcovering or skullcap; also called a *yarmulke* in YIDDISH; worn in recognition that God is above you, and for showing reverence for God.

Kittel. Robe-like white garment worn by men under the CHUPPAH, during the HIGH HOLIDAY period, at the SEDER, and when buried.

Kiyum Mitzvot. The upholding or fulfillment of the commandments.

K'matnat Yado. The principle of not coming before God with empty hands, but according to one's means (from DEUTERONOMY 14:22; 16:1). It refers originally to the sacrificial cult and the pilgrimage festivals.

Kohen. Plural Kohanim. The priest and his descendants, traditionally considered to be directly descended from AARON. The Kohen is held to certain obligations and special ceremonies, and subject to certain restrictions, especially regarding marriage and funerals, in order to prevent his being tainted. Historically he was responsible to arrange for the ATONEMENT of the sins of the community.

Kol Chamira. The formula used to make null and void the CHAMETZ not found, following the attempt to collect and dispose of it for PESACH.

Kol Dikhfin. The PASSOVER SEDER begins with the formula, "Let all who are hungry come and eat. . . ."

Kol HaNe'arim. Literally, "all the children . . .," the final ALIYAH during SIMCHAT TORAH reserved for children.

Kol Nidre. Literally, "all vows," refers to both the opening prayer-chant and the evening of YOM KIPPUR. The prayer asks for release from all vows made henceforth as a historical protective device for Jews forced to make vows to other religions in order to save their lives; while no longer relevant, its haunting melody and memory binds us to the holiday, its mood, and our history.

Kosher. In Hebrew, Kashrut. Dietary laws that regulate the life of an individual Jew. While kosher literally means fit, it can be used to refer to a ritual item that is ritually fit for use, as in a kosher CHANUKIYAH. Glatt kosher is used today to refer to a generally higher or stricter standard of kashrut. Glatt literally means "smooth." It refers only to the lung—it must be perfectly smooth. According to "regular" kashrut laws, some blemishes of the lung are acceptable; by glatt standards, all and any blemishes render the lung (and, therefore, the whole meat) unfit. After inspecting the lung, the rest of the meat must still be inspected, as with "regular" kashrut.

K'vol'o Kakh Polto. Literally, "as it absorbs, so it sheds," an operating principle in the choice of which method to choose when preparing to make utensils KOSHER for PESACH. When considering how the individual item absorbs the CHAMETZ, one will know which process to choose to rid it of the chametz.

Lag B'Omer. Approximately halfway between PESACH and SHAVUOT during the counting of the OMER. It is recognized as the time in which the Hadrianic persecutions somehow ceased; there were celebrations in the SHTETL surrounding recognition of BAR KOKHBA's heroism; and it was the day of death of Rabbi Simon bar Yohai. It is considered a scholar's holiday, today celebrated by school picnics and weddings (since they are prohibited during the omer period); it is alternately referred to as *Lag L'Omer* by SEFARDIM.

Lashon HaKodesh. The holy tongue, referring to the HEBREW language.

Latkes. Potato pancakes, also called *levivot,* part of the CHANUKAH celebration because they are fried in oil.

Lekha Dodi. A mystical prayer that speaks of the Sabbath (as) Bride, sung on Friday evening to welcome Shabbat.

LeShanah Tovah Tikatev(u). "May you be inscribed for a good year," a greeting for Rosh Hashanah.

Levayat HaMet. The mitzvah of accompanying the dead to the grave, by way of funeral and interment.

Levi. Social class distinction (and tribe) in ancient Israel, used to designate assistant priests with certain responsibilities in the Temple; given the second aliyah in the synagogue.

Libun. A process using heat (or blowtorch) in order to make a certain set of utensils kosher for Passover.

Luach. A calendar; specifically referring to either the months of the year, when holidays occur, and which Torah portions are to be read on which week.

Lulav. The festival bouquet with a palm at the center used during Sukkot.

Ma'ariv. The evening liturgy and worship service.

Machzor. A holiday prayerbook.

Maftir. The additional (eighth) aliyah and reading of the Torah in which the last few lines are repeated, typically reserved for the Bar/Bat Mitzvah who then recites the Haftarah; variations may occur in liberal congregations.

Mah Nishtana. The four questions (or *fir kashes* in Yiddish) that are asked by the youngest child during Passover, for which the entire seder is an answer.

Malakh HaMavet. The Angel of Death.

Malkhuyot. Literally, "sovereignty." Refers to the section of the Amidah during the Musaf recited during the High Holidays, acknowledging God's sovereignty in the world.

Mamzer. A technical, legal term, referring to a bastard child born of a forbidden marriage as stated in the Bible (cf. Leviticus).

Ma'ot Chittin. Literally, "wheat money." A requisite charitable contribution over one's normal gift of tzedakah, prior to Pesach in order to make sure poor Jews have a festive seder.

Matanot La'Evyonim. Gifts for the poor, a mitzvah for Purim in which each person is required to give gifts (or charity) to at least two needy people or worthy causes.

Matzah. Unleavened bread, used as the symbol and staple for Passover, often referred to as the *bread of affliction,* referring to the time of Israelite slavery in Egypt. It is said that the Israelites did not have time to allow their bread to rise on escaping Egypt. Specially supervised matzah, called *shemurah matzah,* is watched from the time the wheat is cut or at least made into flour.

Matzevah. Tombstone or monument.

Mechitzah. A divider used in SYNAGOGUES (and gatherings) to separate men from women.

Megillah. Literally, "a scroll." Refers to the books of the Bible kept on single rolled scrolls; generally used to refer to the scrolls of ESTHER and RUTH, which are read during PURIM and SHAVUOT, respectively.

Me'il. TORAH mantle. In modern Hebrew, it is simply a jacket or outer garment.

Mekhirat Chametz. The legal fiction in which one sells all the CHAMETZ remaining in the house (if not destroyed) in preparation for PASSOVER.

Melave Malkah. On Saturday evening, following HAVDALAH, a social party and farewell banquet for the SABBATH Queen.

Menorah. Seven-branched candelabrum used in the ancient TABERNACLE and TEMPLE. The word is used to designate a light bulb in modern Hebrew and the synagogue SHABBAT candelabra. It generally refers to the special MENORAH used for CHANUKAH, also called a CHANUKIYAH. The Arch of Titus menorah has been adopted as the official symbol of the state of Israel.

Menuchah. Rest, especially on the SABBATH.

Meshumad. An apostate who converts from Judaism to another religion.

Meturgaman. Former practice, the person who translates the TORAH from HEBREW into the vernacular during its public reading to ensure understanding.

Mezuzah. Literally, "doorposts." It refers to both the parchment on which portions of the TORAH are written and the case in which it is placed. The mezuzah is set on the doorpost (upper one-third, right side upon entering), taken from DEUTERONOMY 6:9 and 14:20, "Inscribe them on the doorpost of your house and your gates." It also, and somewhat incorrectly, refers to similar-looking jewelry. Also, minor talmudic tractate dealing with the laws related to the writing of the parchment scroll to be placed on the doorpost.

Mikveh. Ritual bath, including "living waters," required for use primarily for conversion by men and for women following the menstrual period; immersion in such a bath is called *tevilah.*

Milchig. In Hebrew, *Chalavi.* YIDDISH term used to refer to those foods that are dairy or to be eaten with dairy, as well as utensils for that purpose; may also be used to refer to a person's culinary state of being.

Milui V'irui. Soaking in cold water, a method for making KOSHER for PASSOVER. Used for glassware that has been used primarily for cold food or drink, it requires three days minimum.

Minchah. The afternoon worship service.

Minhagim. Customs.

Minyan. The quorum of ten adults (men only in traditional Judaism) required for the reciting of prayers limited to community recitation.

Mishebeirakh. Blessing used to honor or pray for the well-being of an individual, often read following the reading of the TORAH during worship services.

Mitzvah. Plural, *mitzvot*. Refers to a specifically designated set of 613 commandments (positive and negative) traditionally acknowledged to have been given by God or decreed by the RABBIS. Generally used to refer to a good deed, especially when pronounced as *mitzveh*.

Mitzvot Shelo Ta'aseh. Negative commandments, behaviors that are forbidden, of the "Thou shalt not" variety.

Mitzvot Ta'aseh. Positive commandments, behaviors that are to be done, of the "Thou shalt" variety.

Mizbe'ach Me'at. Literally, "a small altar," refers to the dinner table at home and represents the sacrificial altar of the TEMPLE.

Mizrach. Literally, "east." A wall plaque used to designate the eastern wall in the house so that one knows the direction to face (toward Jerusalem) during prayer.

Mo'adim LeSimchah. Joyous festivals; also used as festival greeting.

Mohel. The one who performs the ritual of BRIT MILAH.

Motze Shabbat. Saturday evening, after SHABBAT.

Muktzeh. Things that are not be used on SHABBAT, such as work tools, and therefore should not be handled.

Musaf. Literally, "additional prayer"; avoided by REFORM JUDAISM, this is the special prayer recited on those festival days when an additional offering was presented in the ancient TEMPLE.

Ne'ilah. A special concluding prayer, added only on YOM KIPPUR.

Ner Tamid. The eternal light in the SYNAGOGUE, in front of the ARON HAKODESH, which reminds us of the omnipresence of God.

Ner(ot). Candle(s).

Neshamah Yetarah. An extra soul acquired on SHABBAT; according to the RABBIS, its strength allows the individual to experience a taste of REDEMPTION and gain endurance for the difficulties to be encountered in the week to come.

Nichum Avelim. The comforting of mourners.

Niddah. Literally, "she who is separated." A state of ritual impurity of the woman, as a result of the discharge of blood, usually a result of the menstrual period.

Nissu'in. The marriage ceremony part of a wedding, in contradistinction to the engagement.

Omer. First sheaf cut during the barley harvest, which was offered in the TEMPLE as a SACRIFICE on the second day of PASSOVER. Also, refers to a dry measure, one-tenth of an ephah. The counting of the omer *(sefirat ha'omer)* is the period of time between PESACH and SHAVUOT. Its origins are complex and reflect the agricultural life of the Jewish people (cf. LEVITICUS 23:15–16); they link freedom to law and reflect the farmer counting the days as the grain ripens. A state of mourning exists where certain observances are maintained, such as the refraining of the cutting of hair. Weddings are prohibited during this period, except on LAG B'OMER. The days are counted on an omer calendar.

Oneg Shabbat. Literally, "SABBATH joy or delight," refers to the enjoyment of the Sabbath on Friday evening; a reception-like affair in modern synagogues with sweets and coffee, and perhaps a lecture or program.

Orthoprax. A coined term that refers to one who practices ORTHODOX JUDAISM but believes otherwise.

Parashah. The division of the TORAH, the weekly Torah portions, also now called a SIDRA so that the Torah is completely read in one year (according to the BABYLONIAN cycle, which is generally followed) or three years (according to the PALESTINIAN cycle). See also Rabbinical Literature and Commentaries: **sidra.**

Pareve. Specifically refers to food that is neither meat nor milk and therefore can be eaten with either; generally refers to a middle of the road position without taking a stand.

Pasul. Ritually unfit and not to be used, such as a pasul TORAH.

Payas. Or *payot,* earlocks. Hair that is allowed to grow so that a blade might never get near the sideburn area. A custom of the pagans to be avoided assiduously was the engraving of the skin in that area.

Pesach. Passover, paschal offering, springtime festival celebrating the EXODUS from EGYPT following the enslavement of the Israelite people (Exodus 1:1–15:21); one of the SHALOSH REGALIM. Salient celebratory elements include the SEDER and MATZAH.

Pesach Sheni. A second PESACH, to be celebrated when circumstances prevented the celebration of Pesach at its appointed time.

Pesukei DeZimra. Preliminary prayers on SHABBAT morning, selected mostly from PSALMS; also provides some extra time for latecomers before the formal morning services begins.

Pidyon HaBen. Redemption of the firstborn. A ceremony for the firstborn son that symbolically relieves him from service in the PRIESTHOOD because the Jew of priestly descent, the descendent of AARON, was given the responsibility in his stead.

Pitum. The projectile on an ETROG, the pistil of the blossom, without which the etrog is PASUL and unfit for use on SUKKOT.

Piyyut. Plural, *piyyutim.* Medieval liturgical poems written for special occasions and festivals.

Pizmon. Plural, *pizmonim.* Poem praising God; originally used to refer to the first or last line of the first stanza, a sort of refrain that was repeated. Eventually the PIYYUTIM in which these refrains occurred came to be called *pizmonim;* they can be inserted almost anywhere in the liturgy.

Po Nikbar. "Here lies buried," usually found on the headstone of a deceased individual.

Porshen. In following the laws of KOSHER, the removal of arteries and sinews by the butcher.

Purim. Of questionable historicity, from the MEGILLAH (of ESTHER), this late winter, frivolous, joyous festival (in ADAR) commemorates the saving of the Jews of Persia by QUEEN ESTHER and her cousin/uncle MORDECAI from the hands of the vizier HAMAN, in the fifth century B.C.E. The festival is marked by the public reading of Megillat ESTHER, GREGGERS, and HAMANTASCHEN. Given the nature of Purim as a festival marking the saving of the Jews, communities throughout Jewish history have marked similar occasions and called them special Purims with individual names.

Rabbi. Hebrew for "my master." A term used during the first century as a mode of address to authoritative teachers who were ordained members of the SANHEDRIN. The title was used primarily in PALESTINE, whereas BABYLONIANS addressed their teachers as *Rav.* Community religious leader whose office developed in order to teach and judge, a result of the introduction of the notion of ORAL LAW and the disintegration of the power of the PRIESTHOOD with the destruction of the TEMPLE; today, rabbis are generally more localized to SYNAGOGUES.

Rimmon. Plural, *rimmonim;* literally, "pomegranates." Refers to the individual ornaments that adorn TORAH scrolls, in distinction to the keter Torah or *crown,* which covers both rollers of the Torah scroll.

Rosh Chodesh. The first day of the new month, celebrated as a minor holy day; it is observed for one day (if the preceding month had 29 days) or two days (if the preceding month had 30 days). It is celebrated by reciting a short form of the HALLEL PSALMS, reading from the TORAH with four persons given ALIYOT, and adding a MUSAF prayer. The day is also of special significance for women, especially in the modern period, because of the relationship between the menstrual cycle and the lunar calendar.

Rosh Hashanah. New Year festival falling on the first and second days of the month of TISHRI when Jews examine their actions of the preceding year.

Sacred and Profane. An all-encompassing idiom that primarily refers to the division of time between the normal daily schedule and Shabbat and the holidays.

Sandek. From the Greek, meaning "with child." The sandek has the responsibility of holding the child during the brit milah ritual; alternatively referred to as the *kvater* for godfather or *kvarterin* for godmother.

Seder. Literally, "order (of the service)." Refers to the table ceremony held on the first two nights of Passover, which celebrates the holiday and retells the Exodus using the Haggadah. In reform practice, generally only a first seder is held; of late, it has become fashionable to hold a less structured feast-like seder of fruits for Tu Bishevat.

Seged. Ethiopian Jewish festival.

Selichot. Penitential prayers that are recited every day except for Shabbat, following the last Shabbat in Elul and up until Yom Kippur; specifically used to refer to the service of these prayers offered on the midnight of Saturday night prior to Rosh Hashanah, when these prayers are first said.

Sermon. Lecture, a modern transformation of the devar Torah generally given by the rabbi in the context of a worship service; historically, these were limited to Shabbat Shuvah and Shabbat Hagadol.

Seudah Mafseket. The meal before a fast, specifically, before Yom Kippur.

Seudat Havra'ah. The meal of consolation or comfort provided by neighbors for the mourner upon his or her return from the cemetery following interment of the deceased; usually contains foods symbolic of life such as a boiled egg and lentil soup.

Seudat Mitzvah. A celebratory festive meal following the fulfillment of a mitzvah, such as following a wedding, brit milah, bar/bat mitzvah, or completing a tractate of Talmud.

Shabbat. The Sabbath, observed from sunset Friday evening to sundown Saturday evening, marked by rest, worship, and study. One who traditionally observes the legal requirements for Shabbat is called *shomer shabbat* or *shomer shabbos;* its observance is referred to as *shemirat shabbat.* Also, first tractate in the Mishnah order of *Moed,* deals with the rules for Sabbath observance. It also enumerates the thirty-nine specific categories of work that are expressly forbidden on the Sabbath.

Shabbat HaChodesh. The Shabbat prior to the first month of Nisan; the Torah portion describes the fixing of the dates and the regulations for Pesach.

Shabbat HaGadol. Literally, "the great Shabbat," one of the special Sabbaths. This is the Shabbat prior to Pesach, called great because it began the story of the passage of our ancestors from slavery into freedom. It is associated with various traditions throughout history; for example, this was the Shabbat when the Jews of Egypt sprinkled lambs' blood on doorposts to prevent the Angel of Death from stopping by their households during the last plague.

Shabbat Nachamu. The SABBATH of consolation or comfort, the Sabbath following the fast of AV (TISHA B'AV).

Shabbat Parah. Special SABBATH during which we read about the RED HEIFER, the ceremony of the ritual purification of the entire people.

Shabbat Shalom. A Sabbath greeting for well-being; alternatively, *Gut Shabbes* in YIDDISH.

Shabbat Shekalim. Designated because of its special TORAH portion that recalls the contribution of a shekel to the TEMPLE economy, a sort of dues for community membership.

Shabbat Sheni. An artificial legal device that radical REFORM Jews attempted to use (on the model of PESACH SHENI) in order to justify the proposed (and unsuccessful) move of the SABBATH to Sunday.

Shabbat Shuvah. The SABBATH of return (to God); the Sabbath between ROSH HASHANAH and YOM KIPPUR.

Shabbat Zakhor. The SABBATH of remembrance before PURIM: "Remember what the AMALEKITES did unto you . . ." as your ancestor tried to cross the desert.

Shabbes Clock. Refers to a timer that enables modern Jews to abide by traditional Jewish law and still take advantage of lighting, heaters, and the like on SHABBAT.

Shabbes Goy. A practice that permitted a non-Jew to do things for the Jew not permitted on SHABBAT, such as turning on or off lights at the SYNAGOGUE or stoking a fire.

Shabbesdik. An adjective meaning "in the spirit of the SABBATH"; for example, "That outfit is not shabbesdik," or "That kind of talk is not shabbesdik."

Shacharit. Morning worship services, corresponding (in time) to the morning sacrifice at the TEMPLE, traditionally instituted by ABRAHAM, it may be recited anytime during the first quarter of the daylight hours.

Shaddai. The Almighty, referring to God, often used as EL SHADDAI, found in abbreviated form on the outside of the MEZUZAH.

Shaleshudos. The collapsed form of *seudah shelishit,* for the third meal during SHABBAT; it has no KIDDUSH and is often used for words of wisdom, study and song, just before HAVDALAH.

Shaliach Tzibbur. Literally, "the messenger for the congregation." The one who leads the congregation in prayer, usually the CANTOR. Alternatively refers to the BAAL TEFILLAH.

Shalom Aleichem. The traditional greeting, "peace be unto you," especially when you have not seen the individual in some time; the response is *aleichem shalom*. Also refers to the traditional Shabbat evening song, sung when one returns from the synagogue and just sits down to Shabbat dinner; it is a song that invites the angels to come and go in peace.

Shalom Nekevah. In an attempt to provide equal ceremonial status to girls at birth, alternative naming ceremonies have been created. This one corresponds to shalom zakhar; others are *brit banot* and *simchat habat*.

Shalom Zakhar. A ceremony that welcomes the baby boy into the world; on the Friday night preceding the brit milah, friends and relatives gather to celebrate; singing abounds and a rabbi or guest is invited to offer a devar Torah.

Shalosh Regalim. The three pilgrimage festivals on which historically the individual was to make a pilgrimage to the Temple in Jerusalem; it now simply refers to the three festivals of Sukkot, Pesach, and Shavuot.

Shamash. Also called the *Shammos* in Yiddish or Ashkenazi Hebrew, the term refers to both the synagogue beadle and the helper candle used during Chanukah to light the other candles in the chanukiyah.

Shanah. Literally, "year," the twelve-month period of mourning following interment. It is the third and final stage of the mourning process.

Shatnez. The only restriction on clothing, except for issues of modesty, this is the biblical injunction against wearing a garment with a mixture of wool and linen. While there is no obvious reason for this prohibition, it seems to remind us not to violate the ecological integrity of nature.

Shavua Tov. A good week. In Yiddish, *a gut voch*. A greeting used following Havdalah when one begins the regular week anew.

Shavuot. Literally, "the Festival of Weeks," which is observed on the fiftieth day after the first day of Pesach. Because it is the concluding feast of the season, it is called *Atzeret* in the Talmud. Purely a festival of nature, the festival of the offering of the first fruits, it was later connected to the revelation of Torah on Sinai. It is observed by traditional Jews for two days in the diaspora, by liberal Jews and those in Israel for one day.

Shaytl. A sign of modesty, a head covering for married women in the form of a wig.

Shechitah. The ritual process for slaughtering animals for food, according to Jewish law.

Shehechiyanu. A blessing that thanks God for "sustaining us and bringing us to this day"; said on various occasions including bar/bat mitzvah, brit milah, and Purim. It is also recited on the first day of Chanukah, Pesach, Rosh HaShanah, and Sukkot.

Shloshet Yemei Hagbalah. The three days prior to Shavuot for preparing for the holiday; it refers to the period of time during which the people were supposed to prepare for revelation (Exodus 19:10–13).

Sheloshim. The thirty-day period of mourning following interment; it is the second stage of the mourning process.

Shema. Often called the watchword of the Jewish faith, this is the closest thing to a Jewish creed; it proclaims the unity of one God.

Shemini Atzeret. The concluding feast on the eighth day of Sukkot.

Sheva Berakhot. Part of a traditional week-long ceremony, following a wedding, at which time the berakhot are recited during Birkat HaMazon. This is a cluster of seven blessings, also called the *birchot nissuin,* recited over a cup of wine at every wedding ceremony.

Shir HaMaalot. Specifically the song of ascent, Psalm 126, sung before Birkat HaMazon on Shabbat and festivals; also used to refer to a group of Psalms (30–45) generally understood to have been sung by pilgrims as they made the ascent to Jerusalem to celebrate the Shalosh Regalim.

Shivah. The seven-day mourning period following interment.

Shivah Asar B'Tammuz. The seventeenth day of the month of Tammuz, a fast day that commemorates the following: the penetration of the walls of Jerusalem preceding the destruction of the Temple, the breaking of the tablets by Moses when he descended Sinai and saw the Israelites celebrating at the golden calf, the end of daily sacrifices, the Torah scroll being burned by a villain, and Jewish traitors erecting an idol in the Temple.

Shochet. The one who performs Shechitah, ritual slaughtering of animals for food, according to Jewish law.

Shofar. A hollowed out ram's horn, reminding us of the ram offered by Abraham instead of his son (Genesis 22:13); historically used to herald freedom and assemble the community, it is now used for the month preceding Rosh Hashanah as well as during the Yamim Noraim to call attention to the special character of the period and direct us toward repentance. It is a symbol of revelation and redemption, as sounded at Sinai (Exodus 19:16, 19).

Shofarot. Part of the musaf for Rosh Hashanah, a proclamation of God who will sound the shofar at redemption; therefore, speaks of God as Redeemer.

Shomer Mitzvot. Literally, "guardian of the commandments." Refers to one who observes and follows the commandments.

Shomer Shabbat. Literally, "guardian of the Sabbath." Refers to one who observes the Sabbath and follows the Jewish laws relevant to it.

Shtar Piturin. A document of release that allows people to remarry following a divorce.

Shtreimel. Hat, usually fur-trimmed, worn by Polish gentlemen of the eighteenth century and adopted by the Chasidim for their dress.

Shucklin. Back-and-forth swaying movement in prayer, most typical of the traditional Jew.

Shushan Purim. The fifteenth of Adar ordained by the Jews in Persia's capital and in big cities.

Shvut. Regulations that have been imposed on Shabbat to ensure true rest; they include prohibitions against sports, dancing, swimming, boating, and anything that interferes with the spirit of Shabbat.

Siddur. Prayerbook, from the Hebrew word for order, because it establishes the proper order for the recitation of prayers.

Simchat Torah. The last day of the festival of Sukkot, reserved for the "rejoicing of Torah," hence its name, during which time the final portion of the Torah is concluded and the first one is begun. The day is marked by rejoicing and processionals with the Torah in hand.

Siyyum. Conclusion. A reference to the requisite celebrating when one concludes study of, for example, a tractate of Talmud or a book of the Bible.

Skhakh. Thatching used for roofing materials for the Sukkah.

Sofer. A scribe whose responsibility it is to calligraph ritual objects such as a Torah and mezuzah as well as documents such as the ketubah or get.

Spice Box. Ritual object used to keep besamim for use during Havdalah.

Sukkah. Booth or hut, temporary structure built for the celebration of Sukkot in recognition of the temporary dwellings built by our ancestors as they journeyed from Egypt to Canaan; also in recognition of the temporary shelters built in the fields during harvest season. Also, sixth tractate in the Mishnah order of *Moed,* dealing with laws related to the festival of Tabernacles.

Synagogue. Called schul in Yiddish and often referred to as temple in more liberal circles, this is the central house of worship for the Jewish community following the destruction of the Temple; there is evidence that these structures coexisted.

Ta'anit Esther. The fast of Esther, observed just before Purim from dawn to dusk, in commemoration of Esther's fast, which she had imposed on herself in preparation of going uninvited before the King. Esther had also told Mordecai to instruct all the Jews to fast and pray so that she might succeed in her mission. Since the outcome of the fast is known, this is a minor, almost perfunctory fast.

Taharah. The ritual purification of the body after death before burial.

Taharat HaMishpachah. Refers to the body of laws designed to keep the family ritually pure, particularly regarding the sexual relations between husband and wife; most of the relevant rituals are directed toward the woman.

Takhrikhim. Shrouds, white garments used to wrap and dress the deceased for burial; designed so as not to distinguish between rich and poor at death.

Tallit. Prayer shawl, from NUMBERS 15:37–40, reminiscent of the robe-like garment worn by our desert ancestors. Four fringes (TZITZIT) are attached to remind us of our responsibilities to God; worn at morning prayer.

Tallit Katan. A small, four-cornered garment, also called *arba kanfot,* that traditional Jews wear underneath their clothing; worn like the TALLIT to remind us of our responsibilities to God.

Tameh. Something that is ritually impure. A fundamental concept in Jewish law, where an entire order of the MISHNAH *(Tohorot)* is devoted to the subject. A ritually impure person may not touch or eat a holy object or enter the TEMPLE. As a human corpse is the most severe category of ritual impurity, religious law prevents a person who comes into contact with a corpse from having contact with the ancient Temple or its cult.

Tashlikh. A ceremony held near a flowing body of water on the first day of ROSH HASHANAH (on the second day, if the first day is SHABBAT), during which individuals empty their pockets and symbolically cast their sins upon the water.

Tefillah. Plural, *tefillot.* Prayer(s) referring generally to worship.

Tefillin. Phylacteries, or prayerboxes, strapped to the head and arm, worn during daily SHACHARIT, but not on holidays or SHABBAT. They are a sign of the COVENANT between God and the people; in YIDDISH, to don them is to *ley tefillin.* Specifically, they are known as *shel rosh* (for the head) and *shel yad* (for the arm).

Tekiah. Solid, long blast of the shofar. *Tekiah gedolah* is the giant, even longer blast, with an extra push at the end of the note.

Temple. Refers both to the ancient sacrificial cult center and central edifice for divine worship in JERUSALEM; the First Temple was destroyed in 586 B.C.E. and the Second destroyed in 70 C.E. This is the site today of the DOME OF THE ROCK, a Moslem mosque. Used also by REFORM Jews as interchangeable with SYNAGOGUE because the early Reformers rejected a return to Jerusalem if it meant a condemnation of the DIASPORA.

Tena'im. The marriage engagement is formalized by tena'im, the signing of a legal document that sets forth the following conditions: the commitment to marriage, the financial resources each partner will bring to the marriage, the responsibility of each family to the other, and the penalties to be paid if either side were to break off the engagement.

Teruah. The blast of the SHOFAR, an alarm-like sound consisting of nine rapid notes that total approximately the length of a TEKIAH.

Teshuvah. Repentance, a return to the ways of God; whereas one is supposed to do teshuvah all year long, it is the mood of the HIGH HOLIDAY period and the month that precedes it.

Tevah. Coffin, which according to Jewish law is to be all wood and unadorned; also used to refer to NOAH's ark.

Tevilah. Ritual immersion in a MIKVAH for purposes of purification and CONVERSION.

Tikkun. A SOFER's copybook, also used to prepare for the reading of the TORAH because it contains the printed text with vowels parallel to the text without vowels.

Tikkun Layl Shavuot. In observance of SHAVUOT, and in preparation of the REVELATION of TORAH with which the holiday is associated, this is an all-night study period that traditionally included portions from all of the TORAH and the first and last MISHNAH of each tractate of the TALMUD.

Tisha B'av. The ninth of Av, an observance that primarily marks the destruction of both TEMPLES, as well as other mournful periods of Jewish history; referred to as a "black fast." Three other things were to have happened on that day as well: the generation of the desert were told that they would not enter CANAAN and would die in the desert; BAR KOKHBA's fortress was captured by the Romans; and the city of JERUSALEM was plowed under and rendered uninhabitable.

Treifah. That which is ritually unfit, such as food, in contradistinction to KOSHER.

Trop. YIDDISH for the notes of cantillation that direct the reader in chanting the TORAH and HAFTORAH. Called *ta'amei hamikra* in HEBREW.

Tu BiShevat. The fifteenth of SHEVAT, the New Year of the trees, the Jewish Arbor Day. It connects us to Israel because it is the day when the sap begins to run in Israel's trees, promising spring.

Tzitzit. Ritual fringes on the TALLIT or TALLIT KATAN tied with special knots to remind us of God's 613 commandments and our responsibility to keep them. Also, a minor talmudic tractate dealing with the laws for ritual fringes.

Tzom Gedaliah. Fast day commemorating the assassination of Judean governor Gedaliah in 585 B.C.E. With his death, the Jews living in Israel after the destruction of the first TEMPLE were dispersed; in mourning over the EXILE, the RABBIS decreed it to be a public fast.

Unetaneh Tokef. A prayer on ROSH HASHANAH that reflects on its meaning. It speaks to both the essence of the YAMIM NORAIM as well as the Jewish notion of life itself; written in the latter half of the eleventh century by Kalonymus ben Meshullam, head of the Jewish community of Mainz.

Uvda DeChol. Also called *uvdin d'chol.* Anything that may give the SABBATH a workday character (such as the use of the telephone) and therefore prohibited, although not involving direct labor or prohibited work.

Vidui. A confessional, for YOM KIPPUR and the deathbed.

Wimpel. A Torah binding used to hold the scrolls together, under the me'il as an alternative to an avnet. Made from the swaddling clothes of an infant and worn at the brit milah, it is traditionally given to the synagogue in honor of a boy's first birthday; it is sewn together and embroidered with his name, birth date, and a prayer for him.

Yad. Literally, "arm or hand." Used as a pointer for the reading of Torah so that one does not touch the scroll itself.

Yahrzeit. From the Yiddish, the anniversary of one's death; it is commemorated by lighting a twenty-four-hour candle and saying Kaddish Yatom.

Yamim Nora'im. The days of awe, referring to the period between and including Rosh Hashanah and Yom Kippur.

Yichud. The symbolic consummation of one's marriage, just following the wedding ceremony, symbolically represented by the chuppah; many communities allow for private time just after the ceremony in order to recognize it.

Yisrael. An Israelite, the masses of the people, as opposed to the Kohen and Levite; called third to the Torah in a traditional synagogue.

Yizkor. A memorial prayer, the remembrance of the deceased, commemorated during the shalosh regalim on the final day, and Yom Kippur.

Yom HaAtzma'ut. Israeli Independence Day, linked to Yom HaZikaron; its commemoration has matured and developed since 1948.

Yom HaShoah. Day of commemorating the Holocaust; it is observed one week prior to Yom HaZikaron.

Yom HaZikaron. Day of remembrance for Israel's fallen soldiers, observed for the twenty-four-hour period just prior to Yom HaAtzma'ut.

Yom Kippur. Jewish Day of Atonement, generally regarded as the holiest day of the year. It is marked by fasting from sundown of the ninth day of Tishri to sunset of the tenth. On this day, Jews ask for forgiveness for their sins.

Yom Kippur Katan. To emphasize the spiritual character of Rosh Chodesh and renewal, a little Yom Kippur precedes the feast of the new moon; the congregation offers petitions for divine forgiveness, followed by the confessions of sins and Shema Yisrael before the open aron hakodesh.

Yom Tov. A holiday.

Yontif. A collapsed form in Yiddish for yom tov.

Zekher Litziyat Mitzrayim. As a remembrance of the Exodus from Egypt; a reference to some of the rituals we do, taken from Shabbat Kiddush.

Zemirot. Table songs for Shabbat and the festivals.

Zikaron LeMa'aseh Vereishit. As a memory of creation, a reference to some of the rituals we do, taken from the Shabbat Kiddush.

Zikhrano Livrakhah. Of blessed memory, used when speaking of the deceased; idiomatic equivalent of "may he rest in peace."

Zikhronot. Additional proclamations in the MUSAF for ROSH HASHANAH; proclamation of God, Master of Absolute Remembrance and Judge of the Universe.

CHAPTER 2

Bible and Commentaries

The Bible is the oldest and most widely read book in our civilization. It has been in continuous circulation for almost 2,000 years and has been the source of religious ideals and values for countless millions of people. Ever since Sinai, the moral imperatives of the Five Books of Moses and the books of the Prophets have provided great inspiration to social reformers and religious idealists.

Throughout the English-speaking world many famous novelists, poets, and dramatists have studied the Bible for its profound ideas, rich language, and original style. Political ideas and institutions of American life have been shaped by biblical teachings.

Of course, it is in the realm of religion that the Bible is surely of paramount importance. As the holy book of both Judaism and Christianity, its influence has been momentous within the whole ethical framework of Western civilization.

The Bible has been the Magna Carta of the impoverished and oppressed. Historically, no country has had a constitution in which the interests of the people were so highly upheld as they are in the Bible. It is said that the Bible is the most democratic book in the world. And undoubtedly, people throughout the ages have always recognized it as a great spiritual heritage for all of humankind.

This chapter defines the important personalities, places, commentaries, and biblical concepts that will enable many to reach a deeper understanding of the Bible and a richer appreciation of its message.

Aaron. (Thirteenth century B.C.E.) Elder brother of Moses and a leading figure in the events of the Exodus from Egypt. Aaron was Moses's spokesman in his dealings with Pharaoh but was persuaded to make the Golden Calf while Moses was on Mount Sinai. Aaron, as the first priest, was the progenitor of the priestly family, known as a "lover and seeker of peace."

Abel. Second son of Adam and Eve. He was a shepherd, while his elder brother Cain tilled the soil. God favored Abel's animal sacrifice, whereupon Cain in envy killed his brother.

Abraham. First patriarch, Abraham was the founder of the Hebrew nation. According to the Book of Genesis, God made a covenant with Abraham, telling him to leave his own country and promising to give his family (the Hebrews) the land of Canaan. He was the father of Isaac (by Sarah) and Ishmael (by his concubine Hagar). Abraham is the prototype of humility and kindness, famed for his hospitality.

Absalom. Third son of King David. He killed his half-brother Amnon to avenge the rape of his sister Tamar. In rabbinic literature his career is cited as an example of vanity and rebellion.

Adam and Eve. In the Bible, the first man and the first woman. God created Adam by breathing life into "the dust of the ground." Later, God created Eve from Adam's rib. Adam and Eve were placed in the Garden of Eden to tend it, and permitted to eat of the fruit of all the trees, except the Tree of Life and the Tree of Knowledge. Seduced by the serpent, both Adam and Eve ate of the forbidden fruit. For this act of disobedience they were expelled from the Garden.

Adonai. The personal name of the God of Israel is written in the Bible with the four consonants YHWH referred to as the tetragrammaton. Until the destruction of the First Temple in 586 B.C.E., this name was pronounced with its proper vowels. By the third century B.C.E., the pronunciation of

33

the name YHWH was avoided, and Adonai, "the Lord," was substituted for it.

Ahasuerus. King of Persia who figured prominently in the Book of ESTHER. Modern scholarship identifies him with Xerxes (486–465 B.C.E.). Ahasuerus first married VASHTI and later took ESTHER to be his wife and next queen.

Ai. Ancient town, north of JERUSALEM in the vicinity of BETHEL, known in the days of ABRAHAM. An Israelite attack upon it was successful. The people of Ai were killed, their king executed and city burned.

Altar. Place of offerings to a deity. The importance of SACRIFICES in early religion caused the altar to occupy an important position, both in the TEMPLE and in the open.

Amalekite. An ancient people mentioned numerous times in the Bible, known for their hostility to the Israelite people. Shortly after the EXODUS from EGYPT they attacked the Israelites in the desert and defeated the weak and weary. Eventually they were defeated by the Israelite army led by JOSHUA, successor of MOSES. The Amalekites have remained in rabbinic literature as a symbol of everlasting enmity to Israel. HAMAN, the antagonist in the Book of ESTHER, is regarded as a descendant of Agag, king of the Amalekites.

Amos. Eighth-century B.C.E. prophet of JUDEAN origin, Amos was a herdsman. His main center of activity was in the northern kingdom. In his book (the third of the twelve minor prophets), he warns the Israelites of the grave danger from ASSYRIA. Righteousness for Amos was the most important moral attribute of the divine nature.

Angel. Today the word angel is used to describe numerous types of supernatural beings mentioned in the Bible, including CHERUBIM and SERAPHIM. Angels are often sent to earth, sometimes with a human appearance, to bring the message of God to the people. For example, three angels visit ABRAHAM to inform him that his wife Sarah would soon give birth to a son. Names of Angels (Gabriel and MICHAEL) were first mentioned in the book of DANIEL.

Anthropomorphism. The ascription of human form and characteristics to God. The Bible is often anthropomorphic and refers, for instance, to God's hand, fingers, nostrils, and so on.

Antiochus. Name of thirteen Greek kings who ruled Syria in the HELLENISTIC Period. Antiochus IV Epiphanes ruled from 175 B.C.E. to 163 B.C.E., and he was the founder of more new Greek cities than all of his predecessors. As a champion of intense hellenization, his reign marks a turning point in Jewish history. He is the Antiochus generally referred to in the story of CHANUKAH.

Apocalypse. A REVELATION of the future, particularly of the END OF DAYS and the DAY OF JUDGMENT. The sacred books of an apocalyptic nature include the Book of DANIEL.

Apocrypha. Religious writings that are noncanonical, written during the period of the second TEMPLE and some time after its destruction. The oldest books of the Apocrypha are thought to be the books of JUDITH and Tobit.

Archaeology. The scientific investigation of ancient cultures through their material remains. Bible study is illuminated by archaeology both in and outside of Israel. For example, MESOPOTAMIAN discoveries indicate a period of great floods reflected in the biblical flood story.

Ark of the Covenant. The chest in which the two Tablets of the Law (TEN COMMANDMENTS) were kept. Its exact description is given in EXODUS 25:10–22. From the time of MOSES until the construction of the first TEMPLE by SOLOMON, the ark of the covenant was taken out from the HOLY OF HOLIES in case of national need to help the people in battle. During the period of the first Temple, the ark of the covenant found a permanent home in the Holy of Holies and was never removed.

Armageddon. According to Christian tradition, the site of the final and conclusive battle between good and evil (Revelations 16:16).

Authorized Version. Also known as the KING JAMES VERSION of the Bible, this translation was completed in 1611. The Authorized Version was done by a team of approximately fifty translators, and became the appointed version to be read in churches.

Azazel. Name designating the "scapegoat" or the "demon" to whom the scapegoat was sent (LEVITICUS 16). On the Day of Atonement, two goats were prescribed as SIN OFFERINGS for the people. The HIGH PRIEST cast lots and designated one goat "for the Lord" and the other for "Azazel." The latter was sent away into the wilderness.

Baal. Foremost among CANAANITE gods, Baal was not the name of one particular god, but the presiding deity of a given locality. For example, Baal, the god of rain and fertility, was killed each year by the hosts of Mot, the god of drought and death. In the fall Baal came back to life, bringing back the rains. The Bible records how JUDGES and PROPHETS fought Baal worship among the people of Israel. Also, Hebrew for "husband," "owner," or "lord."

Baalzebub. CANAANITE deity adopted by the PHILISTINES. In the New Testament Baalzebub is transformed into Beelzebub, chief of all the demons. Baalzebub in Hebrew literally means "Lord of the Flies."

Babylon. Ancient Asiatic land lying between the TIGRIS and Euphrates Rivers. It is the scene of the biblical story of the Tower of Babel, built by people who aspired to reach the heavens. Babylon was the cradle of ancient civilization and the seat of the great empires. The capital, UR, was the birthplace of ABRAHAM, Israel's first PATRIARCH.

Balaam. Heathen prophet invited by BALAK, king of MOAB, to curse the Israelites. Divinely inspired, Balaam uttered blessings instead of curses (NUMBERS 22:5).

Balak. Thirteenth-century B.C.E. King of MOAB. When the Israelites, wandering through the wilderness, approached his borders, he requested BALAAM to curse them, but the curse was turned into a blessing.

Batsheba. Wife of KING DAVID. In order to marry her, David engineered the death in battle of her husband, Uriah the HITTITE. Batsheba's first son by King David died. Her second son, SOLOMON, succeeded to the throne.

Behemoth. Animal described in JOB 40:24, thought to be the hippopotamus. In rabbinic and medieval lore, the feast from the flesh of the Behemoth was to be a feature of messianic days.

Bel. Babylonian deity; the name is related to the Phoenician word BA'AL. Bel was the chief god of the Babylonians and is mentioned as such by both the PROPHETS ISAIAH and JEREMIAH.

Ben Asher, Moses. Last of a famous family of MASORETES, Ben Asher lived in TIBERIAS and died in JERUSALEM during the first half of the tenth century. He devoted many years to preparing an accurate biblical manuscript incorporating vocalization and accents in accordance with his school of tradition. His version was a model for subsequent copyists and forms the basis of the accepted Bible text, though changes were entered in later centuries.

Ben Sira. (ca. 170 B.C.E.) A JERUSALEM SAGE who belonged to the class of learned SCRIBES. He was the author of the work known as the *Wisdom of Ben Sira,* also called *Ecclesiasticus,* which was translated into Greek by his grandson in 132 B.C.E. and incorporated in the APOCRYPHA. The book contains wise axioms and is similar in form to the biblical book of PROVERBS.

Benjamin. The twelfth and youngest son of JACOB and the second son of RACHEL, who died in childbirth when he was born. The strong mutual devotion of Jacob and BENJAMIN played a prominent part in the events that ended with Jacob's migration to EGYPT.

Bethel. Ancient Israelite city ten miles north of JERUSALEM and formerly called Luz. ABRAHAM erected an ALTAR near the site (GENESIS 12:8); later it was the scene of JACOB's dream, as a result of which it received the name Bethel (literally, "House of God").

Bethlehem. Name of an ancient town located in the Judean hills south of JERUSALEM. Bethlehem (also called Ephrat in the Bible) is the setting of the Book of RUTH, the home of KING DAVID, and the scene of the nativity, according to New Testament tradition of Jesus.

Bible Accents. Called *taamei hamikra* in Hebrew, Bible accents are special signs of cantillation or accents that are placed both above and under the words of the Hebrew Bible. There are those who believe that these accents had been originated by Ezra and the MEN OF THE GREAT ASSEMBLY, who flourished several centuries before the common era. The MASORETES actually set the *taamei hamikra.*

Biblical Criticism. The critical study of the Hebrew Bible, which falls into two categories: (1) literary, or higher criticism and (2) textual, or lower criticism. The former deals with questions of authorship, date of composition, and style. The latter deals with problems of a purely textual nature and attempts to establish the true wording of texts.

Boaz. Husband of RUTH and great grandfather of KING DAVID. Boaz was a wealthy landowner of BETHLEHEM, a benevolent farmer who had a concern for his workers' welfare and a sense of family responsibility.

Book of the Covenant. In EXODUS 24:7, the Book of the Covenant is read by MOSES as the basis of God's COVENANT with Israel, at its ratification at the foot of MOUNT SINAI. This book was probably the Decalogue of Exodus 20:2–17. It has, however, become customary to give the designation of the Book of the Covenant to Exodus 20:22–23:33.

Booths. Small huts erected for the Feast of Tabernacles (in Hebrew, SUKKOT) when for seven days, Jews "dwell," or at least eat in them (LEVITICUS 23:42). The Feast of Tabernacles commemorates the protection that the booths afforded the Israelites throughout their wanderings in the wilderness.

Bow (rainbow). In GENESIS 9:13, God puts a rainbow in the sky as the sign of His COVENANT with NOAH. The rainbow was God's promise that never again would God destroy all flesh by a FLOOD.

Bread of Affliction. Refers to the unleavened flat bread, MATZAH, symbolizing the haste with which the people of Israel had to leave EGYPT. It is traditionally eaten during the Festival of PASSOVER and provides a constant reminder of the poverty and affliction of the Israelites while under the yoke of the Egyptian PHARAOH.

Breastplate. One of the sacred garments of the HIGH PRIEST. It consisted of a square gold frame in which were set twelve gems of different colors, representing the tribes of Israel, and holding the URIM and TUMMIM. Today the term is often applied to the silver ornament (CHOSHEN) placed in front of the TORAH scroll, sometimes made in similar form.

Burning Bush. The desert shrub from which the ANGEL of God appeared to MOSES, prior to his Divine call. The bush was aflame, but miraculously, was not consumed (EXODUS 3:2–4).

Burnt Offering. A kind of SACRIFICE during biblical times where an entire animal was placed upon the ALTAR to be burnt. This offering embodied the idea of the submission of the worshiper to the will of God in its most perfect form.

Cain. Eldest son of ADAM AND EVE and brother of ABEL. After Cain killed Abel, he was condemned by God to wander over the land of NOD, east of Eden.

Caleb. A member of the Kenizzite family and one of the leaders of the tribe of JUDAH during the wandering in the desert. He and JOSHUA were the only spies out of the twelve dispatched by Moses to reconnoiter the land of Canaan who brought back a favorable report. As a reward, they were the sole survivors of the exodus from Egypt to enter the ancient land of Israel.

Canaan. Name for the territory in biblical times that was principally in Phoenicia. It is the land that God promised to Abraham ("Unto your seed will I give this land," Genesis 12:17). Canaan was also the name of the youngest son of Ham, son of Noah.

Canaanites. Inhabitants of the land of Canaan; traditionally descended from Canaan, son of Ham. They were divided into eleven peoples who occupied the area between the Nile River and the Euphrates.

Canon. The authoritative collection of Holy Scriptures that became closed forever to subtraction or addition of other sacred books to the Hebrew Bible. The word "canon," or standard, comes from the Greek *kanones,* or models of excellence.

Cherubim. Winged figures (with human, animal, or bird's head and body), probably derived from a Semitic prototype. Frequently mentioned in the Bible, Cherubim guarded the gates to the Garden of Eden. In the Tabernacle, their images were placed on either side of the Ark of the Covenant. The prophet Ezekiel, in his vision, describes a group of four Cherubim carrying the Divine throne (Ezekiel, Chapter 1).

Chronicles. The name of the last two books in the Hebrew Bible. Chronicles retells the history of the Jewish people from Creation to the close of the Babylonian exile. It concentrates on the history of the Kingdom of Judah and stresses the priestly duties and Temple ritual.

Chumash. From the Hebrew *chamesh* (five), chumash refers to the first five books of the Bible, sometimes called the Five Books of Moses or the Pentateuch. The books of the chumash include Genesis, Exodus, Leviticus, Numbers, and Deuteronomy.

Cloud of Glory. The Divine Cloud (Exodus 4:34–38) of Fire that hovered over the ancient Tabernacle and provided the Israelites with the sign for camping or marching. When it was taken up, the Israelites continued their journey. When it abided, the Israelites encamped.

Coat of Many Colors. The special coat that Jacob gave to his son Joseph. The coat made his other sons jealous and resentful, whereupon they sold him to an Ishmaelite caravan.

Codex. A biblical parchment manuscript that was bound as a book and prepared side by side with a synagogue scroll for the public reading of the Torah. Often illuminated in a variety of colors, a typical codex might also include Masoretic notations and musical accents. A codex was a connecting link between the scroll and the printed book.

Concubine. Marital companion of inferior status to a wife. Concubines mentioned in the Bible include Ritzpah, the concubine of Saul (II Samuel

3:7) and the concubine of Gibeah. Royal concubines were standard among the kings of ISRAEL and JUDAH.

Covenant. A mutually binding agreement between persons or nations. In the Hebrew Bible, God made agreements with NOAH, ABRAHAM, and MOSES. To Noah, the covenantal sign was a RAINBOW, signifying that God would never again destroy the world with a flood. God promised Abraham that he would become the father of a great nation, provided that Abraham went to the place that God showed him. The covenant was sealed by the CIRCUMCISION of all Israelite men. To Moses, God said that the Israelites would reach the PROMISED LAND, but must obey the MOSAIC LAW.

Cubit. In biblical times, measurements were related to the parts of the body. One cubit was the equivalent of the length of a forearm from the elbow to the tip of the middle finger (approximately 18 inches).

D Source. The projects of gathering and assembling the traditions and stories of the Bible were believed by some biblical scholars to be carried out by various groups of people, often called "schools," of writers or editors. The D Source or School derives its name from the Book of DEUTERONOMY, much of which had been prepared by the year 621 B.C.E. In the writings of the D School there is an emphasis upon the keeping of the COMMANDMENTS of the Lord so that the people may enjoy prosperity.

Dan. The fifth son of JACOB, by Bilhah, the handmaiden of RACHEL. The tribe of Dan, known for its fighting men, settled in the area around Ekron in the south of CANAAN and up along the coast north of JAFFA.

"Dan to Beersheba." A popular biblical phrase (e.g., JUDGES 20:1), denoting the entirety of CANAAN, from the north (DAN) to the South (Beersheba).

Daniel. Name of a book found in the section of the Bible known as WRITINGS and of its central character, whose history and visions comprise the book's contents. The prophet Daniel was taken captive to BABYLON and trained for the king's service. When he interpreted some mysterious writing on a wall as symbolizing the downfall of the king, Daniel was cast into a lion's den. Miraculously, he was saved from death.

David. The second king of Israel (ca. 1000–960 B.C.E.). Under David's reign, the tribes of Israel were united and became a nation. One of David's crowning achievements was the capture of JERUSALEM from the JEBUSITES. There he built a new TABERNACLE to which he brought the ARK OF THE COVENANT. Jerusalem came to be called the City of David, the heart of his kingdom and the capital of Israel.

Day of the Lord. The day on which, according to ESCHATOLOGY, God will finally defeat God's enemies and judge all the wicked of Israel for their evil deeds. Israel will be created anew, while paganism will end and the world reign of God will begin.

Dead Sea Scrolls. Ancient manuscripts found in the caves of QUMRAN, seven and one-half miles from JERICHO. The study of the scrolls, including two complete copies of the book of Isaiah, have advanced the study of the Hebrew text of the Bible, as the previously known oldest versions date from the Middle Ages.

Deborah. PROPHET, ca. 1150 B.C.E. She roused the Israelite tribes to revolt under Barak against the CANAANITE king Jabin and Sisera, his ally and commander (JUDGES 4). The song of victory attributed to her (Judges 5) is regarded as one of the oldest compositions preserved in Hebrew.

Deuteronomy. Fifth and last book of the FIVE BOOKS OF MOSES, Deuteronomy has been identified by some scholars as the lost book found in the Temple during the reign of King JOSIAH. Many of the ethical ideas found in the earlier books of the Five Books of Moses reach their loftiest form in Deuteronomy.

Dinah. Daughter of JACOB and LEAH. Her rape by Shechem was avenged by her brothers, SIMEON and LEVI, who annihilated the inhabitants of the town of SHECHEM (GENESIS 34).

Dittography. An error in a manuscript by a SCRIBE who repeats a letter or word that is meant to be recorded only one time.

Divination. An attempt in biblical times to penetrate the future using the methodologies of augury, soothsaying, charming, and conjuring the spirits of the dead. These forms of divination are expressly forbidden in the Bible.

Documentary Hypothesis. A biblical theory that holds that the Bible, instead of a book produced by God through MOSES (a traditional view), was the product of various groups of people who gathered and edited collections of material. These people are often called ''schools'' of writers and editors. The earliest is called the ''J School,'' after the name of the Deity J-H-V-H that appears in the writing of the first school. The others schools are ''E,'' ''P,'' and ''D.''

Dry Bones. In Chapter 37 of the Book of EZEKIEL, the PROPHET finds himself in a valley of scattered dry bones. Under the vivifying effect of the spirit of God, the bones knit together and are covered with flesh and skin. This symbolizes the Divine promise of Israel's rebirth and regeneration as a nation.

E Source. According to the DOCUMENTARY HYPOTHESIS, the biblical source material that was developed from about 750 B.C.E. to 650 B.C.E. This source was so named because its contributions used the Hebrew *Elohim* when referring to God.

Ecclesiastes. One of the five scrolls in the HAGIOGRAPHA section of the Bible. The author (called *Kohelet* in Hebrew and traditionally identified as KING SOLOMON) seeks to discern the purpose of human life with all its trials, but finds no spiritual support in either faith or intellect. The book's motto is ''vanity of vanities, all is vanity.'' The author does insist, however, that God's laws must be kept, whether keeping them results in happiness or tragedy.

Eden, Garden of. The original dwelling place of ADAM AND EVE, containing the TREE OF LIFE and the tree of knowledge of good and evil, from which Adam and Eve were forbidden to eat. When they disobeyed and ate from the forbidden fruit, God banished them from the Garden. In later Jewish literature, the Garden of Eden often refers to the abode of righteous people after death.

Edom. Country in southeastern PALESTINE. The Edomites were of Semitic origin, traditionally descendants of ESAU, and lived by hunting. Traditional enemies of the Israelites, they fought KING SAUL and were defeated by KING DAVID.

Egypt. Hebrew, *Mitzrayim.* Country in northeast Africa. The history of the Jewish people from its very outset has been connected with Egypt. Ruled by a PHARAOH, Egypt figures prominently in many biblical events, including the story of JOSEPH and MOSES and the EXODUS story.

El. A word denoting God, occurring in all Semitic languages. In the Bible it appears relatively rarely for God but is an element in proper names (e.g., SAMUEL, Eleazer).

El Shaddai. Divine name frequently found in the Bible (e.g., EXODUS 6:2). It is usually interpreted as "Almighty."

Elder. Hebrew, *zaken.* In biblical times, a member of the authoritative group of the nation. The elders were influential in shaping the form of government and served as JUDGES and chief representatives of the people down to the period of the Second TEMPLE.

Elijah. PROPHET in the kingdom of Israel (ninth century B.C.E.) known for his opposition to idol worship. According to the biblical account, Elijah did not die but ascended to Heaven in a fiery chariot.

Elisha. Ninth-century biblical PROPHET succeeding ELIJAH. Like Elijah, he wanted to rid Israel of pagan gods. Also known for his acts of kindness and ability to perform miracles, he is said to have divided the waters of the JORDAN RIVER and to have resurrected a child.

Elohim. One of God's biblical names, Elohim (plural of EL) is also used to denote "gods" and idols.

Elohist. Name for a contributing member of the E source.

Enoch. Eldest son of CAIN, grandson of ADAM AND EVE and father of METHUSALEH, the oldest person in the Bible (lived 969 years). The Bible says that Enoch "walked with God," which has been traditionally interpreted to mean that Enoch did not die naturally but was transported to heaven in his lifetime on account of his righteousness.

Ephod. Upper garment worn in ancient Israel for sacred service by the HIGH PRIEST. It was held together by a girdle and two shoulder straps.

Ephraim. Younger son of JOSEPH. Also the name of an Israelite tribe, and a term applied to the more northern of the two Israelite kingdoms (the southern kingdom was called **Judah**).

Ephrata. Wife of **Caleb** and the mother of Hur. It is also an alternate name for the city of **Bethlehem**.

Epic of Gilgamesh. Ancient **Babylonian** creation myth containing several parallels with the biblical narrative, especially the story of the **flood**.

Esau. Son of **Isaac** and elder twin brother of **Jacob**. After Jacob obtained Esau's birthright, Esau became his enemy, seeking to kill him. Twenty years later the two brothers reconciled their differences. The Bible identifies Esau as the progenitor of **Edom**.

Eschatology. Doctrine of the **end of days**, referring to the fundamental changing of the present world by Divine plan at some time in the future. The popular conception of the eschatological era was of a time when the renewed Israelites would defeat their enemies and set up a powerful kingdom. This victorious period is sometimes called the **Day of the Lord**.

Essenes. Religious sect in ancient Israel at the close of the Second **Temple** period. They lived an ascetic life, their chief occupation being farming. The Essenes may have been responsible for the writing of some of the **Dead Sea Scrolls**.

Esther. Central character in the biblical book of the same name. King **Ahasuerus** chose her to be queen in the place of the deposed **Vashti**. She used her influence to save the Jewish people from the hand of **Haman** the Agagite.

Exegesis. The explanation or critical interpretation of the text. The basic Jewish methods of biblical interpretation are the literal (i.e., plain meaning of the text), the homiletical (informal exposition of text), the mystical, and the allegorical.

Exodus. Name of the second of the **Five Books of Moses**. Exodus tells the story of Egyptian oppression of the Israelites, the appearance of Moses, the **ten plagues**, the exodus from **Egypt**, and the giving of the **Ten Commandments** on **Mount Sinai**.

"Eye for an Eye." The biblical principle of justice that requires a punishment equal in kind to the offense. The complete principle is stated in the Book of **Exodus** as "You shall give life for life, eye for eye, tooth for tooth, hand for hand, foot for foot" (**Exodus** 21:24). This was later interpreted by the **rabbis** to mean that money was adequate recompense.

Ezekiel. Third of the major **prophets**, Ezekiel witnessed the destruction of **Jerusalem** and **Judea** and went into **exile** to **Babylonia**. His prophecies have great poetic beauty and mystic power. The most famous chapter (37) describes his symbolic vision of a valley of **dry bones** that are resurrected, symbolizing the rebirth of Israel.

Ezra. One of the two leaders of the return from the Babylonian captivity, a great teacher of the Law, and (presumably) author of the book of Ezra in the Bible. Not the least of his achievements was the custom he began of reading portions from the TORAH on SABBATHS and market days (Mondays and Thursdays).

False Prophet. A spokesperson who claims to be speaking in the name of God but who in truth invents his prophecy, which turns out to be untrue. The authentic prophet JEREMIAH speaks out against false prophecy throughout his book (cf. 14:13 ff; 23:14, 16).

Final Judgment. Sometimes called the Day of Judgment, it refers to the period when God will decide the fate of nations or individuals.

First Fruits. Biblical legislation called for the bringing of the first choice fruits of the field to the TEMPLE (DEUTERONOMY 26:5–10). The first fruits (*bikurim* in Hebrew) could be brought any time between SHAVUOT (also called the Feast of First Fruits) and the Festival of SUKKOT.

Five Books of Moses. The first five books of the Hebrew Bible, traditionally ascribed to the authorship of MOSES. They include GENESIS, EXODUS, LEVITICUS, NUMBERS, and DEUTERONOMY. Other names for the five books include the TORAH, the CHUMASH (from the Hebrew word for five), and the PENTATEUCH (from the Greek words "five books").

Flood. Deluge brought by God to destroy humankind because of its wickedness (GENESIS 6–9). The central figure of the flood narrative is NOAH, the one righteous person on earth, who is commanded to build an ark in which to shelter his family and all living creatures. The biblical flood story is paralleled in other Near Eastern traditions. The most notable is the BABYLONIAN EPIC OF GILGAMESH.

Forbidden Foods. Foods expressly forbidden to be eaten in the Bible due to Divine decree. Included in this list are animals that die of themselves or are killed by another animal, animals that do not have divided hooves and chew their cuds, and fish that do not have both fins and scales.

Former Prophets. The second major part of the Hebrew Bible is called the Prophets, divided into the Former Prophets and the Latter Prophets. The Former Prophets include the books of JOSHUA, JUDGES, SAMUEL I, Samuel II, KINGS I and Kings II. The narrative of these books opens as the Hebrew tribes, under the leadership of JOSHUA, cross the JORDAN RIVER and move into the land of CANAAN. The narrative concludes with the destruction of the Northern Kingdom of Israel and the Kingdom of Judah to the south.

Free-will Offering. Any voluntary sacrificial offering in the Bible, whereby an individual is left free, according to the occasion or his feelings, to decide the kind of prescribed SACRIFICE he wishes to bring. Such offerings might include an animal, bird, or a meal offering (consisting of barley or wheat flour prepared with oil and frankincense). The Hebrew word for offering, *korban,* denotes that which is brought near to God.

Frontlets. A band or phylactery worn on the forehead in biblical times as a reminder of God's unity and dependability as a liberator from slavery to freedom. Today phylacteries (*tefillin* in Hebrew) consist of two black leather boxes fastened to leather straps, containing four portions of the FIVE BOOKS OF MOSES written on parchment.

Gad. Seventh son of JACOB and head of the tribe of Gad, whose territory lay in the Gilead mountains, east of Jordan. The tribe of Gad supplied KING DAVID with some of his best warriors.

Galilee. The northern hill country of Israel extending lengthwise from the VALLEY OF JEZREEL to the foothills of LEBANON, and from the Mediterranean on the west to the JORDAN rift on the east. In biblical times Galilee was occupied by the tribes of NAPHTALI and ASHER.

Gechazi. Servant of ELISHA, whose vulgar behavior is illustrated in the stories relating to his attempt to repel the Shunammite woman (II KINGS 4) and to obtain NAAMAN's gifts by cunning. For the latter offense, he was cursed with leprosy (II Kings 5).

Gehenna. Valley southwest of JERUSALEM opposite the City of David. Children were sacrificed there to MOLECH at a site called Tophet, and the name Gehenna (also known as GEHINNOM) became synonymous with hell—the place where the wicked are condemned after death.

Genesis. The first of the FIVE BOOKS OF MOSES. Genesis tells the story of creation, the FLOOD, and the PATRIARCHS and MATRIARCHS. It closes with JACOB's descent to EGYPT to join his son JOSEPH.

Genizah (Cairo). Depository for used sacred books. One such genizah (meaning ''hidden'' in Hebrew) was discovered in Cairo in the nineteenth century; it yielded a rich supply of manuscripts and fragments, some dating back to the sixth century C.E.

Gershon. Sometimes called Gershom, he was the eldest of LEVI's three sons. During the EXODUS, his Levite descendants were given the task of carrying the TABERNACLE. Gershon is also the name of MOSES' first child, born to his wife ZIPPORAH during the sojourn of Moses in MIDIAN.

Gibeon. Ancient priestly city near JERUSALEM in the territory of the tribe of BENJAMIN (JOSHUA 18:25). Gibeon was the site of a HIGH PLACE where SOLOMON sacrificed and subsequently experienced a Divine vision (I KINGS 3:4–14).

Gideon. A judge of Israel, Gideon fought the MIDIANITES, who were oppressing the Israelites. He defeated them decisively and was offered the kingship, but refused out of loyalty to the principle that God is King of Israel (JUDGES 6–8).

Gilgal. Name of various holy places in ancient Israel. The best known was the first Israelite camp after crossing the JORDAN RIVER, where JOSHUA set up twelve commemorative stones and the Israelites were circumcised after celebrating their first PASSOVER in CANAAN (Joshua 4:19–20).

Gleanings. The remains of the crop after the harvest that are left for the poor (LEVITICUS 19:9–10). The Book of RUTH (2:2) describes the gathering of the gleanings by the poor who are the harvesters.

Gog and Magog. King (Gog) and country (Magog) mentioned in the Bible (Ezekiel 38:9). The prophet Ezekiel foretells the downfall of Gog "in the latter years" after his attack upon the Israelites. Jewish tradition holds that the wars of Gog and Magog will precede the advent of the Messiah.

Golden Calf. Golden idol constructed by Aaron on the demand of the Israelites who had become impatient during Moses' long absence on Mount Sinai. The calf was burned by Moses, who ground the gold to dust and subsequently obtained Divine forgiveness for the Israelites (Exodus 32).

Goliath. Philistine giant from Gath slain by David in single combat (I Samuel 17; 21:10).

Gomer. Wife of the prophet Hosea, known for her unfaithfulness to him. Hosea divorced her but continued to love her. At some later stage he appeared to have forgiven her and taken her back. Gomer is a symbol of the relationship between God and Israel (Hosea 1:3).

Gomorrah. One of the five cities of the Jordan plain destroyed by God in the time of Abraham. The chief of the five cities was Sodom.

Goshen. Fertile district of ancient Egypt allotted by Pharaoh to Joseph's family (Genesis 47:6, 11). It is thought to be situated east of the Nile delta.

Graven Image. A sculptured image with the intent to adore it as a real or surrogate god. The creation of graven images is expressly forbidden in the second of the Ten Commandments (Exodus 20:3–7; Deuteronomy 5:7–10).

Guilt Offering. A type of biblical sacrifice that was offered to God in expiation of evil thoughts or unwitting sins.

Habakkuk. Name of prophet whose book is the eighth of the Minor Prophets. This three-chapter book contains an outcry against the victory of the Chaldeans and the rule of iniquity in the world. It concludes with God's reply and a description of the Day of the Lord.

Hadassah. Another name for Esther, heroine of the Scroll of Esther.

Hagar. Egyptian handmaid of Sarah and mother of Ishmael.

Haggai. Postexilic prophet (ca. 520 b.c.e.) whose book is the tenth of the Minor Prophets. Haggai calls for the rebuilding of the Temple and foretells its glory.

Hagiographa. Meaning "holy writings," the Hagiographa is the Greek word used to designate the third division of the Hebrew Bible, called *Ketuvim* in Hebrew. Books in the Hagiograph include: Psalms, Proverbs, Job, Song of Songs, Ruth, Lamentations, Ecclesiastes, Esther, Daniel, Ezra, Nehemiah, I Chronicles, and II Chronicles.

Half Shekel. The shekel is a silver unit of weight, becoming current as a coin in the time of the Maccabees. In accordance with Exodus 30:13, the

Israelites in the wilderness paid a levy of one half shekel for the maintenance of the sanctuary.

Halleluyah. Hebrew, meaning "praise the Lord," halleluyah is often used as a refrain at the beginning and end of certain PSALMS.

Ham. Son of NOAH. On account of his unseemly behavior toward his father, his descendants, the CANAANITES, were cursed and condemned to servitude (GENESIS 9:20ff.).

Haman. Chief minister of AHASUERUS, king of Persia. His resentment of the Jews led to his scheme of attempted annihilation of them. ESTHER foiled his plans and Haman and his sons were hanged.

Hammurabi. Semitic king ruling in BABYLON (1728–1686 B.C.E.) and known for his famous legal code. There is much resemblance between his code and biblical legislation.

Hananiah. There are many biblical Hananiahs in the Hebrew Bible. Among them are included: (1) leader of the tribe of BENJAMIN (I CHRONICLES 8:24); (2) army commander of UZZIAH, king of Judea; (2 Chronicles 26:11); (3) son of ZERUBBABEL who led the children of Israel from EXILE in Babylon back to JUDEA (I Chronicles 3:19, 21); and (4) leader of Judah who helped rebuild the JERUSALEM walls in the days of NEHEMIAH (Nehemiah 3:30).

Hannah. Mother of SAMUEL and wife of Elkanah. When barren, she vowed that if she became mother of a son, he would be consecrated to the service of God. Her prayer being answered, she brought the child Samuel to serve Eli the priest (I SAMUEL 2:1–10).

Haplography. A scribal error referring to the accidental omission of a letter when copying a biblical text.

Haran. Brother of ABRAHAM and father of LOT. Haran was also a trading town of northwest MESOPOTAMIA, mentioned several times in the Bible with reference to the PATRIARCHS.

Hazor. Name of several ancient sites in Israel. The best known is situated in northeast GALILEE. Hazor was the center of the league led by Jabin, which was defeated by Barak (JUDGES 4).

Heart. In Hebrew, *lev*. Character, personality, will, and mind are modern terms that all reflect something of the meaning of "heart" in its biblical usage (e.g., ECCLESIASTES 1:17; PROVERBS 16:23).

Heave Offering. In Hebrew, *terumah*. General name for an offering to the Sanctuary or to the PRIESTS. It refers to the produce TITHES, the priest's dough offering, and the HALF SHEKEL that had to be contributed to the SANCTUARY.

Hebrew. In Hebrew, *ivri,* denoting either a descendant of Eber, grandson of SHEM (GENESIS 10:24), or one who comes from the other side of the river (Euphrates). ABRAHAM is called "the Hebrew" (GENESIS 14:13), and the term was later sometimes used interchangeably with Israelites (Exodus 9:1, passim).

Hebrew Bible. The authorized Bible of the Jewish people, it consists of thirty-nine books with three main sections: Five Books of Moses, Prophets, and Writings. The Hebrew Bible is also called the Old Testament or the Tanach.

Hebron. In the Bible also called *Kiryat Arba,* ancient city of Judah, south of Jerusalem. Hebron was controlled by the Hittites. Abraham bought from them a plot of land in which to bury Sarah (Cave of Machpelah).

Henotheism. Worship of one god without denying the existence of other gods.

Herod the Great. (ca. 73–74 b.c.e.) King of Judea, son of Antipater and grandson of Antipas, rulers of Edom. Herod captured Jerusalem and destroyed the house of the Hasmoneans. An achievement that brought him great fame was the rebuilding of the Temple (20–19 b.c.e.).

Heth. Son of Canaan and grandson of Ham, he was the acknowledged ancestor of the Hittite tribe.

Hexapla. Bible prepared by Origen of Alexandria. It consists of six columns that include four Greek translations of Hebrew text, the Greek text in Hebrew letters, and a transliteration of the Hebrew words in Greek.

Hezekiah. King of Judea, 720–692 b.c.e. In contrast to his father Ahaz, he attempted to break the country's dependence on Assyria. To this end he freed religious worship from Assyrian influence and purged the Temple of images and pagan altars.

High Place. Place for worship, usually on a hill or mountain, where an altar was built, a pillar erected, and a sacred tree planted in the vicinity. Sanctuaries of this nature were common among the Canaanites and other ancient neighbors of the Israelites.

High Priest. Chief official in the Temple. The office of High Priest was conferred on Aaron and his descendants, who held it until the reign of Herod. High priests performed the sacrificial rites and conducted services in the Sanctuary.

Higher Criticism. A way of studying the Bible critically. This methodology deals with questions of authorship, date of composition, style, and specific interests of the various literary elements that make up the Bible. Baruch Spinoza is generally regarded as the founder of higher criticism.

Hilkiah. High Priest in the time of King Josiah (seventh century). He found a "book of the law" (II Kings 22:8) during the renovations to the Temple. Hilkiah is also the name of the father of the Prophet Jeremiah.

Hittites. Ancient people inhabiting Asia Minor. The Bible connects the Hittites with the Canaanites (Genesis 10:15). Abraham purchased the Cave of MACHPELAH from Hittites and ESAU took wives from among them. The Hittites were one of the seven people from whom the Israelites conquered Canaan.

Holiness Code. Found in LEVITICUS 17–26, this compilation of laws is called the Holiness Code on account of the phrase "for I Adonai, who sanctify you, am holy" (Leviticus 21:8). This code consists mainly of stipulations in connection with the SANCTUARY, the PRIESTS, and the COVENANT community.

Holofernes. ASSYRIAN general in the APOCRYPHAL Book of JUDITH. Judith succeeded in beheading him.

Holy Convocations. An assembly called together for worship at the SANCTUARY. Although it was only on the three PILGRIMAGE FESTIVALS (SUKKOT, PASSOVER, SHAVUOT) that the Israelites were to appear before Adonai at the Sanctuary (LEVITICUS 23:4ff), many would also come on the Day of Atonement.

Holy of Holies. Referring to the most sacred place in the ancient sanctuary that held the ARK OF THE COVENANT with the stone tablets of the TEN COMMANDMENTS. Only the HIGH PRIEST could enter this sacred place.

Hophni. Priest at SHILOH, son of Eli. The Bible describes his evil behavior and his death in battle at the hands of the Philistines (I SAMUEL 1–4).

Horeb, Mount. Mountain at the foot of which MOSES saw the BURNING BUSH (EXODUS 3). In DEUTERONOMY, the name replaces SINAI, and the two mountains have become identical.

Hosanna. Literally, "save now." Hosanna is a refrain, taken from PSALM 118:25, in the special liturgical poems recited during the festival of SUKKOT.

Hosea. Last ruler of the kingdom of ISRAEL (732–724 B.C.E.) before it was engulfed by the rising tide of ASSYRIAN imperialism. Also name of MINOR PROPHET who conceived of the relationship between God and Israel as an almost physical love.

House of David. Referring to the descendants of KING DAVID. The Jewish messianic hope is attached to David's descendants.

House of Israel. Biblical term referring to the whole nation of Israel (e.g., ISAIAH 5:7).

Hur. One of the children of Israel in the desert. In the battle against the AMALEKITES, MOSES had to keep his rod lifted and AARON and Hur held up his hands. Hur was the also the name of one of the five MIDIANITE kings killed by the Israelites in the desert.

Hurrians. Ancient people who invaded Syria and ancient Israel in the seventeenth century B.C.E. They fused Akkadian mythology with their own tradition and were responsible for transmitting its culture to the HITTITES.

I Am That I Am. The answer that Moses receives from God when he asks God for the Divine name in the area of the Burning Bush (Exodus 3:13–14). Often understood as "God will be as God will be," foretelling His promise of Divine power as redeemer and deliverer.

Ibn Ezra, Abraham. (1092–1167 c.e.) Famous Spanish Jewish grammarian and Bible exegete. His Bible commentaries were based on linguistic and factual examinations of the text and occasionally even included hints that foreshadow Bible criticism.

Idolatry. The ancient practice of worshipping idols as gods. Idolatry made the heaviest inroads in the Northern Kingdom, where the worship centered around the golden calves set up by Jeroboam. Judaism was the only religion in the ancient world to oppose idol worship.

Image of God. Referring to God's desire to make humans in God's likeness (Genesis 1:26). This is often understood to mean that human nature is radically different from God's, but humans are capable of approaching God's actions: Divine mercy, love, and justice.

Incense. Materials used to produce fragrant odors that often accompanied burnt offerings. The ingredients are described briefly in Exodus 30:34–38.

Ingathering, Feast of. In Hebrew, *Chag Ha'asiph*. Name given to the Feast of Tabernacles, Sukkot, which falls at the end of the agricultural year (Exodus 23:16).

Inheritance of Daughters. In biblical times, only sons could inherit. The book of Numbers (27, 36) proclaims new legislation that permits daughters to inherit (in the absence of sons), but only when married to a member of their father's tribe.

Isaac. Second of the three patriarchs, his forthcoming birth was announced by angels to his aged parents, Abraham and Sarah. He was saved by Divine intervention on Mount Moriah when Abraham, in obedience to God's command, was about to offer him as a sacrifice.

Isaiah. Prophet in Jerusalem (740–701 b.c.e.). In the book of Isaiah, the prophet protests strongly against moral laxity. His famous vision described a time when "nation shall not lift up sword against nation, neither shall men learn war anymore" (Isaiah 2:4). Modern scholars speak of several Isaiahs (including Deutero–Isaiah and Trito–Isaiah).

Ishmael. Eldest son of Abraham; his mother was Sarah's Egyptian handmaid Hagar. He is traditionally the ancestor of the Arab peoples to whom the name Ishmaelites was applied in the Middle Ages.

Israel. The new name given to Jacob after his night of wrestling at Penuel. Israel also refers to the nation that traces its ancestory back to the twelve sons of Jacob (e.g., Genesis 34:7).

Issachar. Fifth son of Jacob and Leah, and ancestor of the tribe that settled on the west bank of the Jordan near the Sea of Galilee.

J School. According to the DOCUMENTARY HYPOTHESIS, the first school of writers and editors to gather and assemble the oral traditions and experiences of the Israelites. The J School is named after the name of the Deity, J-H-V-H, that appears in the writings of this first school. The school's work was completed about 850 B.C.E.

Jabbok. River flowing into the JORDAN, marking the frontier between the Ammonites and Amorites. JACOB wrestled with the angel by the ford of the Jabbok (GENESIS 32), where his name was changed to ISRAEL.

Jacob. Third of the PATRIARCHS and the younger of the twin sons of ISAAC and REBEKKAH. Jacob cheated his twin brother ESAU out of their blind father's deathbed blessing by impersonating him.

Jacob's Ladder. A ladder that JACOB saw in a dream, with ANGELS of God ascending and descending. In this vision God promised to bless Jacob and to bring his descendants into the PROMISED LAND.

Jair. Israelite hero of the EXODUS period. He captured a group of villages in North Gilead from the Amorites (NUMBERS 32:41). Jair was also the name of an Israelite JUDGE (Judges 10:3) originating from Gilead.

Japheth. Son of NOAH. In his father's blessing, he was promised wide territories. The Bible regards him as the progenitor of fourteen peoples (GENESIS 10:2).

Jashar, Book of. Ancient work mentioned in JOSHUA 10:13, the book seems to have contained poems concerning events and historical personalities from the time of Joshua to the commencement of the Royal Period.

Jason. A HIGH PRIEST (175–172 B.C.E.), son of the high priest Simon II and leader of the hellenizing party.

Jebusites. CANAANITE people who settled in ancient Israel prior to the Israelite conquest. They lived in the vicinity of JERUSALEM, which they called Jebus.

Jedediah. Wife of King Ammon of JUDEA and mother of King JOSIAH (II KINGS 22:1).

Jehoiachin. King of JUDEA and son of JOSIAH, he reigned from 608–598 B.C.E. He was made king by PHARAOH Necoh in succession to his brother Jehoahaz.

Jehoiada. (Ninth century B.C.E.) HIGH PRIEST in JERUSALEM, under whose influence the BAAL cult was prohibited, its sanctuaries destroyed, and the TEMPLE in Jerusalem restored.

Jehoram. King of JUDEA, son of Jehoshaphat (reigned 853–842 B.C.E.).

Jehovah. Traditional but inaccurate Christian reading of the Hebrew Tetragrammaton. It resulted from overlooking the fact that the vowels with which the letters of the Divine name YHVH were provided by the MASORETES are those of ADONAI.

Jehu. King of Israel, reigning from 842–814 B.C.E. While the commander-in-chief of JEHORAM, he conspired with the army and annihilated the royal family, including Jehoram, Ahaziah of Judah, and the queen mother JEZEBEL.

Jephthah. (Twelfth century B.C.E.) Israelite judge, living in Gilead. Before fighting the Ammonites he vowed to sacrifice whatever came first from his home should he return safely. He was met by his daughter and, with her consent, carried out his vow (JUDGES 11).

Jeremiah. (Seventh–sixth century B.C.E.) PROPHET belonging to a priestly family of Anathoth near JERUSALEM, he witnessed the tragic events in the history of JUDEA that ended in the destruction of Jerusalem. His prophecies foretell the doom of his people as punishment for their sins. Jeremiah is the second of the major prophets.

Jericho. Ancient city situated several miles north of the DEAD SEA. The key to JERUSALEM and all CANAAN from the east, it was stormed by JOSHUA and all the succeeding conquerors attacking the land from that direction. Today modern Jericho is an Arab city.

Jeroboam. Jeroboam I was king of Israel from 930–910 B.C.E. To combat the influence of the JERUSALEM TEMPLE, he set up new shrines at BETH EL and DAN that centered around the symbols of the GOLDEN CALVES. Biblical sources are violently hostile to him because he caused the Israelites to sin. Jeroboam II was king of Israel from 784–744 B.C.E. Under his rule the northern kingdom attained the climax of its military and political prosperity.

Jerusalem. The capital of Israel ever since DAVID established his throne there about 1000 B.C.E. Jerusalem has also been called ZION in the Bible, as well as the City of David.

Jeshurun. Poetic name for the Jewish people (DEUTERONOMY 32:15); it literally means "the upright one."

Jethro. MIDIANITE priest and father of ZIPPORAH, wife of MOSES (EXODUS 2–3). After the EXODUS, Jethro visited Moses at Rephidim and advised him on legal administration (Exodus 18). He called a KENITE in the book of JUDGES and is called several names in Exodus, which allows scholars to associate him with the Kenite tribe, even though he is called a Midianite.

Jezebel. Wife of Ahab, she introduced her native BAAL cult into Israel, arousing the anger of the religious elements led by ELIJAH. She is depicted in the Bible (I KINGS 16:31–II Kings 9) as a bloodthirsty woman who persecuted PROPHETS.

Jezreel. Name of two ancient cities. One was located in the territory of the tribe of ISSACHAR (I KINGS 21), and the other was located in JUDAH (JOSHUA 15:56).

JHVH. An ancient name for God, probably pronounced Yahweh, which the Christians pronounced Jehovah.

Joab. (Tenth century B.C.E.) David's nephew and commander-in-chief. A courageous commander, Joab gained a decisive victory over the Ammonites.

Joash. King of JUDEA (836–797 B.C.E.), he restored the TEMPLE. Joash was also the name of another King of Judah (800–785 B.C.E.), who captured JERUSALEM, plundered the Temple, and reduced the country to vassaldom.

Job. Third book in the biblical section called WRITINGS, the theme of Job is divine justice and the problem of suffering of the righteous. In the end, Job learns that people can never really understand the mystery of the Lord's ways. The magnificent poetic description of Job's trials and his patient faith, together with the lofty descriptions of Divine power, make the Book of Job one of the great wisdom books in the Bible.

Joel. Second in the order of the twelve MINOR PROPHETS, the Book of Joel calls the people of JUDEA to repent because the DAY OF JUDGMENT is at hand.

Jonathan. Eldest son of SAUL and devoted friend of DAVID. His bravery in the wars with the PHILISTINES won him great popularity. His close friendship with David, whom he defended against his father's anger, became proverbial.

Jordan River. Chief river of ancient Israel, flowing from MOUNT HERMON to the DEAD SEA. MOSES was not allowed by God to cross the Jordan River into the PROMISED LAND.

Joseph. Son of RACHEL and JACOB, he was the favorite son and was given a COAT OF MANY COLORS. Both a dreamer and an interpreter of dreams, Joseph aroused the jealousy of his brothers and was sold as a slave to an EGYPT-bound caravan. There he quickly rose to power as PHARAOH'S viceroy.

Joshua. The son of Nun, Joshua was chosen to succeed MOSES as leader of the Israelites. He led Israel across the JORDAN, conquered the Jericho fortress, and defeated the hostile CANAANITE tribes. The Book of Joshua is the sixth in the Bible, following the Book of DEUTERONOMY.

Josiah. King of JUDEA (637–608 B.C.E.), he began a program of religious reform, removing foreign cults that had previously taken hold in Judea. In the course of repairing the TEMPLE, the HIGH PRIEST HILKIAH announced the discovery of the book of the Law, which greatly influenced Josiah, who subsequently removed the HIGH PLACES and centralized worship at the Jerusalem Temple.

Jotham. King of JUDEA (751–735 B.C.E.) who defeated the Ammonites and resisted the pressure of the king of Aram to join an anti-Assyrian alliance. Jotham was also the name of the youngest of Gideon's seventy sons and the sole survivor of Abimelech's massacre of his brothers (JUDGES 9).

Jubilee Year. The Bible ordains a rest from agricultural work in ancient Israel once in every seven years (LEVITICUS 25:3ff). Any crops in the seventh year are communal property. The year following seven fallow years—that is, the 50th year—is the Jubilee year (Leviticus 25:8), when cultivation is also prohibited, slaves are freed, and land purchased since the previous Jubilee reverts to its original owner.

Judah. Fourth son of Jacob's first wife, Leah. He was involved in the events that led to Joseph's becoming a slave in Egypt.

Judea. The southerly of the two kingdoms into which ancient Israel was divided in 933 b.c.e. after the death of Solomon, the northerly being the kingdom of Israel. Judea comprised the tribe of Judah, most of Benjamin, and absorbed the tribe of Simeon. Most of the prophets carried out their activities in Judea.

Judges. (Twelfth and eleventh centuries b.c.e.) The Book of Judges spans the period from the death of Joshua to the time of Saul's coronation. During the era of the Judges, Mesopotamian enemies from the north, the Moabites, and the Midianites from Sinai subjugated the Israelites. The judges were called to leadership by the people and their battles eventually extended Israelite mastery of the land. There were sixteen judges in all. Two of them, Deborah and Samuel, were also prophets.

Judith. Book of the Apocrypha, describing the siege of Bethulia and the flight of the Assyrians after Judith succeeded in beheading their general, Holofernes.

Kadesh Barnea. Oasis in the wilderness of Paran and camping place of the Israelites on their journey from Egypt (Numbers 13:26). It was one of the southernmost points of the territory of the land of Israel as envisaged by Moses.

Kedar. Nomadic tribe (Isaiah 21:16) related to the Ishmaelites (Genesis 25:13). They lived in what is now the Arabian desert, and their distinctive black tents (Song of Songs 1:5) were familiar to the Israelites.

Kedron. The Kedron brook begins to the north of Jerusalem and passes the Mount of Olives en route to the Dead Sea. David passed over the Kedron on his way out of Jerusalem during Absalom's revolt (II Samuel 15:23). The reforming kings, such as Hezekiah and Josiah, used the valley as a place for destroying heathen idols and altars.

Kenites. Tribe inhabiting the Negev and the Sinai desert, bordering on the territory of the Amalekites (I Samuel 15:6). The Israelites had a treaty with them from the time of Moses. The Kenite hypothesis is a theory that suggests that Jethro, called a Kenite (in Judges 1:16; 4:11), taught Moses about monotheism.

Keturah. Abraham's second wife, he married her after Sarah's death (Genesis 25:1).

Kimchi, David. (1160–1235) Franco-Spanish exegete and grammarian. He provided Bible students with logical, grammatical explanations of difficult words and passages. His commentary profoundly influenced the Authorized Version of 1611.

Kings, Book of. In the Bible, the First and Second Books of Kings cover the history of the kingdoms of Israel and Judea, from Solomon, 970 B.C.E., to the destruction of Judea by Babylon in 586 B.C.E.

King James Version. Alternately called the Authorized Version, it was King James who took a leading part in organizing a project that would result in a new translation of the Bible. Approximately fifty translators were involved, and in 1611 the new Bible was printed.

Korach. A Levite related to Moses who, together with Dathan and Abiram and 250 Israelite notables, rebelled against Moses and Aaron (Numbers 16) in an attempt to seize away their leadership. However, the earth opened up and swallowed them, and only Korach's sons survived (Numbers 26:11).

Laban. Brother of Rebekkah, father of Leah and Rachel. He gave his sister Rebekkah in marriage to Isaac. Years later, he consented to the marriage of his daughter Rachel to Jacob, but substituted her sister Leah at the wedding. Subsequently he also gave him Rachel in exchange for a further seven years of service by Jacob.

Lamekh. According to one genealogical tree, descendant of Seth and father of Noah (Genesis 5:4–29). According to another (Genesis 4:18–24), he was a descendant of Cain.

Lamentations. Third of the five scrolls in the Hagiographa section of the Bible. It contains five chapters of elegies and mourning over the destruction by the Babylonians of Judea, Jerusalem, and the Temple. According to rabbinic tradition, the author was Jeremiah. Lamentations is read in the synagogue on the fast of Tisha B'av.

Lamps. The central illumination in the Tabernacle and Temple was given by the seven oil lamps included in the menorah, the candelabrum.

"Land of Milk and Honey." A biblical poetic name for the Promised Land. The spies sent by Moses to scout out the land called it "the land of milk and honey" (Numbers 13:27).

Latter Prophets. The Latter Prophets consist of fifteen books that present the teachings of the prophets of Israel. These begin with the three Major Prophets, Isaiah, Jeremiah, and Ezekiel, and conclude with the twelve books of the Minor Prophets. Minor prophets include Hosea, Joel, Amos, Obadiah, Jonah, Micah, Nahum, Habakkuk, Zephaniah, Haggai, Zechariah, and Malachi.

Law. The Torah (Five Books of Moses) is sometimes referred to as the Book of Law. Tables of the Law usually refer to the Ten Commandments.

Leah. Daughter of Laban, and wife of Jacob. She bore him six sons: Reuben, Simeon, Levi, Judah, Issachar, and Zebulun, and a daughter called Dinah. Known as one of the matriarchs.

Leaven. In Hebrew, *chametz*. Fermented dough made from flour of the primary grains (wheat, rye, barley, spelt, oats). Leaven is prohibited during the Passover holiday and was forbidden for use as a MEAL OFFERING in most of the TEMPLE SACRIFICES.

Lebanon. Middle Eastern republic. The Bible refers to the mountains of Lebanon, famed for their cedars (PSALM 92:13).

Lemuel. King of Maasa mentioned in the Book of PROVERBS, who was taught by his mother that kings should not waste their energies pursuing women but should look after the needy and the poor (PROVERBS 31:1–9).

Leprosy. A dreaded disease often described in the Bible (LEVITICUS 13:1ff). Incurring leprosy (believed to be a Divine punishment) debarred both Israelites and priests from fulfilling their duties toward the SANCTUARY.

Levi. Third son of JACOB and LEAH. The tribe of Levi received no allotment of land in ancient Israel because it was set apart to conduct the worship of God. Instead, the Levites received for their maintenance a portion of the TITHES brought by the worshippers to the TABERNACLE.

Leviathan. Legendary sea creature, described in several places in the Bible, and particularly in JOB 40:25.

Levirate Marriage. Marriage with a brother's childless widow. Although it is forbidden to marry a brother's widow where there are children, such marriage is commanded where the brother has left no offspring (DEUTERONOMY 25:5).

Levites. Descendants of LEVI, third son of JACOB. From ages 20 to 50, the Levite was consecrated to render service at the SANCTUARY, where the Israelites worshipped God by bringing sacrifices to the ALTAR. They were gatekeepers, JUDGES, teachers of the Law, temple musicians, and assistants to the PRIESTS.

Leviticus. Third of the FIVE BOOKS OF MOSES, it contains a manual for LEVITES, the priestly ritual of SACRIFICES, the HOLINESS CODE, rules regarding charity, marriage, and laws governing many other aspects of life.

Lord of Hosts. In Hebrew, *Adonai Tzevaot*. One of a large number of biblical appellations for God. It is a title of might and power, and is especially common in the prophetic books of ISAIAH, JEREMIAH, and ZECHARIAH.

Lot. Son of ABRAHAM's brother Haran. He journeyed with his uncle to CANAAN, but as a result of a quarrel they parted company. Lot settled at SODOM, where he was captured by five kings and subsequently rescued by Abraham. The Bible relates his escape from Sodom and the misfortune of his wife, who turned into a pillar of salt.

Lower Criticism. The study of ancient manuscripts and versions of the Bible with the purpose of establishing the most trustworthy text of the Hebrew and Greek Testaments.

Maccabees. Name of the priestly family of the HASMONEANS from the town of MODIN in PALESTINE. They led the struggle (167–160 B.C.E.) against

Antiochus Epiphanes, King of Syria, and succeeded in freeing **Judea** from Syrian oppression. In 165 B.C.E. they cleared and cleansed the **Jerusalem Temple,** and the festival of **Chanukah** was declared.

Machlon. Elder son of Elimelech and Naomi, Machlon and his brother Chilion left their home in **Bethlehem** during a famine and settled in **Moab.** They married Moabite wives, **Ruth** and **Orpah,** and died ten years later.

Machpelah. Cave near **Hebron.** When **Sarah** died, **Abraham** purchased it from Ephron the **Hittite (Genesis** 23). It became the burial crypt of the **patriarchs** and **matriarchs** and a place of pilgrimage.

Mahanaim. Place in **Gilead** where **Jacob** encountered a troop of **angels (Genesis** 32:3).

Major Prophets. Referring to the biblical prophets **Isaiah, Jeremiah,** and **Ezekiel.**

Malachi. Last of the biblical **prophets** (ca. 460–450 B.C.E.). In his book Malachi protests against transgressions in matters of **sacrifice** and **tithes** and complains of mixed and broken marriages. His **eschatology** contains the influential innovation of a vision of "**the Day of the Lord**" preceded by the advent of **Elijah.**

Mamre. Locality in the vicinity of **Hebron** and named after one of **Abraham's** friends **(Genesis** 14:13).

Manasseh. First son of **Joseph** and Asenath **(Genesis** 41:50–51). In blessing Joseph's two sons, **Jacob** conferred on them an equal portion with his own sons in the division of **Canaan.** Manasseh was also the name of the King of **Judea** (692–638 B.C.E.). Depicted in the Bible as one of the worst Jewish monarchs, he introduced pagan practices.

Mannah. Food eaten by the Israelites in the desert **(Exodus** 16:4–35). It was found on the ground every morning except the **Sabbath.**

Marah. The first named Israelite camp after the **Red Sea** crossing. It was called Marah (literally, bitter) because only bitter water was found there **(Exodus** 15:23).

Marduk. Babylonian deity. In mythology he was regarded as the main opponent of the monster Tiamat and as creator of the world and mankind. King of the gods, he determined people's fate at the beginning of the year.

Masoretes. Jewish scribes from 500 to 1000 C.E. who meticulously copied the Scriptures and preserved them. The work of the Masoretes produced the Masoretic Text of the Bible (i.e., the current **Hebrew** text). They set the musical notes for reading, called *ta'amei hamikra.*

Matriarchs. The founding mothers of the Israelites, **Sarah, Rebekkah, Rachel,** and **Leah.**

Mattathias. A **priest** and father of the **Hasmonean** brothers, he waged war on the Syrians. After his death he was succeeded by his son **Judah the Maccabee.**

Meal Offering. An offering made of flour. When used as a THANKSGIVING OFFERING, it was mixed with oil and frankincense and seasoned with salt, but when a SIN OFFERING, it was without oil and frankincense. Part was offered upon the altar, and the rest belonged to the PRIEST.

Mechilta. Oldest rabbinic commentary on the Book of EXODUS.

Megiddo. Ancient city in the JEZREEL Valley, at the foot of the SAMARIAN hills, and the scene of many battles. JOSHUA subjugated the CANAANITE king of Megiddo (JOSHUA 12:21). Its *tel,* or mound, has been the subject of archaeological excavations since 1903.

Megillot. A Hebrew word meaning scrolls. In the Hebrew Bible, SONG OF SONGS, RUTH, LAMENTATIONS, ECCLESIASTES, and ESTHER are designated as the Five Megillot.

Melchizedek. King of Salem. When ABRAHAM returned from his pursuit of five Mesopotamian kings, Melchizedek blessed him in the name of "God the Most High" (GENESIS 14:18-20).

Menorah. Golden seven-branched candelabrum that was one of the most prominent features of the TABERNACLE and TEMPLE. The menorah was the symbol of Judaism in the first century and is frequently portrayed on tombs and monuments.

Meribah. Referring to the place in the Bible (EXODUS 17:7) where the Israelites complained to MOSES because of lack of water.

Messianic Age. Described in the Bible as a time when peace and serenity will fill the world, the wolf will dwell with the lamb, and the leopard shall lie down with the kid (see ISAIAH 11:6ff).

Methusaleh. Biblical figure, son of ENOCH and father of LAMEKH. He died at the age of 969 (GENESIS 5:25-27), the oldest person recorded in the Bible.

Micah. (Eighth century B.C.E.) PROPHET in JUDEA, he speaks for the people against the oppression of the ruling classes, being the first to threaten them with EXILE to BABYLON. His book is one of the twelve books of the so-called MINOR PROPHETS.

Michael. The prince of angels (DANIEL 10:13). As the archangel nearest to God, he is the chief of the Divine messengers and executes God's judgments.

Michal. Younger daughter of Saul and wife of DAVID, she assisted him to escape Saul's jealousy.

Midian. Bedouin tribe related to ABRAHAM (GENESIS 25:2). Its members traveled with caravans of incense from GILEAD to EGYPT. MOSES fled from PHARAOH to Midian and married there the daughter of JETHRO, a Midianite PRIEST.

Minor Prophets. Twelve prophetical books (HOSEA, JOEL, AMOS, OBADIAH, JONAH, MICAH, NAHUM, HABAKKUK, ZEPHANIAH, HAGGAI, ZECHARIAH, and MALACHI) placed in the HEBREW BIBLE after the Book of EZEKIEL. Their dates range between the eighth and the fifth centuries B.C.E.

Miriam. Elder sister of MOSES, who watched as her infant brother was placed in a basket on the NILE. On her suggestion, PHARAOH's daughter, who found the baby, called the child's mother to nurse him. After the RED SEA crossing, Miriam led the Israelite women in a triumphal song and dance.

Moab. Country in what is now known as south TRANSJORDAN. The Moabites were kindred to the Israelites, being traditionally descended, like the Ammonites, from LOT (GENESIS 19:37).

Molech. Name of a pagan deity. The CANAANITES sacrificed human beings, especially firstborn children, to Molech by passing them through fire.

Monotheism. The belief in one God. Monotheism is generally held to be a late development in the history of religion, being preceded by polytheism (belief in many gods). Jewish monotheism is enshrined in the biblical formula (DEUTERONOMY 6:4), "Hear O Israel, Adonai is Our God, Adonai is One."

Mordecai. (Fifth century B.C.E.) Benjamite who served as a palace official at SHUSHAN in the reign of AHASUERUS. His niece ESTHER was wedded to the king. Through her intervention, Ahasuerus learned from Mordecai of an assassination plot against him. Mordecai eventually became chief minister to the king.

Moses. Lawgiver, PROPHET, and founder of the Jewish religion. Moses led the Israelites out of EGYPT on the journey that became known as the EXODUS. Shortly thereafter, he received the TEN COMMANDMENTS from God on MOUNT SINAI.

Myrrh. An ingredient of the holy anointing oil (EXODUS 30:23–33) and prized for its aromatic qualities (PSALM 45:8).

Myth(os). A story about the universe that is considered sacred. Mythological stories deal with great moments in life: birth, initiation, and death. The word "myth" was first applied to the Bible in the eighteenth century when the question of the historicity of the creation story of GENESIS arose. Numerous pagan myths have found their way into the Bible (e.g., God's struggle with the primeval dragon in ISAIAH 27:1; 51:9).

Naaman. (Ninth century B.C.E.) General of Aram-Dammesek, he became afflicted with leprosy and went to Israel to consult Elisha, who cured him. Naaman took soil back to Syria upon which to build an altar to God. This is the only biblical instance of a religious conversion.

Nabateans. Occupants of EDOM in the sixth century B.C.E. Originally nomads, they eventually established a chain of agricultural settlements across the NEGEV.

Nachshon. Chief of the tribe of JUDAH during the EXODUS, brother-in-law of AARON and ancestor of DAVID, who, according to the MIDRASH, was the first to enter the RED SEA.

Nachum. Seventh-century PROPHET who foretold the fall of NINEVEH. His book is one of the twelve MINOR PROPHETS.

Nadab. King of Israel (913–911 B.C.E.) and son and successor of JEROBOAM. While fighting the PHILISTINES, he was assassinated by his rival Baasha (I KINGS 15:25–31). Nadab was also the name of one of Aaron's eldest sons, who along with his brother Abihu sacrificed "strange fire" on the ALTAR. In punishment both were mortally struck by Divine fire (LEVITICUS 10:1–3).

Naphtali. Sixth son of JACOB, his second by Bilhah. The inheritance of the tribe descended from him was in the northern part of CANAAN, including the entire east coast of the SEA OF GALILEE. The tribe was active in the war against SISERA and GIDEON's campaign against the MIDIANITES.

Nathan. A prophet who announced to DAVID that his royal house would be perpetually established. As a protagonist of moral values, he charged David with responsibility for the death of Uriah the Hittite. Later he was prominent in securing the succession for SOLOMON.

Nazirite. Religious devotee who vowed not to drink any liquor, nor to have his hair cut, and to avoid ritual uncleanliness through proximity to corpses (NUMBERS 6:2). Parents could dedicate their children as Nazirites before birth (e.g., SAMSON).

Near East. A region in western Asia and northeastern Africa, often considered the same as the Middle East.

Nebuchadnezzar (or Nebuchadrezzar). King of BABYLON (605–562 B.C.E.). In 586 he captured JERUSALEM, destroyed the TEMPLE, and EXILED the masses.

Nehemiah. (Fifth century B.C.E.) Governor of JUDEA who devoted himself to social reforms, including the stimulation of SABBATH observance, the cancellation of debts owed by the poor, and steps against mixed marriages. His work was decisive in the rebuilding of Judea, and his memoirs form the basis of the biblical Book of NEHEMIAH in the HAGIOGRAPHA.

Nephilim. Semilegendary race created (according to GENESIS 6:4) by the union of the "sons of God" and the "daughters of man." The term was applied hyperbolically to the inhabitants of the land of CANAAN by the spies sent by MOSES to scout out the land (NUMBERS 13:33).

Nile River. River in EGYPT that appears numerous times in the Bible. For example, the infant MOSES was sent away in a basket down the Nile River. In the story of the TEN PLAGUES in Egypt, the Nile River became filled with blood.

Nineveh. Capital of the new ASSYRIAN EMPIRE (from 1100 B.C.E.). JONAH the PROPHET was sent to Nineveh to persuade its citizens to repent.

Noachide Laws. Seven laws that the rabbis hold binding upon all mankind. Six of these laws are negative, prohibiting idolatry, blasphemy, murder, adultery, robbery, and the eating of flesh cut from a living animal. The single positive commandment is that requiring the establishment of courts of justice.

Noah. Biblical figure and hero of the Flood narratives (Genesis 6:ff). He was commanded to build an ark for himself, his wife, and specimens of all living creatures. From his sons, Shem, Ham, and Japheth, sprang the first seventy people from whom humanity was derived.

Nod. A land east of Eden to which Cain was banished by God after Cain had murdered Abel.

Numbers. Fourth book of the Bible, it relates the history of the Israelites in the desert from the second to the fortieth year of the exodus.

Nuzi Tablets. Nuzi was an ancient Mesopotamian city. Excavations have revealed that the town was inhabited by the biblical Horites. More than 4,000 tablets were found in the area, providing a detailed picture of life in an ancient Mesopotamian community.

Obadiah. Fourth of the twelve Minor Prophets, this one-chapter book severely condemns Edom for having refused to assist Jerusalem in her hour of difficulty.

Obed. (Eleventh century b.c.e.) Son of Boaz and Ruth, he was the father of Jesse and the grandfather of King David.

Og. Amorite king, known as King of Bashan. Noted for his stature and physique, he attempted to interrupt the march of the Israelites but was defeated (Numbers 21:33–35).

Old Testament. Reference to the Hebrew Bible (by Christians) in order to distinguish it from the New Testament of Christianity.

Onan. Son of Judah, he married the widow of his brother, but refused to have children by her and is said to have spilled his seed instead.

Onkelos. (First century c.e.) Palestinian proselyte, student of Rabbi Akiva and responsible for the best-known Aramaic translation of the Five Books of Moses, called the Targum.

Ophrah. (Twelfth century b.c.e.) Son of Meonothai, he and his father were leaders of the tribe of Judah (I Chronicles 4:14).

Orpah. Moabite wife of Hilion and sister-in-law of Ruth. She was dissuaded from returning to Judea with her mother-in-law Naomi (Ruth 1).

P School. According to the Documentary Hypothesis, the school of writers and editors so named because the material has a "priestly" point of view. Most of the Book of Leviticus is believed to be the work of this school. The P school is also considered responsible for inserting into the account of the Wilderness Period laws dealing with the privileges and duties of the priesthood (e.g., NUMBERS 18).

Paddan-aram. Name given to the area near Haran in Upper MESOPOTAMIA. ABRAHAM dwelt in this area before emigrating to CANAAN. He also sent his servant Eliezer there to obtain a bride for ISAAC.

Paganism. Belief in false gods.

Palestine. Name properly denoting the land of the PHILISTINES in biblical times, extending along the Mediterranean Sea. The Romans applied the name of Palestine to all of JUDEA.

Paschal Lamb. Refers to the lamb that the Israelites were commanded to SACRIFICE and whose blood was sprinkled on their doorposts in EGYPT prior to the EXODUS. In this way the Israelites were spared the death of their firstborn, since the angel of God passed over those homes on whose doorposts lamb's blood was sprinkled.

Patriarchs. The founding fathers of the Israelites, ABRAHAM, ISAAC, and JACOB.

Peace Offering. SACRIFICE, in the form of cattle or sheep, offered as a thanksgiving, in fulfillment of a vow or a free-will offering (LEVITICUS 3:7–11).

Peleg. Elder son of Eber and a great grandson of SHEM, he was called Peleg, "for in his days the earth was divided" (GENESIS 10:25).

Perez. Twin brother of Zerah, son of JUDAH and TAMAR, conceived by an incestuous relationship between Judah and his daughter-in-law Tamar. Both BOAZ (husband of RUTH) and KING DAVID were among his descendants.

Peshitta. The Syriac translation of the Bible, it served as the Bible of the Christians of Syria.

Pestilence. In Hebrew, *deber*. Refers to all sorts of disasters, and is often linked with the sword and famine (EZEKIEL 6:11, passim).

Pharaoh. Permanent title of the king of EGYPT in ancient times. The word means the "great house," and was originally applied to the royal palace.

Philistines. A seafaring people from the Mediterranean. They dominated the fertile southern coastal plain, which included the cities of GAT, EKRON, ASHDOD, ASHKELON, and GAZA. They were the indomitable enemies of Israel.

Phineas. PRIEST and grandson of AARON. In reward for his zealous action against ZIMRI, he and his descendants were promised the priesthood (NUMBERS 25). Phineas was also the name of a SHILOH priest, second son of Eli. He and his brother Hophni were killed while accompanying the ARK OF THE COVENANT into battle against the PHILISTINES (I SAMUEL 4).

Pisgah. According to DEUTERONOMY 34:1, Pisgah refers to the peak of Nebo. BALAAM prophesied from one of its summits, while from another summit MOSES saw the PROMISED LAND before his death.

Pishon. One of the four streams branching from the river surrounding Eden (GENESIS 2:11). Some have identified it with the Blue Nile of Abyssinia.

Pithom. One of the two places (with RAMESES) where the Israelites built storage cities for PHARAOH during the Egyptian bondage (EXODUS 1:11).

Plagues, The Ten. Afflictions suffered by the Egyptians as a result of PHARAOH's refusal to permit the Israelites to leave the country (EXODUS 7:14–12:34). They were blood, frogs, lice, flies, cattle disease, boils, heavy hail, locusts, darkness, and death of the firstborn.

Polytheism. Belief in or worship of a plurality of gods (antithesis of MONOTHEISM).

Potiphar. Chief of PHARAOH's bodyguard. JOSEPH was sold to him as a slave but became his chief official until imprisoned on a false charge of attempted seduction brought by Potiphar's wife.

Priestly Blessing. Formula for the blessing of the people by the descendants of AARON (NUMBERS 6:24–26). This blessing was given daily by the PRIESTS in the Temple.

Promised Land. The land that God promised to ABRAHAM and his descendants. It is often used synonymously with the Land of Israel.

Prophet. In the Bible, persons who bring a message from God to the people. Their most frequent themes are worship of God, ethical living, and the coming of the MESSIAH.

Proselyte. Referring to a convert to Judaism. A most famous biblical proselyte was RUTH the Moabite.

Proverbs. Biblical book, the second in the HAGIOGRAPHA, it is a collection of moral sayings.

Psalms. First book in the HAGIOGRAPHA section of the Bible, it consists of 150 psalms traditionally ascribed to KING DAVID, often called the Psalmist.

Pseudepigrapha. Noncanonical Jewish literature written during the period of the second TEMPLE and some time after its destruction. The name Pseudepigrapha denotes books ascribed to imaginary authors who take pen names from the great heroes of Israel's history.

Ptolemy. Name of the first Macedonian king of EGYPT and the originator of the Ptolemaic dynasty, all the kings of which bore this name.

Puah. One of the midwives who disobeyed PHARAOH's orders to kill the Hebrew male children at birth (EXODUS 1:15).

Qumran (also Kumran). Site on the northwest shore of the DEAD SEA. The DEAD SEA SCROLLS were discovered in the nearby caves of Qumran.

Rachel. Second wife of JACOB, and one of the four MATRIARCHS of the Jewish people. Jacob wished to wed Rachel but was tricked into marriage with her elder sister LEAH. Rachel was the mother of JOSEPH and BENJAMIN, and died near BETHLEHEM. The biblical image (JEREMIAH 31:15) of the compassionate mother Rachel weeping for her children driven into captivity became a favorite figure in Jewish folklore.

Rahab. JERICHO woman who housed and shielded the spies sent by Joshua (JOSHUA 2). As a reward, both she and her family were spared.

Ramses. Ancient Egyptian city in the NILE Delta area where JACOB and his family settled (GENESIS 47:11). Their descendants were forced to build storehouses for the Egyptian king.

Ras Shamra. Also Ugarit. CANAANITE city of the northern Syrian coast. It was a commercial center in the mid-second millenium B.C.E. Archaeological discoveries there have added substantial knowledge to our understanding of Canaanite culture and religion.

Rashi. Acronym for Rabbi Solomon Yitzhaki ben Isaac (1040–1105). French Bible exegete and great biblical and talmudic commentator. His style is simple and concise, and his objective is to present the direct literal meaning of the text. His commentaries on the Bible and on the TALMUD have become universally popular.

Rebekkah. Wife of ISAAC, daughter of Bethuel and mother of ESAU and JACOB. Her kindness attracted the attention of ABRAHAM's servant Eliezer. She later supported Jacob in his struggle with Esau. She is also considered one of the four MATRIARCHS of the Jewish people, along with LEAH, SARAH, and RACHEL.

Red Heifer. A congregational SACRIFICE whose ashes, when mixed with water, removed impurity created by contact with the dead. The sacrificed animal, a red heifer unblemished and never yoked, was burned outside the camp; those who handled it also required purification (NUMBERS 19).

Red Sea. A branch of the Indian Ocean, it has been identified with the "Reed Sea" crossed by the Israelites during their EXODUS from Egypt (EXODUS 13:18).

Refuge, City of. Places of asylum. The Bible provides for a city of refuge in which an accidental killer was to be safe from the vengeance of the murdered person's kinsman, and where he was required to stay until the death of the reigning HIGH PRIEST (EXODUS 21:13; NUMBERS 35:11ff). There were six cities of refuge in all.

Rehoboam. King of JUDEA (933–917 B.C.E.) and son of SOLOMON by his Ammonite wife Naamah.

Rephidim. One of the Israelites' stopping places between the Wilderness of Zin and the SINAI Desert (NUMBERS 33:14–15). While the people camped there, Moses struck the rock at MOUNT HOREB and a supply of drinking water emerged.

Reuben. Eldest son of JACOB and LEAH. Reuben opposed his brothers' plot against JOSEPH (GENESIS 37) and later volunteered as collateral for BENJAMIN during the latter's visit to EGYPT (GENESIS 42).

Revelation. The act of communication from God to humans and the content of such a communication. The revelation of MOSES on MOUNT SINAI provided the Israelites with the WRITTEN LAW.

Ritual Purity. Ritual purity and impurity are important aspects of biblical law. Ritual bathing could remove the impurity that came from sexual intercourse (LEVITICUS 15:16–18). Purification following childbirth required a SIN OFFERING and a BURNT OFFERING (Leviticus 12:6–8). The most severe degree of ritual impurity came through contact with a corpse, and the purification ritual required the sprinkling of water mixed with ashes of the RED HEIFER (NUMBERS 19:17–19).

Ruth. MOABITE and ancestor of DAVID. After the death of her husband, MACHLON, she accompanied her mother-in-law Naomi back to BETHLEHEM, using these famous words: "Wherever you go, I will go . . . your people shall be my people, and your God my God." The story of Ruth is related in the Book of Ruth, one of the "Five Scrolls" incorporated in the HAGIOGRAPHA.

Sabbath. The day of rest. The Jewish Sabbath is observed weekly from shortly before sunset on Friday until nightfall on Saturday. In the TEN COMMANDMENTS, and in the FIVE BOOKS OF MOSES in general, the emphasis is on the Sabbath as a day of rest and abstention from work, "an everlasting sign between Me and the children of Israel" (EXODUS 31:17).

Sabbatical Year. The Bible ordains a rest from agricultural work in Israel once in seven years (LEVITICUS 25:3ff). Any crops in the seventh year are communal property, and slaves were allowed to go free.

Sacrifice. A cultic act giving tangible expression to a feeling of dependence on the deity. Sacrifices sought to obtain the god's favor and atone for the sins of the sacrificer. While Canaanites sacrificed human beings, the Israelites prepared animal and meal offerings (see also BURNT OFFERING, MEAL OFFERING).

Sadducees. Sect of the Second TEMPLE period, whose name likely derives from ZADOK, the HIGH PRIEST. They adhered very closely to WRITTEN LAW, and had no belief in a future world, RESURRECTION, or IMMORTALITY of the soul.

Samaria. In Hebrew, *Shomron*. Capital of the Northern Kingdom of Israel, founded ca. 880 B.C.E.

Samaritans. People with their capital at SAMARIA, descended from the tribes of EPHRAIM and MANASSEH. The religion of the Samaritans is a modification of SADDUCCEAN Judaism, except that the whole Bible for the Samaritans is the FIVE BOOKS OF MOSES. Samaritans also believe that the TEN COMMANDMENTS were given by God on MOUNT GERIZIM.

Samson. Israelite JUDGE, son of Manoah of the tribe of DAN (JUDGES 13–16).

A NAZIRITE from birth, he excelled in strength (the secret of which was his long hair). Ultimately, he fell into PHILISTINE hands as a result of the deceit of Delilah, who betrayed the secret of his strength.

Samuel. PROPHET and last Israelite JUDGE (eleventh century B.C.E.). He chose SAUL to be the first king. The two books of Samuel in the Bible describe the founding of the Kingdom of Israel and the reigns of King SAUL and King DAVID.

Sanctuary. A place set apart for the worship of God or gods. Israel's first sanctuary was the movable tent known as the TABERNACLE, where the ark containing the tables of the COVENANT was housed (EXODUS 25:8). With the settlement of Israel in the land, DAVID planned and SOLOMON completed a permanent TEMPLE in JERUSALEM.

Sarah. Wife of ABRAHAM, mother of ISAAC, and one of the four MATRIARCHS of the Jewish people.

Satan. Usually identified with the devil or the prince of the demons. In the Bible, Satan is no evil spirit, but belongs to the Divine household like any other angelic being, his function being that of accuser (JOB 1:6). In I CHRONICLES 21:1, Satan develops into a more hostile and destructive tempter.

Saul. (Eleventh century B.C.E.) Selected by SAMUEL to be Israel's first king, he defeated the Ammonites and fought successfully against the PHILISTINES, MOABITES, and AMALEKITES. His last battle was with the Philistines. Badly defeated, his sons slain by the enemy, he fell upon his sword and killed himself (I SAMUEL 8–31).

Scribe. In the Judean monarchy the king's scribe is the highest official in the land. EZRA is described as "scribe of the law of the God of Heaven." Later the term scribe came to refer to a professional copier of manuscripts and official documents. The term MASORETE was applied to certain scribes who assumed responsibility for determining the biblical text and preserving the traditions about its spelling, wording, and meaning.

Scriptures. A body of writing considered as authoritative, often referring today to the Bible.

Selah. Term found frequently in the Book of PSALMS, generally agreed to mean some sort of musical or liturgical sign.

Seleucids. HELLENISTIC royal dynasty established by Seleucus Nicator, a general of ALEXANDER THE GREAT.

Semites. Peoples speaking tongues akin to Hebrew (e.g., ASSYRIANS, Arameans, etc.).

Sennacherib. King of ASSYRIA (705–681 B.C.E.) who engaged in constant wars with Elam and BABYLON.

Sepphoris. Ancient city in the GALILEE, and seat of the patriarchate from the time of JUDAH THE PRINCE until its removal to TIBERIAS in the early third century C.E.

Septuagint. Name for the first translation of the HEBREW BIBLE into Greek, derived from the number "seventy," after the seventy rabbis who did the translation (250 B.C.E. in ALEXANDRIA, EGYPT).

Seraphim. Referring to a class of ANGELS. In ISAIAH 6:2, they appear as members of the celestial court surrounding the Divine Throne. They appear to have led in Divine worship, with one chanting the refrain "Holy, holy, holy is the LORD OF HOSTS, the whole earth is filled with His glory."

Serpent. From the period of GENESIS, the serpent symbolized an ancient power. For provoking Eve to eat the fruit of the TREE OF KNOWLEDGE, it was cursed to crawl on its belly.

Servant of the Lord. Term used by ISAIAH. According to Isaiah 42:2–4, the Servant is to preach Divine truth to the gentiles. In Isaiah 52:12–13, the Servant is portrayed as suffering vicariously. This passage has evoked considerable controversy. The Servant of the Lord has been identified with the people of Israel, the MESSIAH, and the prophet Isaiah himself. In Christian tradition, it has been identified as Jesus.

Sforno, Obadiah ben Jacob. (1475–1550) Italian physician and Bible commentator. His biblical commentaries rely on plain meaning (*peshat* in Hebrew) and sometimes on philosophy, but include no linguistic observations.

Shechem. Ancient CANAANITE town, originally situated between MOUNT GEREZIM and Mount Ebal. The biblical PATRIARCHS camped there, and it was pillaged by SIMEON and LEVI (GENESIS 34). Later, Shechem was in the territory of EPHRAIM, a levitical city and a CITY OF REFUGE.

Shekel. A silver unit of weight, and a coin in the time of the MACCABEES. In accordance with EXODUS 30:13, the Hebrews in the wilderness paid a levy of one-half shekel for the maintenance of the SANCTUARY.

Shem. One of the three sons of NOAH. According to the Bible, the nations of Elam, Asshur, Arpachshad, and Aram originated from Shem. The term SEMITE is believed to have originated from Shem.

Sheol. According to the Bible, the dwelling of the dead (GENESIS 37:35; ISAIAH 38:10), situated far below the earth.

Shewbread. Twelve loaves of fine white flour that were laid into two rows on the golden table in the inner shrine of the TEMPLE. They were later divided among the PRIESTS (LEVITICUS 24:1–9).

Shibboleth. Hebrew for "sheaf of corn." Word used by JEPHTHAH to test the nationality of wayfarers near the JORDAN RIVER. In EPHRAIMITE dialect the word was pronounced "sibboleth," and this enabled Jephthah to identify the Ephraimites, with whom he was in strife.

Shiloh. First cult center of the Israelites after the conquest of Canaan under Joshua. Situated north of Jerusalem, both the Ark and the Tabernacle were kept there during the period of the Judges, serving as the central national shrine.

Shittim. One of the names given to the final Israelite encampment before they crossed the Jordan, opposite Jericho (Numbers 25:1; Joshua 2:1).

Shunem. Ancient place in the territory of the tribe of Issachar, and home of the wealthy woman ("the Shunammite") whose dead son was revived by Elisha (II Kings 4).

Shushan. Capital of Elam and subsequently of Persia, it was the place of the royal palace mentioned in the Book of Esther (Esther 2:18).

Sifra. Oldest rabbinic commentary on the Book of Leviticus.

Sifri. Oldest rabbinic commentary on the Books of Numbers and Deuteronomy.

Siloam. Pool in the vicinity of Jerusalem receiving water from the Gihon spring. To assure the city's water supply in case of attack, Hezekiah cut a tunnel through which the water of the Gihon spring flowed into the pool at Siloam (II Kings 20:20).

Simeon. Second son of Jacob. Out of zeal for the reputation of his sister Dinah, he and Levi slaughtered the male inhabitants of Shechem and took the women and children as captives (Genesis 34).

Sinai Covenant. Refers to the revelation of God to the Children of Israel on Mount Sinai, giving them the Ten Commandments. The covenant made here between God and the Israelites played a major role in molding the people into one nation serving one God.

Sin Offering. Sacrifice brought in atonement for a sin committed unwittingly (Leviticus 4:1–3). It was also brought after childbirth, leprosy, and the completion of the Nazirite vow. This offering was either an animal or a bird.

Sisera. General of Jabin, Canaanite king who dwelt at Hazor. He conducted the war against the Israelites under Barak and Deborah.

Slave. The Bible recognized the institution of slavery, but made detailed provision for its humane legislation. An Israelite slave would be a slave for a limited period, with freedom at the seventh year of service or at the jubilee year. Non-Jewish Canaanite slaves were normally acquired by purchase from neighboring peoples. These slaves were a type of proselyte. Males had to undergo circumcision, and women were subject to the laws binding to Jewish women.

Sodom and Gomorrah. Two evil cities of the Jordan plain that God destroyed with a rain of fire and brimstone. Although Lot and his daughters escaped destruction, Lot's wife looked back and became a pillar of salt.

Solomon. King of Israel (ca. 961–920 b.c.e.), son of Davɪᴅ and Bᴀᴛsʜᴇʙᴀ. Solomon is known for his wisdom, his many wives, his great wealth, and for building the Tᴇᴍᴘʟᴇ in Jᴇʀᴜsᴀʟᴇᴍ. Some have also attributed the Book of the Soɴɢ ᴏꜰ Soɴɢs to Solomon's authorship.

Son of God. Son (*ben* in Hebrew) is commonly used in Semitic languages to denote membership of a class, as "son of Israel" for an Israelite. Son of God in Hebrew means "godlike" rather than the son of God. In Psᴀʟᴍ 29:1 and 89:6, the "sons of God" form God's heavenly train. In the Bible the term "son of God" also refers to human beings standing in a relation of special intimacy to God, such as kings (cf. Psalm 89:27–28). In the Aᴘᴏᴄʀʏᴘʜᴀ, the term is also applied to the Mᴇssɪᴀʜ.

Son of Man. Epithet applied in the books of Eᴢᴇᴋɪᴇʟ and Dᴀɴɪᴇʟ to a man of God in his relation to God. Ezekiel is termed Son of Man in his vision of the Divine Chariot (Ezekiel 2:1), and Daniel is so called by the angel Gabriel (Daniel 8:17).

Song of Songs. First of the Five Scrolls incorporated in the biblical Hᴀɢɪᴏɢʀᴀᴘʜᴀ, consisting of a collection of poems about sexual love and courtship. The composition of the book has been attributed to King Soʟᴏᴍᴏɴ.

Source Criticism. Referring to a kind of Bible study that examines the sources used by its author and the way in which these sources were utilized or combined by him.

Store Cities. Towns where provisions such as grain, oil, and wine were placed in storehouses by the central government and held as reserve supplies. The Israelites helped to build the Egyptian store cities of Pɪᴛʜᴏᴍ and Rᴀᴍsᴇs (Exoᴅᴜs 1:11).

Succoth. Second station of the Israelites during the Exoᴅᴜs.

Sumer. Region of southern Bᴀʙʏʟᴏɴɪᴀ named after a non-Semitic people that migrated there in prehistoric times and founded a series of city-states. Its culture was the basis of Babylonian civilization.

Supercommentary. Commentaries mostly on the chief commentators of the Pᴇɴᴛᴀᴛᴇᴜᴄʜ, such as Rᴀsʜɪ and Iʙɴ Eᴢʀᴀ. Composed soon after the appearance of the original commentaries, the largest number of super-commentaries are on Rᴀsʜɪ.

Tabernacle. The portable sᴀɴᴄᴛᴜᴀʀʏ set up by Mᴏsᴇs in the wilderness according to Divine instructions (Exoᴅᴜs 26–27). Its chief architects were Bezalel and Oholiab. The most important part of the tabernacle was the Hoʟʏ ᴏꜰ Hoʟɪᴇs, containing the Aʀᴋ, the seven-branched ᴍᴇɴᴏʀᴀʜ, the table of sʜᴇwʙʀᴇᴀᴅ, and the golden ᴀʟᴛᴀʀ for incense. The name Tabernacle is also applied to the ʙᴏᴏᴛʜs erected in the wilderness by the Israelites, commemorating the festival of Sᴜᴋᴋᴏᴛ.

Tamar. Wife of Er, and later of Er's brother, Onan, the sons of Jᴜᴅᴀʜ. Tamar is also the name of Davɪᴅ's daughter, who was raped by her half-brother Amnon (II SAMUEL 13). Amnon was slain for his action by ABSALOM.

Tanakh. Referring to the HEBREW BIBLE, from the initial letters of TORAH, NEVI'IM, and KETUVIM: "PENTATEUCH, PROPHETS, and HAGIOGRAPHA."

Targum. The ARAMAIC translations of the Bible. The most important of these is the translation of the FIVE BOOKS OF MOSES by ONKELOS, the PROSELYTE (first century c.e.). The "Jonathan Targum" is a freer translation of the Bible, ascribed to Jonathan ben Uzziel. An earlier fragmentary version is known as the "Jerusalem Targum."

Tarshish. Biblical town bordering on the Mediterranean Sea. The prophet JONAH embarked on a ship sailing to Tarshish (Jonah 1:3) from Jaffa in order to flee to a distant land (ISAIAH 66:19).

Tekoah. Town south of BETHLEHEM, birthplace of the minor prophet AMOS.

Tel el-Amarna. Arabic name of the site of the capital of PHARAOH Amenhotep IV in Middle Egypt. In 1887 many cuneiform tablets were discovered there.

Temple. Central edifice for Divine worship in Israel until 70 c.e., situated on MOUNT MORIAH in JERUSALEM. The First Temple, built by SOLOMON, was a shrine for the ARK, the sacred vessels, and offerings, with a hall for worshippers. This Temple was destroyed in 586 B.C.E., and a Second Temple was built seventy years later.

Ten Commandments. Alternately called the Decalogue. According to the Bible, the Divine laws spoken by God to MOSES and written on two tablets of stone (EXODUS 20:2–17; DEUTERONOMY 5:6–21).

Terach. Father of ABRAHAM, he left UR of the Chaldees to travel to the land of CANAAN with his son and nephew LOT. Legend depicts Terach as a devout idolator challenged in his beliefs by ABRAHAM.

Teraphim. Images of domestic deities used for divination. Possession of them indicated rights to general property ownership. RACHEL stole teraphim from her father's house (GENESIS 31:19).

Terebinth. A turpentine tree, and one of the trees under which sacrifices and offerings were made "because their shade is good" (HOSEA 4:13).

Thanksgiving Offering. SACRIFICE brought by an individual as a token of thanks to God.

Theophany. Referring to any visible manifestation of a deity. One of the greatest theophanies in the entire Bible was the appearance of God to MOSES atop MOUNT SINAI.

Throne of God. The Divine seat. Visions of the Throne of God are reported in various biblical books (I KINGS 22:19; EZEKIEL 1, passim).

Thummim. Along with the URIM, a sacred means of divination used by the early Hebrews. It was attached to the BREASTPLATE of the HIGH PRIEST.

Tiamat. Refers to one of the deities in the BABYLONIAN creation story.

Tigris. River in southwest Asia, it was regarded as one of the four rivers emerging from the GARDEN OF EDEN (GENESIS 2:4).

Tikkun Sopherim. Hebrew for "scribal emendation." Term applied to eighteen emendations (changes) of the Bible attributed to the SCRIBES. Their purpose was to prevent expressions that appeared to represent the Deity irreverently. The term Tikkun Sopherim (or simply Tikkun) also refers to an unpointed copy of the printed PENTATEUCH used for practice in reading the TORAH scroll.

Timbrel. A kind of tambourine used as an accompaniment to singing and dancing (EXODUS 15:20).

"Time to be born, time to die." A phrase in the Book of ECCLESIASTES. The passage begins, "To everything there is a season, and a time to every purpose under heaven" (i.e., there is an appropriate moment for all things to take place).

Timnah. Concubine of ESAU's son Eliphaz; she bore him AMALEK.

Tithe. A tenth part of the produce, set aside as a religious offering. This custom has ancient biblical origins, dating back to ABRAHAM, who gave "a tenth of all" to MELCHIZEDEK (GENESIS 14:18–20).

Torah. In its narrow meaning, the PENTATEUCH, also called the FIVE BOOKS OF MOSES. It is also known in Jewish tradition as "the Written Law."

Tower of Babel. Building intended to reach to heaven erected by the descendants of NOAH after the FLOOD. God frustrated the work by confusing their languages, thus leading to the diversity of tongues (GENESIS 11:1–9). Scholars today have seen a similarity between the tower and the Sumerian Ziggurat, or step-temple.

Tree of Life. One of the two trees specified in the GARDEN OF EDEN (GENESIS 2:9). Whoever ate of it lived forever. After Adam and Eve ate of the forbidden Tree of Knowledge of Good and Evil, they were expelled from the Garden, lest they also eat of the Tree of Life.

Tribes of Israel. Twelve clans into which the Israelites were divided in biblical times. They derived from the sons of JACOB—REUBEN, SIMEON, LEVI, JUDAH, ISSACHAR, ZEBULUN, JOSEPH, BENJAMIN, DAN, NAPHTALI, GAD, and ASHER. MOSES conferred the priestly office on the Levitical tribe, and divided the tribe of Joseph into the tribes of EPHRAIM and MANASSEH.

Triennial Cycle. Referring to the ancient Palestinian custom of reading the TORAH scroll over a period of three years, rather than completing it in one year in accordance with the ancient BABYLONIAN rite. Reading the Torah scroll according to the triennial cycle has been revived in numerous congregations today.

Unleavened Bread. Flat bread eaten by the Israelites upon their hurried EXODUS from Egypt.

Ur. Ancient Babylonian city, and the home of Abraham before his family's departure for Haran.

Urim and Thummim. Sacred means of divination used by the early Israelites. They were attached to the breastplate of the high priest. The divination involved the use of two stones that could answer questions on occasions fateful for the nation.

Uzziah. King of Judea (ca. 780–740 b.c.e.) who conquered and defeated the Philistines. He also rebuilt the seaport of Eilat.

"Valley of the Shadow of Death." An expression in Psalm 23 ("The Lord is my Shepherd"), it symbolizes the perils of life from which God protects believers. Modern scholars have understood the Hebrew as an emendation that reads the "valley of shadows."

Vashti. Persian queen and wife of Ahasuerus. The Book of Esther describes her divorce after she refused to appear at a banquet thrown by her husband.

Veil. Part of the Tabernacle, its purpose was to form a partition between the Holy of Holies and the remaining part of the tabernacle.

Versions of the Bible. Term referring to different translations of the Bible (e.g., Septuagint, Vulgate, and Targum).

Vocalization. Referring to the placing of vowels into the biblical Hebrew text, usually associated with the work of the Masoretes.

Vulgate. Fourth-century c.e. Latin translation of the Bible made in Palestine by Jerome.

Wave Offering. Near Eastern practice of showing the offering to the deity. Wave offerings were used for both animal and grain offerings. The waving was only a preliminary to offering up the material on the altar fire (Exodus 29:24, 26; Leviticus 7:30).

Wisdom Literature. Term applied to certain biblical books (Proverbs, Job, Ecclesiastes, and Psalms 37, 49, and 73) and apocryphal works (Ben Sira, Wisdom of Solomon, IV Maccabees). Wisdom in these books is based on fear of God and knowledge of the commandments.

Wisdom of Solomon. Apocryphal book, belonging to the Wisdom Literature. Its contents praise wisdom and are ascribed to Solomon.

Zadok. Priests, descended from Aaron, and chief priest of King David. Many aristocratic priestly families claimed kinship with this family (also see Sadducees).

Zaphenath–paneach. The Egyptian name given to Joseph by Pharaoh in Genesis 41:45. It means "the god speaks."

Zebulun. Sixth son of Jacob and Leah. His descendants, the tribe of Zebulun, received territory in the Valley of Jezreel.

Zechariah. PROPHET (sixth century B.C.E.), whose prophecies are concerned with contemporary events and foretell the ingathering of the exiles and the expansion of JERUSALEM. His book is one of the Twelve Books of the MINOR PROPHETS.

Zedekiah. King of JUDEA (597–586 B.C.E.), son of JOSIAH. Conspiring with Egypt, the BABYLONIANS invaded his kingdom and captured JERUSALEM.

Zelophehad. Israelite of the tribe of MANASSEH who died in the desert. He left five daughters and no son, and his daughters claimed their paternal portion of the PROMISED LAND. As a result, new laws were written permitting daughters to inherit (in the absence of sons), but only when married to a member of their father's tribe (NUMBERS 27, 36).

Zephaniah. Seventh-century B.C.E. PROPHET whose prophecies were mostly ESCHATOLOGICAL. Described in his book (one of the MINOR PROPHETS) is the DAY OF THE LORD, when God will punish all of the wicked and will be universally acknowledged.

Zeresh. Wife of HAMAN, chief minister of King AHASUERUS of Persia.

Zerubbabel. Grandson of JEHOICHIN, he was one of the first Jews to return to JUDEA from BABYLON.

Zilpah. Handmaid of LEAH, who gave her to JACOB as wife. She was the mother of both GAD and ASHER (GENESIS 30:9–13).

Zimri. Ninth-century King of Israel and general in the service of Elah.

Zin, Wilderness of. Desert traversed by the Israelites during the EXODUS on the journey from the RED SEA to REPHIDIM (EXODUS 15:1).

Zion. Jebusite stronghold in JERUSALEM, captured by DAVID and identified with the City of David (II SAMUEL 5:6–7).

Zipporah. Wife of MOSES and daughter of JETHRO, PRIEST of MIDIAN. On traveling to Egypt with Moses, she saved his life by circumcizing their son (EXODUS 4:24–26).

Ziv. Biblical month (I KINGS 6:1), known today as IYAR.

Zoar. Biblical town where LOT fled to find safety (GENESIS 19:23).

Zohar. Mystical biblical commentary on sections of the FIVE BOOKS OF MOSES and parts of the HAGIOGRAPHA (SONG OF SONGS, RUTH, LAMENTATIONS). The Zohar dwells on the mystery of creation, and explains the stories and events in the Bible in a symbolic manner.

CHAPTER 3

Rabbinic Literature and Commentaries

Just as the Bible is the foundation of Judaism, the rabbinic books are the steel pillars that support the intellectual and spiritual structures of Jewish life. The Talmud, the rabbinic codes of law and their commentaries, is the product of centuries of spiritual, intellectual, and cultural activity. All forms of contemporary Judaism are derived from rabbinic teachings, including ethics, jurisprudence, ceremonial laws, ritual and liturgy, philosophy, science, geography, and politics.

The Talmud served as a full and complete explanation of Jewish traditions and rituals. However, it was found that the "ocean of the Talmud" was so vast that it became difficult to locate all the specific references on any one subject. The Rabbis then began to codify the laws and set them in order, according to subject areas, so that one would be able to find them more easily. Among the most famous codes is the *Mishneh Torah,* written by Rabbi Moses ben Maimon (better known as Maimonides). The most popular and respected code of Jewish law, the *Shulchan Arukh* (the Prepared Table), was written by Rabbi Yosef Caro. Today this book still serves as one of the basic keys to Jewish law and tradition.

From the sixteenth century on, the major method of interpreting Jewish law became the Responsa. Individuals would ask a rabbi a question on a current problem; the rabbi would give his answer, called a responsum, basing his reasoning on supporting statements in earlier law codes.

This chapter highlights salient concepts related to rabbinic law and its commentaries, including the tractates of the Talmud, rabbinic personalities, and books of the Codes, together with their commentaries and methods of interpreting Jewish law.

Abba. Literally, "father." Honorary title given to a number of tannaitic scholars (e.g., Abba Shaul, Abba Binyamin). Also, the name of several AMORAIM (e.g., Rav).

Acharonim. Hebrew for "latter ones." Designation for recent rabbinic authorities as distinguished from the RISHONIM, early authorities. The dividing line is placed between the eleventh and sixteenth centuries C.E.

Aggadah. Part of the TALMUD that complements the legal parts (HALAKHAH), stressing its ethical and inspirational meanings. The Aggadah includes picturesque similes, epigrams, proverbs, metaphor, wordplay, and dramatic colloquy.

Agunah. A deserted woman whose husband's death may be suspected but not proved. Therefore, she is forbidden to marry, according to traditional Jewish law.

Akiva. (ca. 40–135 C.E.) Great talmudic storyteller and leader of his people. According to legend, he began his Jewish education at age 40, and his collecting and arranging the whole ORAL LAW according to subjects laid the foundation for the editing of the MISHNAH.

Am Ha'aretz. Literally, "people of the land." Talmudic term referring to the common people who did not adhere to the rabbinic regulations with regard to the laws of purity, tithes, and so on. It later acquired the connotation of "ignoramus."

Amora. Plural, *amoraim.* Title given to Jewish scholars in PALESTINE and BABYLONIA in the third through the sixth centuries C.E. The *amoraim* continued the work of the TANNAIM, the creators of the MISHNAH. Their work was eventually incorporated into the GEMARA.

Amram Gaon. Intellectual leader, head of the SURA academy (856–874 C.E.) and author of RESPONSA.

Arabic. A semitic language that is cognate to HEBREW. Today Arabic is the prevailing language of Saudi Arabia, Jordan, Lebanon, Syria, Iraq, and parts of North Africa.

Arakhin. Hebrew for "estimations." Fifth tractate of the Mishnah order of Kodashim. It discusses the valuation, for purposes of redemption, of men and things that are vowed to the sanctuary (cf. Leviticus 27:2–29).

Aramaic. Semitic language known since the ninth century b.c.e. as the speech of the Arameans and adopted as speech by various non-Aramean peoples including the Jews after the Babylonian captivity. The Talmud is written in Hebrew and Aramaic.

Arba'ah Turim. Hebrew for "four rows." Great legal code written by Jacob ben Asher, a thirteenth-century codifier. The book is divided into four parts: (1) *Orach Hayyim,* dealing with daily conduct, (2) *Yoreh Deah,* including dietary laws, (3) Even Ha'Ezer, governing personal and family matters; and (4) Choshen Mishpat, dealing with civil law.

Arukh. Medieval lexicon covering the Talmud and Midrashim, written by Nathan ben Jehiel in 1101.

Arukh HaShulchan. Authoritative law code dealing only with the laws that have practical importance. It was written by Jehiel Epstein, a nineteenth-century rabbinic authority.

Avadim. Hebrew for "slaves." Minor talmudic tractate dealing with the laws related to Hebrew slaves.

Av Bet Din. Hebrew for "father of the court." Vice-president of the Supreme Court in Jerusalem during the Second Temple. The Av Bet Din handled court procedure. Today the Av Bet Din often refers to the head of a Jewish religious court (Bet Din).

Avodah Zarah. Hebrew for "idolatry." Eighth tractate in the Mishnah order of Nezikin, it deals with regulations related to idols and idolatry.

Avot. Hebrew for "fathers." Tractate of the Mishnah in Nezikin having no Gemara. It contains pithy sayings and ethical teachings of the rabbinic sages from the third century b.c.e. to the third century c.e. The tractate is alternately called *Pirkei Avot,* Ethics of the Fathers.

Avot deRabbi Natan. Small tractate that provides an expansion to the tractate of Avot. It is ascribed to Rabbi Nathan the Babylonian.

Avraham ben David (Ra'avad). (1120–1198) French talmudist, known for his strictures *(Hassagot)* on Maimonides' Mishneh Torah. He feared that Maimonides's code would supplant the study of Talmud.

Babylonian Talmud. The first source book of Jewish law, with over 2,000 scholarly contributors. It is composed of the Mishnah, a six-volume work written in Hebrew and edited by Judah the Prince (200 c.e.), and the Gemara, which explains the Mishnah, completed in approximately 500 c.e. and written in Aramaic.

Baraita. A tannaitic source that is not part of the MISHNAH.

Bat Kol. Hebrew for "daughter of a voice." In rabbinic literature it denotes a Divine voice that could manifest itself to an individual or a group. Occasionally a bat kol gave heavenly approval to a religious legal decision under debate.

Bava Batra. Aramaic for "last gate." A talmudic tractate in the Order of NEZIKIN, dealing with real estate laws, inheritance, partnerships, and legal documents.

Bava Kamma. Aramaic for "first gate." A talmudic tractate in the Order of NEZIKIN dealing with damages caused by property or agents (e.g., by an ox or fire).

Bava Metzia. Aramaic for "middle gate." A talmudic tractate in the Order of NEZIKIN, dealing with the laws of chattel, lost and found property, fraud, interest, and so on.

Bekhorot. Hebrew for "firstlings." Fourth tractate in the MISHNAH order of KODASHIM, dealing with laws related to the firstborn, both people and animals.

Benei Brak. Small town in JUDEA, hometown of RABBI AKIVA and the seat of his YESHIVAH.

Berakhot. Hebrew for "blessings." First tractate of the MISHNAH order of ZERAIM, dealing with the reciting of the SHEMA, blessings, and prayer in general.

Bet HaMidrash. Hebrew for "house of study." School for higher rabbinic learning where students gathered for study, discussion, and prayer. In the Talmud, Bet HaMidrash refers to an academy presided over by a distinguished rabbinic leader.

Bet Hillel. A school of TANNAIM during the first century C.E., known for its more lenient teachings, which became accepted in most cases of Jewish law. Bet Hillel is usually juxtaposed with the other great school of its time, Bet SHAMMAI, known for its more stringent view.

Bet She'arim. Town in Galilee, seat of the SANHEDRIN for most of the life of Rabbi JUDAH THE PRINCE. Most of his editing of the MISHNAH was done in Bet She'arim.

Betzah. Hebrew for "egg." Seventh tractate in the MISHNAH order of MOED. Its original name was YOM TOV (festival day), and it deals with a myriad of laws related to Jewish festivals.

Bikurim. Hebrew for "first fruits." Eleventh and final tractate in the Mishnah order of ZERAIM, it deals with the offerings of first fruits in the Temple (EXODUS 23:19; DEUTERONOMY 26:1–11).

Binyan Av. Analogy, or an interpretation based on induction. It is one of the fundamental talmudic principles of biblical interpretation.

Bruriah. Wife of RABBI MEIR (second century C.E.), she is one of the few women mentioned in the TALMUD who participated in legal discussions.

Caesarea. A coastal settlement founded in the fourth century B.C.E. After the BAR KOKHBA revolt it became home to important Torah scholars and even had its own YESHIVAH. The disciples of Rabbi JUDAH THE PRINCE lived there, and parts of the JERUSALEM TALMUD were edited there.

Caro, Yosef. Spanish sixteenth-century codifier known for editing Judaism's most authoritative law code, called the Shulchan Arukh (Hebrew for "the prepared table"), also known as the CODE OF JEWISH LAW.

Chagigah. Hebrew for "festival offering." Twelfth tractate in the MISHNAH order of MOED, dealing with TEMPLE sacrificial offerings during the three PILGRIMAGE FESTIVALS.

Charity. Hebrew, *tzedakah*. The Jewish concept of charity relates to righteousness and justice, since helping the needy is considered a religious obligation. By talmudic times each community had a *kuppah,* or charity fund, which was used to defray the cost of meals for the poor.

Chaver. Literally, "an associate," it refers to a person who became a member of a group dedicated to the meticulous observance of *mitzvot.*

Chazakah. Hebrew for "taking hold." In general, this talmudic term refers to the act of taking possession of property.

Chazal. A term referring to the talmudic sages (acronym).

Chullin. Hebrew for "profane matters." Third tractate in the MISHNAH order of KODASHIM, dealing with the laws of ritual slaughtering and other regulations connected with the preparation of animal food.

Code of Jewish Law. Authoritative law code written by YOSEF CARO, a sixteenth century legal codifier. It is still recognized today by traditional Jews throughout the world.

Cordoba. Spanish city where Moses ben Enoch established Spain's first talmudic college.

Dayan. Hebrew for "judge." Judge of a rabbinical court, qualified to adjudicate money matters and problems of civil law.

Demai. Hebrew for "dubious produce," with reference to tithes. Third tractate in the MISHNAH order of ZERAIM, dealing with the requirements for tithing produce where there is doubt regarding whether the proper TITHES have been given.

Derekh Eretz Rabbah. A small tractate at the end of the MISHNAH order NEZIKIN, dealing with laws of personal status, moral sayings, and so on.

Derekh Eretz Zuta. A second small tractate at the end of the MISHNAH order NEZIKIN containing moral sayings.

Din. Hebrew for "judgment" (see **BET DIN**). The term refers to a law, a legal decision, or a lawsuit.

Eduyyot. Hebrew for "testimonies." Seventh tractate in the **MISHNAH** order of **NEZIKIN**. Containing only mishnah, the book consists of personal testimonies of sages regarding legal rulings that they had received from their teachers.

Eger, Rabbi Akiva. (1761–1837) Scholar and **RABBI** of the city of Posen. In his notes, called *Gilyon HaShas,* he points out problems and difficulties in the commentaries accompanying the **TALMUD** or in the remarks of other commentators.

Eliezer b. Hyrcanus. **TANNA**, pupil of Rabbi **YOCHANAN BEN ZAKKAI**, and teacher of **RABBI AKIVA**. Known for his phenomenal memory, he set up an academy at Lydda (Lod).

Elisha b. Abuyah. Second-century C.E. **TANNA**, teacher and friend of **RABBI MEIR**. After his adoption of heretical opinions, he was called *Acher* ("the other").

Eruvin. Hebrew for "amalgamations." Second tractate in the **MISHNAH** order of **MOED**, dealing with the laws of the **ERUV** (a technical term for the rabbinic provision that permits the alleviation of certain **SABBATH** prohibitions).

Exilarch. In Aramaic, *Resh Galuta,* head of the exile. Title of the head of **BABYLONIAN** Jewry. He appointed **JUDGES** and was the court of final appeal.

Fez. City in Morocco producing many rabbinical scholars, including Rabbi Isaac Alfasi. **MAIMONIDES** also lived there for a few years.

Gamliel the Elder, Rabban. President of the **SANHEDRIN** and grandson of **HILLEL**.

Gaon. Plural, *geonim.* Title born by the heads of the two large academies in **BABYLONIA** and in **SURA** and **PUMBEDITA,** between the sixth and the eleventh centuries C.E. They both explained the law and established new laws.

Gaon of Vilna. Elijah ben Solomon Zalman (1720–1797). Talmudist famed for his scholarship, who founded an academy in Vilna. His works include commentaries on the Bible and annotations on the Bible, **MIDRASH,** and **ZOHAR.**

Gemara. A commentary on the **MISHNAH** by a group of later scholars known as the **AMORAIM,** who sought to reconcile the varying opinions of conflicting opinions in the **MISHNAH**. The **GEMARA** was edited in the year 500 C.E.

Gemilut Chasadim. Referring to deeds of lovingkindness (e.g., hospitality to strangers, visiting the sick, burying the dead). The **MISHNAH** lists this type of kindness among those things "the fruit of which a man enjoys in this world while the principal remains for the world to come" (MISHNAH *Peah* I.1).

Gerim. Hebrew for "PROSELYTES." Minor tractate appended to the TALMUD, containing legal statements related to the acceptance of proselytes and the manner of conversion.

Gezerah. A decree of regulation, initiated by the sages, that prohibits something that was once permitted (see TAKANAH).

Gezerah Shavah. A verbal analogy, a fundamental principle of biblical interpretation. If the same word or phrase appears in two places in the Bible, and a particular law is explicitly stated in one of these places, then one may infer on the basis of "verbal analogy" that the same law applies in the other case as well.

Gittin. Hebrew for "bills of divorce." Fifth tractate in the MISHNAH order of NASHIM, dealing with the laws of divorce.

Glossaries. From the word "gloss," referring to commentators (from the tenth century onward) on the Bible and TALMUD who explain words by giving their equivalents in the vernacular language in HEBREW script. The most famous glossator was RASHI, who gives over 3,000 different glosses on the Bible and Talmud. Some are in German, but most are in French, and are used today as an important source of knowledge of Old French.

Haggahot HaBah. Referring to proposed emendations in the text of the GEMARA, in RASHI's commentary, and in the TOSAFOT. Its author is Rabbi Yoel Sirkes, a seventeenth-century Polish scholar.

Haggahot HaGra. A method of emendation similar to HAGGAHOT HABAH, but the language is more vigorous. Its author is Rabbi Eliyahu HaGaon, known as the GAON OF VILNA.

Hai Gaon, Rav. Gaon in PUMPEDITA and last of the Babylonian GEONIM (939–1038).

Halakhah. The legal part of talmudic literature in contrast to AGGADAH, the nonlegal elements.

HaMaor. Referring to the commentary of Rabbi Zerahyah HaLevi (twelfth century), which consists of glosses and criticisms of decisions of the RIF.

HaRan. The interpretation of Rabbenu Nissim ben Reuven of Spain (fourteenth century). His book is an extensive commentary on the legal decisions of the RIF.

Hekdesh. Any property that a person consecrates for use in the TEMPLE or as a SACRIFICE.

Hermeneutics. The study of the methodological principles of interpretation of the Bible. Various collections of these principles existed in TANNAITIC times, including the seven rules of HILLEL, the thirteen principles of RABBI ISHMAEL, and the thirteen rules of Rabbi Eliezer ben Jose HaGalili.

Hillel. Sometimes called "The Elder," he was a first century B.C.E. scholar and founder of the school known as BET HILLEL. He was the ancestor of a dynasty of patriarchs that held office until the fifth century.

Horayot. Hebrew for "decisions." Tenth tractate in the MISHNAH order of NEZIKIN, dealing with decisions related to religious law made in error by the SANHEDRIN or the HIGH PRIEST (LEVITICUS 4:1–21).

Ishmael's Principles of Logic. Thirteen principles of logic created by the second-century TANNA Ishmael ben Elisha. These principles were used by the talmudic sages to help explicate verses in the PENTATEUCH.

Jerusalem Talmud. Compilation of the laws and discussion of the AMORAIM in Israel, mainly in the ACADEMY of TIBERIAS. Much smaller in length than the BABYLONIAN TALMUD and considered less authoritative, its final form was completed sometime at the beginning of the fifth century C.E.

Jerusalem Targum. An ARAMAIC translation of the PENTATEUCH, often attributed (probably erroneously) to Jonathan ben Uzziel, a Palestinian TANNA.

Judah the Prince. (ca. 135–ca. 220) Patriarch of Palestinian Jewry and redactor of the MISHNAH. He was usually referred to in rabbinic literature simply as "Rabbi."

Kal Vachomer. An *a fortiori* inference, and a fundamental principle of rabbinic exegesis. This is a rule of logical argumentation by means of which two cases are compared, one lenient and the other more stringent. The Kal Vachomer principle asserts that if the law is stringent in a case where we are usually lenient, then it will certainly be stringent in a more serious case.

Kallah. Late Hebrew tractate dealing with marital relations.

Karet. A divine punishment (of a short life) for serious transgressions.

Kelim. Hebrew for "utensils." First tractate in the MISHNAH order of TOHAROT, which discusses the ritual uncleanliness of vessels (cf. LEVITICUS 11:32; NUMBERS 19:14).

Keritot. Hebrew for "excisions." Seventh tractate in the MISHNAH order of KODASHIM, dealing with the punishment of KARET.

Ketubot. Second tractate in the MISHNAH order of NASHIM, dealing primarily with the money to be received by a wife in case of divorce or widowhood.

Kiddushin. Hebrew for "betrothals." Seventh and last tractate in the MISHNAH order of NASHIM, dealing with regulations related to marriage.

Kilayim. Hebrew for "diverse kinds." Fourth tractate in the MISHNAH order of ZERAIM, dealing with the prohibitions of mingling different kinds of plants, animals, and clothing (LEVITICUS 19:19).

Kinnim. Hebrew for "bird nests." Eleventh and last tractate in the

MISHNAH order of KODASHIM, dealing with the regulations for the bringing of an offering after childbirth (LEVITICUS 12:8).

Kinyan. A mode of acquisition, a formal procedure to render an agreement as legally binding. After the act of kinyan occurs, the object is legally the property of the purchaser.

Kodashim. Hebrew for "holy things." Fifth order of the MISHNAH, consisting of eleven tractates that deal with the laws of ritual slaughter, sacrifice, and other TEMPLE-related objects.

Kutim. (1) Talmudic term for SAMARITANS. (2) Refers to any person or group rejecting the ORAL LAW. (3) A minor tractate in which the relationships among Samaritans, Jews, and Gentiles are discussed.

Ma'amadot. Hebrew for "stands" or "posts." Groups of Israelites attending the TEMPLE SACRIFICE. The people were divided into twenty-four lots of PRIESTS, LEVITES, and Israelites, each being assigned a specific time to serve in the Temple. Each went in his appointed week of service.

Ma'aser Sheni. Hebrew for "second TITHE." Eighth tractate in the MISHNAH order of ZERAIM, dealing with tithes eaten in JERUSALEM (DEUTERONOMY 14:22–27).

Maharil. (ca. 1525–1609) Known as Judah Low ben Bezalel, he was chief rabbi of Moravia, much admired for his rabbinic learning. He wrote many books of rabbinic commentary.

Maharsha. A combination of two works by Rabbi Shmuel Eliezer Edels (1555–1631), a Polish rabbi. The two works are called *Chiddushei Halakhot* and *Chiddushei Aggadot,* covering almost the entire TALMUD.

Maharshal. Work by Rabbi Shlomo Luria, a sixteenth-century Lublin rabbi. This rabbinic work consists of textual emendations, many of which are now incorporated within the editions of the TALMUD itself.

Makhshirin. Hebrew for "predisposings." Eighth tractate in the MISHNAH order of TOHOROT, dealing with the laws of ritual impurity in connection with foods that are susceptible to such impurity when wet (LEVITICUS 11:24, 38).

Makkot. Hebrew for "stripes." Fifth tractate in the MISHNAH order of NEZIKIN, it deals with lashings administered by court decree (DEUTERONOMY 25:1–3), false witnesses, and CITIES OF REFUGE (NUMBERS 35:9–28).

Mamzer. Hebrew for "bastard." Referring to any child of a forbidden relationship.

Masoret HaShas. Refers to parallel texts and cross-references to identical passages elsewhere in the TALMUD. It is printed in small letters on the inside margin of a page of Talmud.

Megillah. Hebrew for "scroll." Tenth tractate in the MISHNAH order of

Moed, dealing with the reading of the Scroll of Esther and regulations for the care of synagogues and holy objects.

Megillat Ta'anit. Hebrew for "Scroll of the Fast." Early Aramaic work listing month by month the days in the calendar that commemorate miracles and joyous events on which it is forbidden to fast.

Me'ilah. Hebrew for "trespass," that is, in regard to holy things. Eighth tractate in the Mishnah order of Kodashim, dealing with the laws concerning profane use of things for holy purposes (Leviticus 5:15–16).

Meir, Rabbi. Second-century Palestinian tanna and student of Rabbi Akiva. His Mishnah formed the basis of the accepted Mishnah of Judah the Prince. His wife Bruria was a scholarly authority.

Meir of Rothenberg. (ca. 1220–1293) Outstanding rabbinic authority of his generation whose legal decisions influenced Jewish law throughout Europe.

Me'iri. (ca. 1249–1306) French Talmudist who wrote a masterful commentary on the Talmud called *Bet HaBechirah.*

Mekhilta. Name applied to certain midrashic works (e.g. the oldest midrashic commentary to the Book of Exodus is called the Mekhilta). Mekhilta is also used as a synonym for *masekhet,* that is, tractate of the Mishnah or Talmud.

Men of the Great Assembly. A body of 120 scholarly men whose decisions constituted the supreme authority in matters of religion and law during the period of the Second Temple.

Menachot. Hebrew for "meal offerings." Second tractate in the Mishnah order of Kodashim, dealing with preparation of the meal offering (Leviticus 2:1–14).

Middot. Hebrew for "measures." Tenth tractate in the Mishnah order of Kodashim, describing the architecture of the Second Temple.

Midrash. Refers to the nonlegal sections of the Talmud and the rabbinic books containing biblical interpretations in the spirit of the aggadah (i.e., legend).

Midrash Rabbah. Collection of aggadic midrashim to the Pentateuch and the Five Megillot.

Midrash Tanchuma. Midrash attributed to Rabbi Tanchuma bar Abba, also known as *Yelammedenu,* from the characteristic opening phrase in each sermon, *yelammedenu rabbenu* ("let our master teach us"). The discourses center around the opening verse of each Bible portion of the week.

Mikraot Gedolot. An edition of the Bible published in Venice (1524–1525) by Daniel Bomberg. It became the "accepted" version of the Bible, "the Masoretic Text," upon which everyone has since relied and which all have copied and imitated.

Mikvaot. Hebrew for "ritual baths." Sixth tractate in the Mishnah order of Tohorot, dealing with the rituals related to ritual bathing (Leviticus 14:8; 15:5).

Minhag. Referring to a custom or observance within a given sector of Jewry.

Minor. A child who has not reached maturity (*katan* in Hebrew).

Minor Tractate. Talmudic books whose subject matter does not generally have a place in the Mishnah and Talmud.

Mishnah. Legal codification, expounding the Bible and constituting the core of Oral Law, compiled and edited by Rabbi Judah the Prince in the early third century. The Mishnah is arranged in sixty-three tractates and has six divisions: Zeraim (agriculture), Moed (festivals), Nashim (marriage), Nezikin (damages), Kodashim (sacrifices), and Tohorot (purity).

Moed. Hebrew for "set feast." Second order of the Mishnah, consisting of twelve tractates dealing with the laws related to the Sabbath, festivals, and fast days.

Moed Katan. Hebrew for "minor festival." Eleventh tractate in the Mishnah order of Moed, dealing with the type of work permitted during the intermediate days of Passover and the Feast of Tabernacles. The tractate also deals with the laws of mourning on festivals.

Nachum of Gamzo. Second-century tanna who made significant contributions to midrashic exegesis. His comment on every apparent misfortune was the later proverbial *gam zeh letovah* (this too is for the good).

Nashim. Hebrew for "women." Third order of the Mishnah, consisting of seven tractates dealing with marriage, divorce, and the laws of vows and Nazirites. The tractates include: Yevamot (sisters-in-law), Ketubot (marriage deeds), Nedarim (vows), Nazir (Nazirite), Sotah (woman suspected of adultery), Gittin (divorce), and Kiddushin (betrothals).

Nazir. Hebrew for "nazirite." Fourth tractate in the Mishnah order of Nashim, dealing with the laws concerning Nazirite vows (Numbers 6:1–21).

Nedarim. Third tractate in the Mishnah order of Nashim, dealing with regulations concerning vows.

Nega'im. Hebrew for "plagues of leprosy." Third tractate in the Mishnah order of Tohorot, dealing with the laws concerning various types of leprosy.

Nehardea. Babylonian town, home of the exilarch and of the senior Babylonian academy.

Ner Mitzvah. Provides reference to the primary halakhic works that treat the subject matter of the Gemara. The Ner Mitzvah, alternately called *Ein Mishpat Ner Mitzvah,* usually refers to the halakhic works of the Mishnah Torah, Sefer Mitzvot Gadol, and the Shulchan Arukh.

Nezikin. Hebrew for "damages." Fourth order of the MISHNAH, divided into BAVA KAMMA, BAVA METZIA, and BAVA BATRA. It deals with money matters and all damages that are decided by the courts. It also contains a tractate containing ethical teachings (AVOT).

Niddah. Hebrew for "menstruous woman." Seventh tractate in the MISHNAH order of TOHOROT, dealing with ritual impurity as a result of menstruation and childbirth (LEVITICUS 12:1–5).

Ohalot. Hebrew for "tents." Second tractate in the MISHNAH order of TOHOROT, dealing with ritual impurity as a result of contact with a corpse (NUMBERS 19:13–20).

Onkelos. First-century Palestinian PROSELYTE, best known for his ARAMAIC translation of the PENTATEUCH.

Oral Law. Referring to interpretation and analysis of the WRITTEN LAW handed down orally from generation to generation.

Orlah. Hebrew for "uncircumcized fruit." Tenth tractate in the MISHNAH order of ZERAIM, dealing with the law forbidding the use of the fruit of trees or vineyards for the first three years after planting (LEVITICUS 19:23).

Parah. Hebrew for "heifer." Fourth tractate in the MISHNAH order of TOHOROT, dealing with the regulations concerning the RED HEIFER (NUMBERS 19).

Pardes. Mnemonic word formed by the initials of the four main types of biblical interpretation. They include *peshat* (literal meaning), *remez* (allegorical and philosophical), *derash* (aggadic), and *sod* (secret and mystical).

Peah. Hebrew for "corner." Second tractate of the MISHNAH order of ZERAIM, dealing with the setting aside of the corners of one's field for the poor (LEVITICUS 19:19).

Pesachim. Hebrew for "PASCHAL LAMBS." Third tractate in the MISHNAH order of MOED, dealing with the regulations related to the holiday of PASSOVER.

Pikuach Nefesh. The rabbinic concept that states that the effort to save a human life supersedes and takes precedence over all the commandments of the TORAH, with the exception of idolatry, murder, and forbidden sexual relations.

Piyyut. Hebrew liturgical poetry that began in PALESTINE in the years 300–500 C.E. Among the great early poets were Yose ben Yose and Eleazar Kalir.

Pnai Moshe. A commentary on the JERUSALEM TALMUD written by Moses ben Simeon Margoliot, an eighteenth-century Lithuanian rabbi.

Posek. A Hebrew term for a scholar whose intellectual efforts were concentrated on determining the Jewish law in practice, in contrast to those commentators who applied themselves to study for its own sake.

Prosbul. A legal document annulling the cancellation of debts during the SABBATICAL year. It was developed by HILLEL despite the Bible's standing rule that prohibits the maintaining of debts during the JUBILEE YEAR.

Pumbedita. BABYLONIAN city and seat of a famous ACADEMY founded by Judah ben Ezekiel in the middle of the third century C.E.

Rabban. Variant form of RABBI used as a title of honor in early mishnaic times to a select group of scholars (e.g., YOCHANAN B. ZAKKAI).

Rabbana. Hebrew for "our master." Title applied to scholars from the family of the EXILARCH in BABYLONIA.

Rabbenu Gershom (Meor HaGolah). Tenth-century rabbinic authority and one of the TALMUD's first commentators, he corrected many copyists' errors. His legal decisions and regulations were accepted by European Jewry. They included a ban on polygamy and divorcing a woman without her consent.

Rabbenu Hananel. Eleventh-century North African rabbi who composed one of the TALMUD's first commentaries. Unlike RASHI's commentary, his deals with the interpretation of whole sections, clarifying the principal contents.

Rashbam. Nickname for Samuel ben Meir, a French scholar who, like his grandfather RASHI, was both a BIBLE and TALMUD commentator.

Rashi Script. Semicursive form of Hebrew characters principally used for writing and printing rabbinical commentaries, especially that of RASHI.

Responsa. Written replies given to questions on all aspects of Jewish law by qualified authorities from the time of the later GEONIM to the present day.

Rif. Nickname for Rabbi Isaac ben Jacob Alfasi, an eleventh-century talmudic scholar. His compendium of legal discussions of the BABYLONIAN TALMUD, *Sefer HaHalakhot,* is the main collection of its type prior to the work of MAIMONIDES.

Rishonim. Hebrew for "first ones." A general term denoting older authorities, including commentators of talmudic law of the GAONIC period up to the time of the compilation of the CODE OF JEWISH LAW.

Rosh (Rabbenu Asher ben Yehiel). Nickname of Asher ben Yehiel, a talmudic codifier whose RESPONSA are a primary source for the history of the Spanish Jews of the fourteenth century. His decisions *(Piskei Ha-Rosh),* a compendium of Jewish law, are still standard.

Rosh Hashanah. Eighth tractate in the MISHNAH order of MOED, discussing regulations related to the sanctification of the new moon and the blowing of the ram's horn on the festival of Rosh Hashanah.

Saboraim. Hebrew for "reasoners." Name given to the BABYLONIAN scholars from approximately 500–700 C.E. Some modern scholars have ascribed most of the compilation of the TALMUD to the Saboraim.

Sanhedrin. Fourth tractate in the MISHNAH order of NEZIKIN. It deals with courts of justice and judicial procedure, especially with reference to criminal law.

Sefer Mitzvot Gadol. A compendium of Jewish law written by Rabbi Moshe of Coucy (thirteenth century).

Sefer Mordechai. Written by Rabbi Mordechai ben Hillel Ashkenazi, a thirteenth-century scholar, the book is an original work of halakhic commentary containing halakhic material from the GEONIM to the great RABBIS of Germany.

Semachot. Hebrew for "joyful occasions." Minor talmudic tractate, euphemistically called *Semachot,* but also known as *Evel Rabbati* (Hebrew for "great mourning"), dealing with death and mourning customs.

Shammai. A RABBI (first century B.C.E.) and contemporary of HILLEL. He was the founder of a school, known as Bet Shammai, whose scholars usually took a more rigorous and stringent point of view than those of the BET HILLEL.

Shas. Hebrew initials of *shisha sedarim,* the six orders of the MISHNAH that form the basis of the TALMUD. Today the term is used synonymously with Talmud.

Shekalim. Hebrew for "shekels." Fourth tractate in the MISHNAH order of MOED, dealing with the half-SHEKEL tax collected during Second TEMPLE times for the maintenance of Temple worship.

Sherira Gaon, Rav. (906–1006) PUMPEDITA GAON who wrote numerous commentaries on the Bible and various talmudic tractates. His famous *Letter of Sherira Gaon* contains a wealth of information on the history of the CHAZAL and the development of Jewish law.

Shevi'it. Hebrew for "seventh year." Fifth tractate in the MISHNAH order of ZERAIM, dealing with the laws of the SABBATICAL year (EXODUS 23:11).

Shevuot. Hebrew for "oaths." Sixth tractate in the MISHNAH order of NEZIKIN, dealing with the various types of oaths (LEVITICUS 5:4) and the laws applying to one who becomes aware of being unclean (LEVITICUS 5:2–3).

Shiltei HaGibborim. Commentary of Rabbi Yehoshua Boaz (author of MASORET HASHAS), a sixteenth-century talmudic scholar. This book supplements the work of the RIF.

Shimon ben Shetah. First-century sage, noted for introducing compulsory general education for all Jewish boys. He also instituted the KETUBAH, the Jewish marriage contract, in order to make it more difficult for a husband to secure a divorce (BABYLONIAN TALMUD, SHABBAT 14b).

Shimon HaTzadik. Simon the Just, third-century High PRIEST in JERUSALEM, one of the last survivors of the GREAT ASSEMBLY. He was the first sage of the ORAL LAW to be mentioned by name. One of his most famous sayings stated, "The world rests on three things: on Torah, on Temple service and on benevolent deeds" (AVOT 1:2).

Shmuel HaNaggid. Samuel ibn Nagrela, tenth-century Spanish statesman, poet, and talmudist. He wrote grammatical works and an introduction to the TALMUD now printed in the standard editions.

Sidra. A halakhic discourse related to the Bible portion of the week that was delivered weekly (usually on Sabbath afternoons) by a scholar during talmudic times.

Sifra. Oldest rabbinic commentary on LEVITICUS.

Sifri. Oldest rabbinic commentary on NUMBERS and DEUTERONOMY.

Simlai, Rabbi. Third-century AMORA who was a renowned authority in AGGADAH. Simlai is the author of the statement (MAKKOT 23b) that the TORAH contains 613 commandments.

Soferim. Hebrew for "Scribes." Minor talmudic tractate containing a collection of laws governing TORAH scrolls and how they must be written, as well as laws of reading the Torah and HAFTAROT.

Sotah. Hebrew for "errant wife." Sixth tractate in the MISHNAH order of NASHIM, dealing with the laws concerning the woman suspected of adultery (NUMBERS 5:11–31). It also discusses which liturgical readings may be recited in any language and the rite of the heifer, *egla harufah* in Hebrew, whose neck is broken in the event of unusual murder (DEUTERONOMY 21:1–9).

Sura. BABYLONIAN city where RAV founded an ACADEMY in the early third century C.E. The academy was in existence for eight centuries.

Ta'anit. Hebrew for "fast." Ninth tractate in the MISHNAH order of MOED, dealing with the designation of fast days in time of drought.

Takanah. Any regulation that supplements the law of the TORAH. These regulations came into being to regulate the observance of many commandments and, in particular, civil matters. Some regulations are attributed to MOSES (public reading of the Torah), to EZRA (courts are to sit every Monday and Thursday), and so on. Also, a regulation that creates a new legal category, or a law that permits something that was once prohibited (cf. GEZERAH).

Talmid Chakham. Hebrew for "student of a sage." Person learned in talmudic study; generally refers to a wise pupil.

Talmud. Hebrew for "teaching." Name applied to the BABYLONIAN TALMUD and Palestinian Talmud, in which are collected the records of academic discussion and judicial administration of Jewish Law by generations of scholars during several centuries after 200 C.E. The Talmud consists of the MISHNAH together with the GEMARA, a commentary on the Mishnah.

Tam, Rabbenu. Jacob ben Meir, twelfth-century French scholar, grandson of RASHI. An outstanding rabbinical authority of his day, his commentary often attempted to correct textual corruptions in the TALMUD.

Tamid. Hebrew for "perpetual offering." Ninth tractate in the Mishnah order of Kodashim, it deals with the laws related to daily burnt offerings (Exodus 29:38) and Temple organization and priestly duties.

Tanna. Plural, *tannaim.* Teachers mentioned in the Mishnah or Baraita, living during the first two centuries c.e. Also, the term applied during talmudic times to the academy reader of tannaitic texts.

Tarfon, Rabbi. First-century tanna who took a leading part in the discussions at Yavneh.

Tayku. Hebrew for "let it stand," that is, the question raised in the previous passage remains unsolved. The Hebrew acronym stands for the words *Tishbi yitaretz kushyot u she'alot* (the Messiah will ultimately solve all difficult questions).

Temurah. Hebrew for "exchange." Sixth tractate in the Mishnah order of Kodashim, dealing with the regulations concerning the exchange of an animal consecrated for sacrifice (Leviticus 27:10, 33).

Terumot. Hebrew for "heave offerings." Sixth tractate in the Mishnah order of Zeraim, dealing with heave offerings due to the priest from both the Israelite and the Levite (Numbers 18:8, 25ff).

Tevul Yom. Hebrew for "one who has bathed that day." Tenth tractate in the Mishnah order of Tohorot, dealing with ritual uncleanliness that remains until sunset after ritual bathing (Leviticus 15:7–18).

Tikkun Olam. Hebrew for "improvement of the world." Certain rabbinic ordinances that were instituted to prevent difficulties for people. These ordinances were instituted to make the world a better place.

Tohorot. Hebrew for "purifications." Sixth and last order of the Mishnah. The name is a euphemism for ritual uncleanliness and all the tractates of the order deal with laws of impurity. The tractates in the order include Kelim (vessel), Ohalot (tents), Nega'im (leprosy), Parah (heifer), Tohorot (purifications), Mikvaot (ritual baths), Niddah (menstruating woman), Makhshirin (preparations), Zavim (people suffering from secretions), Tevul Yom (immersed during the day), Yadayim (hands), and Uktzin (stems).

Torah Or. A reference apparatus for biblical quotations written by Rabbi Yehoshua Boaz.

Tosafot. Hebrew for "Addenda." Critical and explanatory notes on the Talmud by French and German scholars of the twelfth to fourteenth centuries (known as tosaphists). They frequently criticize and modify Rashi's talmudic commentary.

Tosefta. A supplement to the Mishnah, containing six orders with the same names as those of the Mishnah. Its paragraphs are called *baraitot*.

Tractate. In Hebrew, *Masakhet.* A treatise of the Mishnah or Talmud.

Uktzin. Hebrew for "stalks." Twelfth and last tractate of the Mishnah order of Tohorot, dealing with ritual purity brought to a harvested plant when its roots, stalks, or pods come into contact with an unclean person or thing.

Usha. Settlement near HAIFA, it was the seat of the SANHEDRIN.

Vilna. Town in Lithuania. Its best known scholar is Elijah ben Solomon Zalman, known as the GAON OF VILNA.

Vow. A religious obligation undertaken voluntarily by an individual. In talmudic law its two types include (1) a promise to make a charitable gift to the TEMPLE; and (2) a promise not to eat specified food or not to derive any benefit from specified property.

Yadayim. Hebrew for "hands." Eleventh TRACTATE in the order of TOHOROT, dealing with rabbinic enactments related to the ritual impurity of hands.

Yavneh. City south of JAFFA where RABBI YOCHANAN BEN ZAKKAI opened an ACADEMY. There he reestablished the SANHEDRIN, which sat in Yavneh until the BAR KOKHBA revolt.

Yevamot. Hebrew for "levirates." First TRACTATE in the talmudic order of NASHIM, dealing with the status of the widow of a man who has died childless and whose brother must contract levirate marriage.

Yochanan ben Zakkai. First-century Palestinian TANNA and pupil and intellectual heir of HILLEL. Most of his sayings are in the field of ethics and AGGADAH.

Yoma. Aramaic for "day." Fifth TRACTATE in the order of MOED, describing the TEMPLE service on the DAY OF ATONEMENT and dealing with laws relating to the fast and REPENTANCE.

Yose HaGelili. First-century TANNA, colleague of RABBI AKIVA and one of the leading scholars of his day.

Zavim. Hebrew for "suffers from flux." Ninth chapter in the talmudic order of TOHOROT, dealing with ritual uncleanliness caused by a flux.

Zeraim. Hebrew for "seeds." First order of the MISHNAH and TALMUD, dealing with the laws of prayers and agricultural laws. Its eleven TRACTATES include BERAKHOT (blessings), PEAH (corner of field), DEMAI (doubtfully tithed), KILAYIM (mixtures), SHEVI'IT (sabbatical year), TERUMOT (contributions, the priests' portion of the harvest), MA'ASEROT (TITHES), MA'ASER SHENI (second tithe), CHALLAH (Dough), ORLAH (uncircumcised fruit), and BIKURIM (first fruits).

Zevachim. Hebrew for "animal sacrifices." First TRACTATE in the Talmudic order of KODASHIM, discussing the laws related to animal sacrifices.

Zugot. Hebrew for "pairs." Term applied to five generations of RABBIS preceding the TANNAIM. They are (1) Yose ben Joezer and Yose ben Johanan; (2) Joshua ben Perahia and Nittai the Arbelite; (3) Judah ben Tabbi and SHIMON BEN SHETAH; (4) Shemaiah and Avtalyon; and (5) HILLEL and SHAMMAI.

CHAPTER 4

World Jewish History and Geography

Following the destruction of the First Temple in 586 B.C.E., when the Jewish community was exiled to Babylonia, and probably before, Jews began their journey through the world, in time and place. While many Jews returned to the land of Israel at the conclusion of the Exile in 538 B.C.E., others stayed in Babylonia and traveled elsewhere. Following patterns of economic development, recession, and anti-Jewish actions, Jews have moved from country to country seeking refuge and security. During the Jewish journey throughout history, Jewish communities have been established in almost every country. The noted American Jewish historian Jacob Rader Marcus has called this unique status of the Jew "omniterritoriality."*

In these countries, Jews have interacted with the national cultures, contributing to and simultaneously absorbing some of their salient elements, reshaping them and making them their own. World Jewish history expresses constant tension between ecstatic joy and deep disillusion. This chapter traces the Jewish people through the history of the world, through their glory days, such as the Golden Age of Spain, as well as through the dark and dreary periods of the expulsion from Spain and the Holocaust.

Central Conference of American Rabbis Journal, Volume 99, 1989, pp. 111–114.

Academies. Schools of higher learning, established by the RABBIS in the rabbinic period, in order to discuss rabbinic teachings; it was here that rabbinic literature took its shape. The discussions that took place in the academies were eventually codified into the MISHNAH, TALMUD, and related literature. Well-known academies include SURA and PUMBEDITA.

Aklyas. Also known as Aquila (second century C.E.), translator of the Bible into Greek. His translations are preserved in fragments only, often joined together with ONKELOS because the TALMUD and TOSEFTA often refer to them together.

Alby, Council of. Held in Alby in 1254, in southern France, for the purpose of exterminating adherents of the Christian sect Albigenses; as a result, barbarous decrees were launched against the Jews. In 1320, during the Pastoureaux riots, the Jews of Alby were annihilated.

Aleppo. Second largest city in Syria, in the center of northern Syria. There have been Jewish settlements there since Roman times. In 1947 the SYNAGOGUES were destroyed and most of its community forced to leave. A special prayer custom, called the *Aram–Zobah* rite, existed there and was brought to Israel by immigrants.

Alexander the Great. Arrived in PALESTINE in 331 B.C.E., a glamorous figure in Jewish legend, especially after he lifted the yoke of Persian occupation. He attempted to bring Greek culture to the Middle East; following his death, his empire fell to pieces.

Alexandria. Founded and named by ALEXANDER THE GREAT to honor himself, at the mouth of the NILE, this city resembled modern New York—big, busy, and cosmopolitan without much national background, although a center of HELLENISTIC culture and sophistication. The Jewish community was large, of considerable dignity even as second-class citizens, and highly assimilated through a cultural interchange.

93

Allgemeine Zeitung des Judenthums. Literally, "General Journal of Judaism," a German–Jewish periodical published in Leipzig and eventually in Berlin between 1837 and 1922. It was one of the first modern such periodicals in Central Europe and the first to discuss current events rather than merely literary matters.

Alliance Israelite Universelle. Founded in Paris, France, in 1860 with ADOLPH CREMIEUX as its president, a direct outgrowth of the MORTARA incident. Beginning in 1862, it concerned itself especially with the much-neglected Jews of North Africa and the Middle East, providing them with a network of schooling and vocational training. Like other organizations of its kind, it served the national interests of its country of origin in undeveloped areas. It was the first such organization to represent world Jewry on a political basis.

Anatevka. An imaginary SHTETL from the writings of SHOLOM ALEICHEM, which epitomized the life of the Jew of Eastern Europe.

Anilewicz, Mordecai. (1919–1943) A twenty-four-year-old Zionist who convinced WARSAW GHETTO leaders that military resistance offered them their only chance for survival; he led the uprising in 1943.

Anschluss. Literally, the annexation of Austria by Germany in 1938.

Anti-Semitism. A term taken from the linguistic categorization of languages, used to refer to anti-Jewish sentiments. It was probably coined in late 1870 by Wilhelm Mari, a German journalist, who wrote "The Victory of Judaism over Germandom." In it he claimed that German history was a struggle between Semitic aliens (the Jew) and active Teutonic stock, which the Jews were winning with disastrous consequences.

Apion. (First century C.E.) Anti-Jewish propagandist in Alexandria, who provoked agitation. FLAVIUS JOSEPHUS wrote against him.

Apologetic. Discourse that is meant to defend a position under attack from another community.

Arbeit Macht Frei. "Work makes you free," written over the entrance to DACHAU.

Archives Israelites de France. A monthly periodical issued in France, edited by Isidor Cahan, which presented a radical–liberal point of view.

Aryan Myth. Originally a term used by philologists to group languages, this racist form of ANTI-SEMITISM was the assertion by the Nazis that those of Aryan ancestry were superior human beings; consequently, all others, including Jews, were inferior. This led them to the FINAL SOLUTION.

Assembly of Jewish Notables. In 1806 Napoleon convened this assembly from France and Italy to define the Jewish position regarding the relationship between its Jewish citizens and the state, as well as in order to establish a new set of Jewish institutions. The Assembly was presented with such questions as: Did Jewish marriage and divorce procedures conflict with French law? Were Jews permitted to marry Christians? Did

Jews consider France their country and Frenchmen their brothers? The Assembly responded cautiously, realizing that it would not overtly disagree with the emperor of France, knowing full well that while he was moving them to equality, he was concerned about the allegations against the Jews of DUAL LOYALTY.

Assyrian Empire. Beginning in the fifteenth century B.C.E., the ancient nation of Assyria in northern MESOPOTAMIA emerged as a major Near Eastern power. As local city-states began to collapse, the Assyrians made annual military expeditions that eventually destroyed the independent states in the area. The Empire was a major political and military force until its decline in the seventh century B.C.E. It had moved as far south as Egypt.

Auschwitz. The largest of the death camps established by the Nazis, located in a small town in Galicia near the border of Upper Silesia. One to two million Jews, sent from all over Europe, were killed there by cyanide gas (Zyklon B). Auschwitz also served as a forced labor camp; when the Jews arrived, a small number of them were selected to be worked to death in nearby factories.

Auto da Fe. Literally, "act of faith." Ceremony accompanying the pronouncement of judgment by the Inquisition, and followed by the execution of the sentence. Broadly, it refers to the burning of heretics. Jews and heretics were sentenced in these public spectacles.

Babi Yar. One of the largest single massacres of the Jews during World War II, which took place outside Kiev in German-occupied Russia, at the end of September 1941. At least 34,000 Jews were marched out of town, forced to dig a pit, stripped, machine-gunned, and buried by the local ANTI-SEMITES, urged on by the EINSATZGRUPPEN.

Babylonian Exile. Between the years 587 and 538 B.C.E., following the destruction of the First TEMPLE by NEBUCHADNEZZAR, the Jews were dispersed from JERUSALEM and forced to live in BABYLONIA. It ended when Cyrus, king of Persia, took control of MESOPOTAMIA and ended the Babylonian state, allowing the Jews to return to Jerusalem and rebuild the Temple. While exiled in Babylonia, Israelite culture achieved a remarkable degree of self-awareness and creativity.

Bar Kokhba Rebellion. (132–135 C.E.) A MESSIANIC revolt led by Simon bar Kosiba (called by some sources Bar Kokhba, "son of the star," a messianic allusion to NUMBERS 24:17). The revolt was triggered by Hadrian's HELLE-NIZING in JUDEA, which included a ban on CIRCUMCISION and a plan to turn JERUSALEM into a PAGAN city. The revolt failed even amid heavy Roman casualties, and Hadrian outlawed Judaism throughout the land and prohibited Jews to live in Jerusalem, which he had renamed *Aelia Capitolina.* In 135 C.E. Bar Kokhba and his followers made their final stand against the Romans at BETAR, situated on a hill southwest of JERUSALEM. In 138 C.E., on the ninth of AV, Betar was captured by the Romans and the city was razed.

Basel Program. The demands of Zionism, as formulated at the First

Zionist Congress held in Basel, Switzerland, in 1817. "Zionism aims at establishing for the Jewish people a publicly and legally assured home in PALESTINE. For the attainment of this purpose, the Congress considers the following means suitable: (1) the promotion of the settlement of Jewish agriculturists, artisans, and tradesmen in Palestine; (2) the federation of all Jews into local or general groups, according to the laws of various countries; (3) the strengthening of the Jewish feeling or consciousness; and (4) preparatory steps for the attainment of those governmental grants, which are necessary for the achievement of the Zionist people."

Beilis, (Menachem) Mendel. In 1911, a Kievian Jew was brought to trial by the Russian government on the charge of ritual murder (the BLOOD LIBEL); he was exonerated.

Bene Israel. Jewish community in India, led by the *Mucaddam,* the secular leader, and the *Cazi,* the religious leader.

Benjamin of Tudela. A great medieval Jewish traveler of the second half of the twelfth century. He recorded all his travels, giving a full account of the cities and the scholars he encountered.

Bergen-Belsen. Nazi CONCENTRATION CAMP near Hanover, Germany, originally established as a transit camp in part of a prisoner of war camp—in order to exchange Jews for Germans in allied territory.

Bilu. From the HEBREW for "House of Jacob, come and let us go up." As a reaction to the 1881 POGROMS in Russia, a group of Russian Jews pioneered a modern return to the land of Israel. While this ideology was originally not connected to any one country and was only a nationalistic response to assimilation, it soon became a general return to Israel.

Birobidzhan. The colloquial name for the Jewish Autonomous Region in the Russian S.F.S.R., selected by the Soviets for Jewish settlement, thought by some to be an alternative to the ZIONIST idea. It was eventually brutally ended during the Stalinist purges of the 1930s and 1940s.

Black Death, The. The bubonic plague, which some modern scholars believe may have killed more than one-third of the population of Europe. It was widely believed that the plague occurred as a result of the Jews having poisoned the wells with a mix of animal and human parts, as well as from the Host. The butchery of Jews between 1348–1350 was unprecedented when it began in southern France and swept through Switzerland and western Germany.

Black Hundreds. Armed street gangs with clandestine government backing in Russia who attacked Jews in dozens of towns and cities in the late nineteenth and early twentieth centuries.

Blessed is the Match. "Consumed in Kindling Flame" A poem by HANNAH SENESH, freedom fighter who was killed by a secret court during World War II in Hungary, after she had parachuted in to help save European Jewry.

Blood Libel. A form of ANTI-SEMITISM, accusing the Jews of killing Christian children in order to use their blood to make PASSOVER MATZAH. It first appeared in the English town of Norwich in 1144, and shows up throughout European history until the twentieth century.

B'nei Mosheh. A short-lived, semisacred society that pledged complete devotion to the renaissance of HEBREW in the late nineteenth century, led by AHAD HA'AM.

Boethusians. A religious/political sect that existed in the century just prior to the destruction of the Second TEMPLE. They closely resembled the SADDUCEES and may even have been a part of them; they were loyal to the Herodians.

Breslau Seminary. The first modern theological seminary, called the Juedisch-Theologisches Seminar, established in 1854 by ZECHARIAH FRANKEL. It was a center of scholarship and spiritual activity until 1938.

Buchenwald. German CONCENTRATION CAMP, considered the worst prior to World War II. It was originally built for criminals, then used for political prisoners and Jews. It became a forced labor camp for war production in 1942, and was especially known for its pseudomedical experiments on inmates.

Bund, The. The General Jewish Workers Union in Lithuania, Poland, and Russia, shortened form of *Algemeyner Yidisher Arbeter Bund in Lite, Poyln un Rusland;* a Jewish socialist party founded in Russia in 1897, associated with YIDDISH autonomism and secular Jewish nationalism. After the Russian Revolution in 1917, a part of the Bund joined the Jewish section of the Communist party. In Poland, the Bund showed considerable strength, establishing schools and conducting cultural work in the Yiddish language. Remnants of the Bund are still active in Israel, some European countries, and the United States.

Center of the World. Referring to JERUSALEM, a long-held perspective on Jewish life.

Cherem. A kind of excommunication that deprives the individual Jew of social intercourse with his coreligionists.

Chmielnicki, Bogdan. A Cossack chief and leader of a revolt in the Ukraine in 1648, during which Jews were slaughtered. When the Polish king died and his successor tried to negotiate with Chmielnicki, the opposing forces from all sides attacked the Jews until the fighting stopped in 1667.

Chuetas. A term of abuse for CRYPTO-JEWS or MARRANOS in Majorca. They lived in a separate and distinct community from the rest of the population.

City Without Jews. Written by Hugo Bettauer in 1926, a provocative novella that is a slightly veiled satire on the ANTI-SEMITIC policies of Vienna.

Concentration Camp. Camps built by the Nazis to bring together all of the Jews, and then put them to forced labor and death.

Concerning the Civic Amelioration of the Jews. This important volume was written in 1781 by Wilhelm Dohm, the Prussian counselor of state who was influenced by MOSES MENDELSSOHN. In it he blamed Christian society for the degraded conditions of the Jewish people, arguing strongly for EMANCIPATION.

Conversos. CRYPTO-JEWS in Spain, another name for MARRANOS beginning in 1391.

Council of the Four Lands. The central institutions of Jewish self-government in Poland and Lithuania from the middle of the sixteenth century until 1764.

Court Jews. A position of privilege, it provided medieval princes with commercial and financial services, essentially in Central Europe from the end of the sixteenth century forward.

Cremieux, Isaac Adolphe. (1796–1880) French lawyer and statesman who refused to take the humiliating oath MORE JUDAICO and eventually fought to get it eliminated; president of the ALLIANCE ISRAELITE UNIVERSELLE.

Crypto-Jews. Persons who remained faithful to Judaism while outwardly practicing another religion they were forced to accept; they came into existence in the seventh century in Spain.

Cyrus. King of Persia who reigned from 559–529 B.C.E. He ended the BABYLONIAN EXILE after he defeated Babylonia and allowed the Israelites back to JERUSALEM.

Dachau. Town near Munich where a CONCENTRATION CAMP was built nearby in 1933. It served as a model for all of the other camps built by the Nazis and existed until it was captured by the American forces in 1945. Here the Germans first began their pseudo-scientific experiments. During World War II, over 150 branches of the main camp were set up in Germany and Austria and also called Dachau.

Damascus Blood Libel. Sometimes referred to as the Damascus Affair. In 1840, Christian and Muslim anti-Jewish feelings, aggravated by the political struggle of the period, mounted together when a friar and his Muslim servant disappeared. Although they were probably murdered by tradesmen, since they were involved in questionable business practices, the Jewish community was accused of the BLOOD LIBEL. A false witness claimed to have seen the murder take place, community members were tortured, and sixty-three children were seized, leading to world outcry. Eventually the remaining living prisoners were released; the event resulted in the establishment of the ALLIANCE ISRAELITE UNIVERSELLE.

Dhimmi/Dhimma. An Arabic word that refers to the relationship between the protector, *dhimma,* and the protected, the *dhimmi;* it establishes the legal status of the Jew or Christian who lives in the Muslim state.

Diaspora. Greek word meaning "dispersion." Following the destruction of the TEMPLE, Jews were dispersed in lands throughout the world; this dispersion outside of Israel is referred to as the diaspora. It is sometimes used interchangeably with GALUT, or in contradistinction to it. It has been applied since classical times to any Jewish settlement outside of Israel.

Doctor's Plot. One of the most dramatic anti-Jewish purges in the Soviet Union. Just before Stalin died in 1953, his regime "unmasked" a group of prominent Moscow physicians, mostly Jews, in an alleged conspiracy to assassinate Soviet leaders.

Doenmeh. Following the failure of SHABBATAI ZEVI, this set of his adherents embraced Islam.

D.P. (displaced person). Following the liberation of the CONCENTRATION CAMPS at the end of World War II, the individuals there, whose homes and lives had been destroyed, were termed displaced persons. They were kept in camps until they could be integrated back into society or helped to emigrate.

Dreyfus, Captain Alfred. (1859–1935) In a celebrated case of ANTI-SEMITISM that gained worldwide attention, this French army officer (the only Jewish officer on the French General Staff) was court-martialed and eventually acquitted of sending a secret military document in 1894 to the military attaché of the German embassy in Paris. Defended by, among others, French author Emile Zola, Dreyfus became the center of one of the most famous cases in legal history, and a crucial point in the battle against modern anti-Semitism. He had been convicted of treason because the French government suppressed evidence, fearing that the army would be discredited. His exoneration in 1906 represents not only a victory over anti-Semitism but the final defeat of monarchical and clerical elements in French politics. It also led to the separation of church and state.

Dubnow, Simon. (1860–1941) Historian and political idealogue, he was particularly known for his sociological interpretation of Jewish history, noting that the Jewish people developed in an interactive state with any environment in which it found itself throughout history.

Dura-Europos. An ancient city on the Euphrates that is well known because of a SYNAGOGUE discovered there in 1932.

Dybbuk, the. Sometimes spelled Dibbuk; from the word "to cleave." An evil spirit that, according to Jewish folklore, enters the living person and causes mental illness. The classic interpretation is in a 1916 play by S. An-sky that inspired other productions, including a film by the same name.

Ebionites. From the Hebrew *evion,* poor. An early Jewish–Christian sect that clung to the precepts of the TORAH.

Edict of Toleration. In 1782, the Holy Roman Emperor Joseph II issued the *Toleranzpatent* for the Jews of Vienna and Austria, granting them freedom of trade and industry and eliminating restrictions regarding housing and ghettoization. The year before he had eliminated the Jewish badge and the Leibzoll.

Eichmann, Adolf. (1906–1962) Nazi who was chiefly responsible for the Nazi scheme to exterminate all of European Jewry; captured while living in exile in Argentina in 1960, he was abducted by the Israelis, brought to trial, and eventually executed.

Einsetzgruppen. German S.S. "action groups" who were sent to murder Jews, Soviet officials, and gypsies in occupied territory behind the German lines to the East. Local ANTI-SEMITES were encouraged by the Einsetzgruppen to stage POGROMS.

Elbogen, Ismar. (1874–1943) Historian who was involved in the organizational work of German Jewry until he immigrated to New York (following the onset of Nazism). He taught simultaneously at THE JEWISH THEOLOGICAL SEMINARY, HEBREW UNION COLLEGE, Jewish Institute of Religion, and DROPSIE COLLEGE.

Elephantine. Situated on the southern end of a small island in the NILE, it came into prominence in the modern era when a discovery of documents known as the Elephantine Papyri was made there.

Emancipation. The attainment of equal rights before the law, the logical consequence of the principle that a nation should have a uniform system of law for all its citizens.

Ethnarch. Greek word for ruler of the people. The title was given to leaders of the Jewish people in classical times to implicitly deny their independent status "as a king." It was conferred on Simon the HASMONEAN. Later it was used to refer to the head of the DIASPORA Jewish community, for example, ALEXANDRIA in the first century B.C.E.

***Exodus* (1947).** This refugee ship took a sensational journey that gained the attention of the world. Under the auspices of the HAGANAH in 1947, it began with 4,584 Jewish refugees from Europe who were not permitted to land in HAIFA, then PALESTINE. Seized by the British, they were huddled off to France, where they had embarked. The refugees refused to land and France refused to coerce them. Eventually, they were sent back to the British Occupation Zone in Germany where they found themselves in D.P. camps once again. Leon Uris wrote a best-selling novel called *Exodus*. It tells the story of the landing of immigrants in Palestine (Israel) amidst the British blockade following the end of World War II.

Fagin. In Charles Dickens's *Oliver Twist,* the corrupt Jewish ringleader of the orphaned children who led them into a life of crime.

Falasha. For stranger, derogatory name for Ethiopian Jews.

False Messiah. Individual who claims to be the MESSIAH.

Fertile Crescent. An area in the Middle East consisting of a narrow belt of agriculturally valuable land shaped like a huge horseshoe. Its boundaries are northward along the Mediterranean Coast, eastward across Syria and

Iraq, and southward ending at the Persian Gulf. The Fertile Crescent has been settled for more than 6,000 years and is one of the earliest homes of civilized people. It is considered the birthplace of Jewish history.

Final Solution, The. The Nazi plan to exterminate the Jews.

Fourth Philosophy. A revolutionary group, established when Roman rule was instituted in Judea in 6 c.e., that refused to pay a tax to the empire. The groups that took their own lives on Masada were part of the revolutionary group.

Frank, Jacob. (1726–1791) False messiah, founder of a sect that bore his name (Frankists), as the last stage of the movement started by Shabbatai Zevi.

Frankel, Zechariah. (1801–1875) Rabbi and scholar, he became chief rabbi at Dresden in 1836. From 1854 until his death he directed the Breslau Rabbinical Seminary, which endeavored to combine Jewish religious tradition with the European Enlightenment.

Friedlaender, David. (1850–1934) An advocate of assimilation, this communal leader and author in Berlin fought for equal rights for Jews. He advocated a joining together of Protestants and enlightened Jews, rejecting Christian dogma and Jewish ritual precepts. He is considered by some to be a forerunner of Reform Judaism.

Galut. Literally, exile. A somewhat perjorative term that refers to Jews living outside of the land of Israel, often used interchangeably with diaspora.

Geiger, Abraham. (1810–1874) Rabbi and early leader of Reform Judaism, well-known for his conflicts with Solomon Tiktin, whom he served as assistant in Breslau. He was active in the synods held by Reform rabbis in Frankfurt and Breslau and a founder of the Breslau Seminary.

General Privilege. As part of a decree of Frederic II of Prussia in 1750, this small group of Jews was given economic and residential rights. Most other groups were very limited.

Ghetto. A city section where Jews were forced to live, usually surrounded by fence or wall, separated from the rest of the city. The term was probably first used in 1516 to designate a quarter of Venice near a foundry (ghetto), declared to be the only sector open to Jews for settlement.

Giudecca. Italian for Jewish quarter. Once Jews were allowed to live in Venice, the term referred specifically to an isolated island in Venice, separated by walls, gates, and drawbridges.

Glukel of Hameln. Eighteenth-century German Jewish woman whose diaries shed light on the economic status of the Jews in that period.

Golden Age of Spain. A period from the eleventh to thirteenth centuries, when Jewish life and scholarship flourished, primarily under Muslim rule.

Graetz, Heinrich. (1817–1891) Historian and Bible scholar, well known for his multivolume *History of the Jews,* written from the perspective of the MISSION OF ISRAEL.

Grand Sanhedrin. Established by Napoleon in 1807, this assembly of RABBIS and lay people was called together to confirm its responses of the ASSEMBLY OF JEWISH NOTABLES; the members of the Grand Sanhedrin pledged loyalty to the emperor and rejected all Jewish law that brought conflict with political requirements of citizenship.

Habiru. Sometimes Abiru. Resembling the biblical word for HEBREW, this word is found in Near Eastern sources, referring to a social stratum living on the fringe of settled society; the PATRIARCHS' clans may have been part of this group.

Hasmoneans. Following the revolt of the MACCABEES, a Hasmonean dynasty was established as a religious authority to lead the people, so-called from the name of one of the ruling family's ancestors; three generations ruled JUDEA, beginning with Simon (ca. 140 B.C.E.).

Hellenism. The influence of Greek culture, blended with Near Eastern elements in the context of continuing social change throughout the area.

Hep! Hep! Riots. From the rallying cry of the rioters. These riots against the Jews, which took place in German cities and the countryside in 1819, were used to postpone EMANCIPATION to the distant future.

Hirsch, Baron Maurice de. (1831–1890) German financier and philanthropist who, as the originator of the JEWISH COLONIZATION ASSOCIATION, was the first to plan for resettlement of the Jews on a large scale.

Hofjude. German COURT JEWS who provided German princes with valuable services by being military contractors, arranging for loans and the extension of credit, managing the mint, providing the court with precious stones and fine clothing, and founding new industries; their status allowed them to settle in areas previously prohibited to Jews.

Host Desecration Libel. Another form of ANTI-SEMITISM, accusing Jews of conspiring to steal and pierce the wafer of the Host in order to torture the body of Jesus.

Hyksos. An Egyptian term for foreign rulers; some scholars believe that their domain over the area made JOSEPH's rule possible.

Immanuel of Rome. (ca. 1261–1328) Poet, known in Italian as Manoello Giudeo, "Immanuel the Jew." It is thought, although not substantiated, that he was a physician with a high post in the community, occasionally responsible for the correspondence of the Jewish community in Rome.

Infamous Decree. *Decret infame.* Issued by Napoleon on March 17, 1808, this order restricted the economic activity and freedom of movement of the Jews in the eastern province of the empire for ten years.

Intertestamental Period, The. The period between the canonization of the Hebrew Bible and the New Testament.

Isavists. Messianic movement in the seventh-eighth century c.e. in Persia founded by Obadiah Abu Isa Al-isfahan, who claimed to be the Messiah.

Israelitische Landeskanzlei. Localized central office of the community of Hungary in the nineteenth century, representing the non-orthodox majority.

Israelitische Landessekretariat. Localized central office of the community of Hungarian Jews in the nineteenth century, representing the orthodox community.

Instituto Convitto Rabbinico. Also called Collegio Rabbinico Italiano. Italian rabbinical college, inaugurated in Padua in 1829 as the first modern institution of its kind.

J'accuse. Newspaper article written by Emile Zola, noted French writer, during the Dreyfus Affair in which he accuses France, not Dreyfus.

Jacobson, Israel. (1768–1828) In 1810, the Jewish merchant of Seesen, Prussia, erected his own synagogue and took the initiative of establishing modest reforms including confirmation, paving the way to the development of Reform Judaism.

Jewish Antiquities. Series of volumes by the chronicler Flavius Josephus that proves the Jews are an ancient people. A sort of apologetic, it details Jewish life in the diaspora; it also recalls events in the Bible, but not as they are recorded there.

Jewish Chronicle, The. English newspaper established in 1841, the oldest Jewish periodical in existence; it swallowed its principal competitors, *Hebrew Observer* and the *Jewish World,* along the way.

Jewish Colonization Association (JCA). Established by the Baron Maurice de Hirsch in 1891 as a philanthropic association to assist Jews to emigrate and settle them with productive employment.

Jewish Cultural Reconstruction. Organization founded in 1947 in New York by nearly all Jewish organizations worldwide to deal with Jewish cultural and religious property confiscated by the Nazis and recovered by the U.S. military.

Jewish National Councils. Established as representative organs of Jewish minority in Czekoslovakia, Austria, and Russia.

Jewish Quarter, The. The existence of separate streets or sections of a city for Jews, usually determined by law.

Jewish Quarterly Review (JQR). Originally published in London and then in Philadelphia, this learned journal was established in 1889 by Israel Abrahams and Claude Montefiore.

Jewish Race. Anti-Semites maintain that there is a Jewish race and strive to prove it by establishing similarities in physical characteristics.

Jewish Telegraphic Agency (JTA). A worldwide Jewish news service established by Jacob Landau in The Hague in 1914; it eventually moved to the United States in 1935, where it was reorganized.

Jewish Wars, The. Series of volumes by the chronicler Flavius Josephus, detailing the history of war between Rome and the Jewish people; contains some distortion of fact since Josephus wanted to impress the new Roman rulers.

Jews College. Rabbinical seminary in London founded in 1855. Originally established to train English-speaking rabbis and laymen, it also served until 1879 as a secondary school for boys. Beginning in 1883, its students graduated from London University.

Josephus Flavius. (ca. 38–100 c.e.) Chronicler, historian, and chief representative of Jewish Hellenistic literature, known for his works the *Jewish Wars* and *Jewish Antiquities*.

Judaea Capta. From the Latin, meaning "Judea taken"; a coin issued by Vespasian and his immediate successors featuring a female bound in chains under a palm tree.

Judengasse. German for the Jewish quarter or ghetto.

Judenrat. German for the Jewish National Council that headed the Jewish community; established by the German occupying forces during World War II, responsible for enforcing Nazi orders.

Judenrein. (or *Judenfrei*) German for "cleansed free of Jews"; the Nazis used the term to refer to the Final Solution.

Judenstaat. Written by Theodor Herzl in 1896 to advocate the need for and creation of a Jewish state.

Judeo–Christian. Refers to the early Christian period in which groups like the Ebionites clung to Jewish law and messianism.

Juderia. Jewish quarter in Spain.

Judezmo. Jewish folk language, related closely to Ladino, developed around the first century c.e. in the center of the Iberian Peninsula.

Judghanites. Pre-Karaite sect eventually absorbed by those who were influenced by Eastern Islamic tendencies.

Judischer Kulturbund. An organization that existed in Nazi Germany from 1933 to 1941, established to give Jewish actors, writers, and musicians access to public hearings when Nazi decrees barred them.

Juedishen Glaubens. Literally "Jewish faith," full name *Central Verein Deutscher Staatsbuerger Juedishen Glaubens,* abbreviated C.V., for Cen tral Union of German Citizens of Jewish Faith. Founded in Berlin in 1893 to safeguard Jewish rights in the midst of rising German ANTI-SEMITISM.

Kahal. Literally, "the community," referring to the infrastructure and community ruling council of the Jewish community in Europe.

Kairawan. Also spelled Kairouan. Town in Tunisia; its ACADEMY was well known, especially because of its correspondence with the Babylonian academies.

Kapo. Jewish prisoner in charge of other inmates in a Nazi CONCENTRATION CAMP.

Khazars, The. A sovereign group in Eastern Europe of the general Turkish type in the seventh to tenth centuries; its leaders adopted Judaism.

Kiddush Hashem. Literally, "sanctification of the divine name." Eventually refers to martyrdom.

Kishinev, the Pogrom of. The capital of the Moldavian S.S.R., it became known to the world as a result of two POGROMS, April 1903 and October 1905, preceded by poisonous anti-Jewish campaigns.

Kley, Eduard. (1789–1867) German teacher and preacher of REFORM JUDAISM, composer of numerous hymns.

Kristallnacht. Literally, "the night of broken or shattered glass," for Nazi anti-Jewish attacks on November 9–10, 1938. The named developed because of the windows of Jewish stores and homes that were broken throughout Germany, ostensibly a retaliation for the assassination by a Jew of Ernst Vom Rath, third secretary of the German embassy in Paris. Marked the turning point in the treatment of German and Austrian Jewry.

Ladino. Spanish folk language of the Jews.

Landesrabbinerschule. Rabbinical seminary in Budapest, Hungary, established in 1877 amid controversy and infighting between the ORTHODOX; a state institution funded by state-imposed taxation on the Jewish community.

League for the Attainment of Equal Rights for the Jewish People in Russia. This group met illegally in 1905, and consisted of middle-class liberals and ZIONISTS in favor of civil, political, and national rights, the freedom of natural and cultural self-determination, a comprehensive KEHILLAH autonomy, and free choice of language and school education.

League of Anti-Semites, The. Also called the Anti-Semitic League, it was a political party established in Germany focusing on racial and economic issues. Solely committed to racial anti-Semitism, it was established in Germany in 1879 by Wilhelm Marr, who introduced the term ANTI-SEMITISM to the German public (after it had been recently coined).

Leibzoll. Body tax, in Central Europe in the Middle Ages. Whenever a Jew entered a town he was subject to pay this body or head tax at the town gate in order to gain entry.

Levi, Primo. Twentieth-century Italian writer who wrote of his experiences during the HOLOCAUST.

Levi Yitzchak of Berdichev, Rabbi. Chasid who was well known for his arguments with God in the midst of his community.

Levinsohn, Isaac Baer. Beginning in the 1820s in the PALE OF SETTLEMENT, a product of the ENLIGHTENMENT, he advocated secular education and vocational diversification in manual labor and agriculture yet was always respectful of Jewish tradition.

Levita, Elijah. (ca. 1468–1549) A German Jew living in Italy who taught Hebrew to important Christian humanists. He wrote about the system of vowels and accents in the MASORETIC TEXT.

Limpieza de Sangre. Purity of blood, first advanced by the enemies of the CONVERSOS in the fifteenth century. It became an obsession in Spain in the sixteenth and seventeenth centuries to exclude anyone without a Christian genealogy from guilds and colleges as well as military and religious orders.

Luftmenschen. From the German, "man of the air." A reference to a rootless person, a term coined by Max Nordau to refer to the masses of Eastern European Jews with no stable or productive occupation.

Luzzatto, Moses Hayyim. Italian Jewish pietist, poet, and playwright; he lived in the eighteenth century and wrote about religious and secular themes.

Luzzatto, Samuel David. (1800–1865) Italian Jew who was probably the most erudite HEBREW philologist of the nineteenth century. He was critical of what he called the "EMANCIPATION complex," which he felt obsessed the students of the science of Judaism.

Ma'amad. Council of elders in a SEFARDI community, corresponds to the KAHAL in the ASHKENAZI community (*see Rabbinic Legal Literature and Commentaries:* MA'AMADOT).

Ma'ase-Buch. A vast collection of stories and folktales handed down by word of mouth and later recorded in YIDDISH.

Magid. Wandering preacher and storyteller, especially active in eighteenth-century Poland in the nascent CHASIDIC movement.

Majdenek. CONCENTRATION CAMP and extermination camp on the outskirts of Lublin, Poland, where at least 125,000 Jews were killed in 1942–1943.

Manasseh ben Israel, Rabbi. (1604–1657) Outstanding Jewish writer of seventeenth-century Amsterdam who was born of a Portuguese MARRANO family. He published defenses of Judaism to the Christians and participated in efforts to resettle Jews in England.

Mapu, Abraham. (1808–1867) Lithuanian whose early life on a farm informed his colorful Hebrew romances, which depicted lush pastoral scenes in ancient PALESTINE. His work was influential in raising the banner of Lithuanian Jewish nationalism.

Mara deAtra. The RABBI of the local community.

Marrano. Literally, "swine." The term enters Jewish history in the mid-fifteenth century to refer to CONVERSOS by their enemies. Eventually the term lost its negative connotation and became a badge of honor among Jews.

Maskilim. Those who accepted the ENLIGHTENMENT and worked to further it.

May Laws. In 1882, the Russian Minister of the Interior issued this set of "temporary rules," which came to this name because of the month they were issued. These laws curtailed Jewish residences in villages, even in the PALE OF SETTLEMENT, reversing the more liberal policy toward the Jews in the previous era. They also started quotas on gymnasia and universities so that students were forced to travel abroad for their education, doctors and lawyers were deprived of their positions, and people could not expand businesses.

Melitzot. A type of rhymed prose, found in medieval Spanish-Jewish literature.

Mellah. JEWISH QUARTER in Morocco. Term first appeared in Fez in the fifteenth century.

Memorbuchen. European memory books, kept in local synagogues, in which the names of Jews were inscribed following their deaths in various POGROMS and massacres. These led to YIZKOR books issued by modern SYNAGOGUES near the HIGH HOLIDAYS.

Menachemists. Or Menachemites. Messianic movement in Kurdistan in the twelfth century, followers of David Alroy (called Menachem).

Mendele Mocher Seforim. (1835–1917) An important YIDDISH writer of eastern Europe who, like SHOLOM ALEICHEM, used realism, irony, and satire to depict the virtues and limitations of the intense Jewish environment in which he was raised. He emphasized the humble heroism of typical SHTETL figures.

Meor HaGolah (Rabbi Gershon of Mayence). (Tenth century) Called the "light of the exile," one of the most famous of the early teachers. Among his surviving legal opinions is his RESPONSUM prohibiting polygamy.

Mesopotamia. Region of western Asia, in what is now Iraq, known as the "cradle of civilization." People living in Mesopotamia included the Akkadians, Sumerians, HITTITES, and ASSYRIANS.

Mikhoels, Solomon. Stage name for Solomon Vorsi (1890–1948), murdered in Russia in 1948 by the secret police as part of the Stalinist purges. He directed the Jewish State Theatre in Moscow from 1929. His murder touched off the systematic liquidation of all Jewish cultural institutions.

Molcho, Solomon. (Sixteenth century) A man from Lisbon affected by MESSIANISM, he circumcised himself, took this name, and went to Solonika to study KABBALAH. Eventually Molcho announced that the messianic kingdom would come in 1540. He was burned at the stake in 1532 by Emperor Charles V.

Montagu, Lily. (1874–1963) Social worker, pioneer of LIBERAL JUDAISM in Great Britain, involved as a founder of the WORLD UNION FOR PROGRESSIVE JUDAISM.

Montefiore, Claude. (1858–1938) Theologian and leader of LIBERAL JUDAISM in England, founder of the *Jewish Quarterly Review* and president of the WORLD UNION FOR PROGRESSIVE JUDAISM; an opponent to ZIONISM.

Montefiore, Sir Moses. (1784–1865) English Jewish philanthropist and community worker, related by marriage to the Rothschilds, who amassed a fortune as a stockbroker and investment banker. He used his position and his finances to struggle for Jewish EMANCIPATION in England, and contributed funds for economic development, schools, and orphanages in PALESTINE. He bought land there for agricultural enterprises and encouraged colonization. He endowed hospitals, established the first girls' school in JERUSALEM, and built SYNAGOGUES. In 1837 he was knighted by Queen Victoria. Many places in Israel bear his name, including YEMIN MOSHE in Jerusalem and Shechonat Montefiore in TEL AVIV. During his lifetime, he was the principal spokesman for world Jewry, always ready to help a community in need. He is remembered most for resolving the DAMASCUS Affair and BLOOD LIBEL.

More Judaico. In eighteenth-century central Europe, when Jews testified in general courts, they were forced to take this special oath, worded to emphasize their "untrustworthy" nature.

Mortara, Edgar. This Jewish child was kidnapped in Italy in 1859 for the purpose of forced baptism, which led to outcry around the world, and the formation of the BOARD OF DELEGATES OF AMERICAN ISRAELITES.

Morteira, Rabbi Saul. (ca. 1596–1660) RABBI, born in Italy, who worked as a scholar in Amsterdam, where he was a CHAKHAM of the Bet Ya'akov community. Although a teacher of BARUCH SPINOZA, he was a member of the BET DIN that excommunicated him.

Moscato, Judah. (ca. 1530–1593) One of the most important rabbis and authors of the Italian renaissance, he became chief rabbi of the Mantua community in 1587.

Mourners for Zion. In Hebrew, *avelei Zion.* Primarily KARAITES who deprived themselves of wine, meat, and other luxuries. They settled in JERUSALEM in order to pray continually that Israel's sins be forgiven in an appeal to God for REDEMPTION. They mourned the destruction of the TEMPLE and the Jewish state.

Musta'rabim. Arabic-speaking Jews living in the Middle Ages were sometimes referred to by this name.

Nagid. Although first used by SHMUEL HANGID (ca. 993–1056), this title of prince was soon adopted by leaders of regional Jewries in the Muslim world.

Nathan the Wise. A play (1779) by the philosopher and litterateur Gotthold Ephraim Lessing in which Nathan, the Jewish protagonist, epitomized wisdom, kindness, and nobility.

Neofiti. Italian for Neophytes. Names given to Jews in southern Italy who, at the end of the thirteenth century, were forced to convert. Many of them secretly clung to their Judaism, but by the sixteenth century, they were no longer distinguishable.

New Christians. Another name for CONVERSOS, MARRANOS. Medieval Spanish Jews forced to convert, beginning particularly in the last quarter of the fourteenth century.

Nuremberg Laws. In 1935, at a Nazi national convention in this city, the Reichstag took away the citizenship of all German Jews, reducing them to second-class citizens, removing the EMANCIPATION of the previous century.

Nuremberg Trials, the. Officially called the International Military Tribunal at Nuremberg (November 20, 1945–October 1, 1946). The heads of the Nazi regime, captured by the Allies, were tried.

Operation Exodus. Following Soviet glasnost and perestroika and the potential for mass emigration of Soviet Jews, funds and human resources were mustered (beginning in 1989) in order to mobilize the rescue efforts.

Organization for Rehabilitation through Training (ORT). Originally called Society for Manual Work among Jews, then Society for Spreading Work Among Jews. An agency closely associated with the AMERICAN JEWISH JOINT DISTRIBUTION COMMITTEE, this organization was established in 1880 for the establishment and development of vocational and agricultural schools, agricultural colonies, and model farms, and to provide vocational training to DISPLACED PERSONS. Today it provides similar services around the world and particularly in Israel.

Pact of Omer. Dating from ca. 800 C.E. Signs of DHIMMI subordination were generally incorporated into this pact, which prohibited Jews and Christians from taking converts, building synagogues and churches, and making a public display of their rituals. Jews and Christians could not live in houses higher than those of Muslims, carry weapons, or ride horses (only donkeys).

Pale of Settlement. The code of 1804 by Alexander I (reigned 1801–1825) codified Jewish status in Russia and defined those territories of western Russia in which Jews were permitted to reside legally. It eventually came to be known as the Pale of Settlement and shortened to the Pale.

"Partisans' Song." Sung by the underground who fought the Nazis during World War II: "Never say you walk the final road."

Peretz, I(saac), L(eib). (1852–1915) A peer of Sholom Aleichem and Mendele Mocher Seforim, perhaps the paradigmatic Yiddish writer of his era. While he wrote in Hebrew, Polish, and Russian, his many literary contributions were in Yiddish, in a sophisticated style touched by the pain and pressure of Warsaw and its Jewish community. He was a traditional and sensitive Jew who embraced the Enlightenment. He was probably best known for *Bontsche Shweig* and *Even Higher.*

Pfefferkorn, Johannes. An early sixteenth-century Jewish convert who denounced Jewish practices and called for the destruction of the Talmud. He was engaged in a controversy over his position with Johannes Reuchlin, a German humanist and Hebrew scholar.

Pharisees. Jewish religious and political party during the Second Temple Period, considered the bearers of traditional Judaism. They instituted centers of learning and synagogues for worship.

Phoenicia. Considered, in part, a part of Canaan, it included most of what is now Lebanon, stretching from Akko (in Israel) north along the east coast of the Mediterranean Sea.

Pogrom. The wanton destruction of Jewish property and Jewish people, often part of clandestine government policy, particularly in Western and Central Europe.

Polemics. A written or oral dialogue defending one's position or ideology, in particular, Judaism, against claims that have been made by an opposition, such as Christianity—especially significant during periods of missionary activity to convert the Jews.

Poll Tax. Another burden placed upon Jews because of their status in society, particularly true of Jews who lived under Muslim rule.

Prisoners of Conscience. A term that developed during the 1970s referring to the Soviet Jews who were kept in Russia, often in prison or in Siberia, and refused the right to emigrate.

Protocols of the Elders of Zion. Anti-Semitic document that claims that the Jewish community has a plan to take over the world; first appeared in Russia at the turn of the century.

Rabbanites. From the tenth century onward, this term was used to refer to those Jews who accept the oral law as equally binding as the written law.

Rabbiner-Seminar für das orthodoxes Judenthum. A modern orthodox rabbinical seminary established in 1873 in Berlin by Azriel Hildesheimer in order to promote *Torah im Derech Eretz* (the combination of Torah study and a knowledge of modern culture); closed in 1938 following Kristallnacht.

Radanites. Jewish merchant groups who traveled from their headquarters in France through eastern Europe, to the Middle East, then India and China; especially active between the eighth and eleventh centuries.

Rapaport, Nathan. (1911–) Sculptor, born in Warsaw, Poland, best known for patriotic monuments, such as that of the defender of the WARSAW GHETTO, MORDECAI ANILEWICZ, which stands in front of Kibbutz Yad Mordecai in Israel.

Refuseniks. Russian Jews who have been refused exit visas to emigrate, primarily to Israel, after they have made applications for them.

Reparations. Monies paid by the German government as a gesture of compensation for the property confiscated during the Nazi period.

Resh BeiRabbanan. Head of the YESHIVAH in Egypt, also known as *resh haseder,* in the early Middle Ages.

Resh Kallah. In BABYLON, the president of the students assembled to study in ADAR and ELUL, second only to *resh sidra.*

Resh Metivta. Alternative name for GAON, from the ACADEMIES of BABYLONIA.

Resh Pirka. The archipherecite, the official leader of Palestinian Jewry, a head of the ACADEMY. This word was used in the early centuries of the common era.

Reuben, David. In the era of MESSIANISM, following the expulsion of Jews from Portugal and Spain, he claimed to have been sent from a distant Jewish kingdom of lost biblical tribes. He visited Italy and Portugal, where he created a stir among the MARRANOS.

Righteous Teacher. The leader of the ESSENES' community at QUMRAN, may have been the model on which Jesus of Nazareth based his career.

Ritual Murder. The charge by ANTI-SEMITES that Jews kill young Christian boys in order to use their blood to make PASSOVER MATZAH; part of the BLOOD LIBEL.

Rossi, Azariah dei. (1521–1578) A writer and early historian who published a work, *Meor Einayim* (Light to the Eyes), containing the results of his inquiries into the ancient Jewish past, a nomad nation at the time. He was the first to rediscover the writings of PHILO and JOSEPHUS and to bring to bear the historical evaluation of TALMUDIC legend through non-Jewish sources. His work was banned by then-contemporary Jewish authorities and did not receive recognition until the nineteenth century.

Rothschild Family. German Jewish financiers who established branches of their bank in Vienna, Paris, and London, where they arranged government loans on a large scale. It is of special significance that the family did not ASSIMILATE into European nobility, but instead remained committed to and active in Jewish philanthropies.

Rothschild, Lionel de. (1808–1879) The first Jew to take a seat in the British House of Commons (in 1858), he led the struggle for EMANCIPATION in Great Britain.

Russo, Baruchiah. Leader of the DOENMEH.

Salanter, Israel. (1810–1883) Israel Ben Ze'ev Wolf, founder of the MUSAR movement.

Schutzjude. Protected Jews; those who paid a tax to and were protected by the emperor of Rome, beginning in the thirteenth century.

Secret Jews. Those who were forced to behave publicly like Christians while practicing Judaism in secret, beginning in the fourteenth century.

Shneur Zalman of Lyady. (1745–1813) Founder of CHABAD CHASIDISM, and patriarch of the rabbinic dynasty that continues to lead the community.

Shoah. Literally, consumed by fire. HOLOCAUST, refering to the destruction of six million European Jews between the years 1938–1945.

Sholom Aleichem. (1859–1916) Also spelled Sholem, the pen name of Shalom Rabinovitz, a YIDDISH author who used humor as a vehicle to communicate his social criticism; he is especially well-known for his Tevye stories.

Shtadlan. The Jewish community representative who had access to secular community leaders; the exact function of this leader was determined by the country and circumstance in which the individual lived.

Shtetl. Small communities in Eastern Europe with a unique sociology, culture, and life-style, usually Jewish towns related to larger cities or those that made up the PALE OF SETTLEMENT. Often the socioeconomic structure of the shtetl was negatively determined by POGROMS and the like; there was a pervasive intimate life-style with an emphasis on the traditional ideas of piety, learning, and charity.

Shylock. In Shakespeare's *Merchant of Venice,* the Jewish usurer, whose name has become a negative stereotype.

Sicarii. A term used by JOSEPHUS FLAVIUS for dagger men, those who used ambush as their military maneuver. Jewish patriots who actually resisted the Roman government in the first century C.E.

Steinschneider, Moritz. (1816–1907) Considered to be a founder of modern Jewish scholarship, he was instrumental in the creation of modern Jewish bibliographic research.

St. Louis, S.S. Sometimes referred to as the Voyage of the Damned, this boatload of refugees from Nazi-occupied Europe went from country to country seeking refuge and was not given asylum. Eventually the boat returned to Europe and most of its passengers perished in CONCENTRATION CAMPS.

Syrkin, Nachman. (1868–1924) Considered to be the first ideologue of social Zionism—the realization of ZIONISM through cooperative mass settlement by Jewish workers, the proletariat.

Tarbut. Hebrew for culture. Refers to a cultural organization that maintained schools in Eastern Europe between the two World Wars.

Theresienstadt. A town in Czechoslovakia. While it functioned as a CONCENTRATION CAMP between 1941 and 1945, it was shown to the International Red Cross as a model of "humane treatment" as news of Jewish extermination began to spread to the West.

Tiktin, Solomon. (1791–1843) Member of rabbinic family who succeeded his father in the rabbinate of Breslau and Silesia. He was involved in a controversy with the REFORM movement when he and his son launched a campaign against ABRAHAM GEIGER.

Treaty of Versailles. Established a mandate system after World War I for the administration of former overseas possessions of Germany and parts of the Turkish Empire. PALESTINE was assigned to Great Britain, with a primary purpose to establish a national home for the Jewish people.

Treblinka. One of the main death camps built by the Nazis during World War II, known until that time only as a railway station northeast of Warsaw.

Wannsee Conference. Held at the central interpol office in Wannsee, Berlin, on January 20, 1942, and convened by Hermann Goering, this Nazi conference determined the coordination of all activities of the Nazi Party and the S.S. to bring about an efficient FINAL SOLUTION.

Warsaw Ghetto Uprising. Led by MORDECAI ANILEWICZ, the underground in the Warsaw ghetto fought back the advancing German forces beginning on April 19, 1943. The uprising, which lasted for two months, had a powerful moral effect on Jews and non-Jews who had previously thought that all of the Jews went to their deaths without a fight.

Whirlwind. The term by which some survivors of the HOLOCAUST refer to the Holocaust.

Wiesenthal, Simon. (1908–   ) Nazi hunter from Vienna.

World Jewish Congress. An association of Jewish organizations throughout the world whose mission is to ensure the survival and nurture the unity of the Jewish people; officially established in 1936 under the leadership of STEPHEN S. WISE and Nahum Goldmann.

Yellow Badge. A sign that Jews were required to wear that designated them as Jews. The yellow star was required during the Nazi period, but prior generations of Jews in various countries were required to wear other signs, including different vestments in the Muslim world, a piece of yellow taffeta over the heart in the thirteenth century in England, and a wheel for a short period in France around the same time.

Zealots. A name probably first recorded by JOSEPHUS FLAVIUS to describe the Jewish resistance party who fought against the Romans in the first century C.E.

Zevi, Shabbatai. (1626–1676) A self-appointed MESSIAH and leader of the movement called Shabbateanism, named for him. The largest and most significant messianic movement in Jewish history since the failed BAR KOKHBA rebellion, it climaxed in 1666 when Zevi converted to Islam.

Zhid. A Russian term of derision referring to Jews.

Zion Mule Corps. During World War I, a battalion of muleteers who served under Joseph Trumpeldor at Gallipoli in support of the Allied efforts. Made up of Jewish refugees from PALESTINE in Egypt.

CHAPTER 5

American Jewish History and Geography

In 1654, twenty-three refugee Jews arrived aboard the *St. Charles/ Catherine* in Dutch New Amsterdam from Recife, Brazil, just conquered by the Portuguese. This began what has been called the greatest period of civilization in the history of Judaism. The waves of immigration that eventually followed this modest beginning contributed to the building of a diversified community replete with its own autonomous streams and factions. Today, the American Jewish population numbers some six million. From shore to shore, Jews have made their way to America's small towns and large urban centers, making their impact felt in every walk of American life. Often, they came to this country to escape persecution and pogroms—as well as economic insecurity—often disembarking in New York City, building up its Lower East Side. They spilled over to cities throughout the Eastern seaboard and made their way to the American heartland by way of numerous orchestrated immigration plans such as the Galveston Movement.

In 1924, when the Johnson Immigration Act was passed into law, severely restricting immigration, the American Jewish community was forced to create its own unique amalgamated identity. This was the first time that Judaism was expressed in a free and democratic society, operating in an environment that tolerated and encouraged religious and political pluralism. The people, places, institutions, and organizations listed in this chapter helped shape that identity. This chapter is the itemized story of a people as it has traversed the land and history of the America it has called home for numerous generations.

Acculturation. The process of adopting the traits of another culture, in this case, secular American society; in other words, becoming "American."

Adler, Cyrus. (1863–1940) Scholar and social worker, Adler was active in the founding of the JEWISH PUBLICATION SOCIETY and the reorganization of the JEWISH THEOLOGICAL SEMINARY under the presidency of SOLOMON SCHECHTER, the founder of the UNITED SYNAGOGUE OF AMERICA. He was also the president of DROPSIE COLLEGE, as well as a founding member of the AMERICAN JEWISH COMMITTEE. Adler was especially adept at interpreting the needs of traditional Jews to wealthy American Jews, moving in Jewish scholarly and American government circles.

Adler, Felix. (1851–1933) Philosopher and educator, Adler founded the Society for ETHICAL CULTURE, which advocated an ethic apart from any religion or dogma. He worked for various social causes such as maternal and child welfare, vocational training schools, medical care for the poor, labor problems, and civic reform.

Adler, Jacob. (1855–1926) YIDDISH actor who settled in New York (indirectly from Odessa) in 1890; his most memorable part was as SHYLOCK in Shakespeare's *Merchant of Venice,* which he played in Yiddish among an English-speaking cast.

Adler, Samuel. (1809–1891) A rabbi and scholar who participated in the founding of the REFORM Movement as a participant in the early rabbinical conferences. He came to America from Worms, Germany, in 1857 to become rabbi of Congregation Emanu-el in New York City, forming a theological seminary there. He also founded the Hebrew Orphan Asylum.

Agro-Joint. Established by the AMERICAN JEWISH JOINT DISTRIBUTION COMMITTEE with the cooperation of the Jewish Colonization Association and ORT; active in the first half of the twentieth century in the economic rehabili-

117

tation of declassed Russian Jews by moving them into agriculture and industry.

Albert Einstein Medical School. Established in 1955 at Yeshiva University, New York City, by its president Samuel Belkin.

Allen, Woody. (1935–) Actor, writer, and director whose personification and self-perception of the Jewish anti-hero is considered by some to be self-hating.

Alrightnik. One who believes that all is right with the world or everything will turn out "all right" even in the face of disaster.

Altman, Benjamin. (1840–1913) Department store magnate, founder of B. Altman and Co.; a pioneer in providing social, medical, and recreational benefits for employees. He was also a patron of the arts.

Am Olam. Literally, "eternal people." Back-to-the-soil movement aimed to realize the ideal of a collective life on the soil but without making Palestine their objective; it launched, unsuccessfully, a score of joint farming projects in the late nineteenth century in the United States, led by Herman Rosenthal.

American Council for Judaism. Anti-Zionist group, founded in 1942 and active in the third quarter of the twentieth century. It consisted of a small minority of laypersons and rabbis, primarily Reform, led by Lessing Rosenwald and Rabbi Louis Wolsey. They feared that Zionism would lead to the old accusation of dual–loyalty, and acted in response to a Central Conference of American Rabbis resolution supporting the establishment of a Jewish Army in Palestine.

American Federation of Polish Jews. Formed in 1908 as the Federation of Polish Jews in America, an organized group of Polish landsmanshaftn, mobilized to provide relief to the pauperized people in Poland in the years between World War I and II.

American Hebrew, The. New York weekly published in 1879 by Philip Cowen, written with a viewpoint favoring Orthodoxy over Reform, often taking an anti-Zionist position. It tried to nurture relations between Jews and non-Jews. Independent publication ceased in 1956 when it joined to form the *American Examiner.*

American Israelite. An Anglo-Jewish weekly newspaper originally called *The Israelite,* established in 1854 by Isaac M. Wise as a platform for his ideas; it is still published in Cincinnati today.

American Jewish Archives. Primarily located on the Cincinnati campus of Hebrew Union College—Jewish Institute of Religion, with branches on the other campuses of HUC–JIR; a historical repository on Jews in the Western Hemisphere, established in 1949 by Jacob Rader Marcus.

American Jewish Committee (AJC). Established in 1906 by an elitist group of Jewish leaders, following the dissolution of the Jewish Alliance of America. Its purpose, according to its own articles of incorporation, was to "prevent the infraction of the civil and religious rights of the Jews, in any part of the world; to render all lawful assistance and to take appropriate remedial action in the event of threatened or actual invasion or restriction of our rights, or of unfavorable discrimination with respect thereto; to secure for Jews equality of economic, social and educational opportunity; alleviate the consequence of persecution, and to afford relief from calamities affecting Jews, wherever they may occur."

American Jewish Conference. An attempt in 1943 to mobilize the American Jewish community in order to denounce the WHITE PAPER of 1939 and demand unrestricted immigration to Palestine.

American Jewish Congress. Founded in 1918, in reaction to the then-current elitist, predominantly anti-ZIONIST leadership of the AMERICAN JEWISH COMMITTEE, as a movement for a democratically elected organization that would declare the will of the community regarding the demand for minority rights of Jews in Eastern Europe and a Jewish future in Palestine.

American Jewish Historical Society. Founded in 1892 in response to a call issued by CYRUS ADLER, "to collect and publish material bearing on the history of the Jews in America." It is currently located on the campus of BRANDEIS UNIVERSITY.

American Jewish Relief Committee. Organized in 1914 by the AMERICAN JEWISH COMMITTEE, with LOUIS MARSHALL as chairman, in order to raise funds and distribute monies for the relief of victims from World War I.

American Jewish Year Book. Beginning in 1899 and published by the JEWISH PUBLICATION SOCIETY, this annual volume serves as a record of events, here and abroad, of institutions and of individuals of note in the American Jewish community.

American Mizrahi Organization. The religious wing of the ZIONIST movement, established in 1903, with similar societies having been established a year earlier throughout the world.

American Zionist, The. Periodical published by the ZIONIST ORGANIZATION OF AMERICA, originally called *The New Palestine,* whose mission is to develop positive public relations on behalf of the state of Israel.

Americanization. To make or become American, especially following the process of immigration.

Angoff, Charles. (1902–1979) Novelist and editor, born in Russia, moved to the United States in the 1920s. Known for his ability to weave into the story of his hero a whole panoply of American–Jewish character types, ranging from the YIDDISH-speaking immigrant to his post-World War II Americanized descendants.

Anti-Defamation League (ADL). A defense agency established in 1913 as part of what is now the INTERNATIONAL ORDER OF B'NAI B'RITH; its purpose is to collect data and to fight ANTI-SEMITISM and anti-Jewish discrimination.

Antin, Mary. (1881–1949) A nonfiction writer born in Poland, who moved to the United States as an early teen, and expressed the immigrant's admiration for the land of freedom. She is best known for *The Promised Land,* which reflected the MELTING POT THEORY of AMERICANIZATION.

Ararat. Named for the first dry land where the biblical NOAH's ark rested, this tract of land, called a "CITY OF REFUGE for the Jews," was situated near the Great Lakes and the outlet of the Erie Canal, on Grand Island in the Niagara River northwest of Buffalo, New York. It was acquired by MORDECAI MANUEL NOAH in 1825 as the site for Jewish settlement as a pilot project for the restoration of PALESTINE.

Arbeiter Ring. Literally, "the Workman's Circle," established in 1950 by socialists in order to maintain influence over the labor movement. It provided the benefits of a fraternal order while also conducting a program of educational, social, and recreational activities for its members and a network of YIDDISH afternoon schools for their children. Steeped in the spirit of socialist idealism, it later created English-speaking branches.

Asch, Sholem. (1880–1957) YIDDISH writer, also known to the world at large. An immigrant to the United States in 1914, he won recognition as one of the foremost American novelists through the translation of his works. He was best known for his series on the central figures of the development of Christianity, as a result of which he lost a significant portion of his Jewish following. His work infused Yiddish literature with warmth and happiness, trying to liberate it from the oppressiveness of the SHTETL.

Ashinsky, Aaron Mordecai. (1866–1954) Born in Poland, he was an ORTHODOX RABBI and religious Zionist leader devoted to the cause of Jewish education. Primarily known for his work in Pittsburgh, Pennsylvania, he was one of the founders of the AMERICAN MIZRAHI ORGANIZATION and the UNION OF ORTHODOX RABBIS.

Ashkenazim. Jews who live in, or whose ancestry comes from, Central and Eastern Europe; refers literally to Ashkenaz, the medieval term for Germany.

Assimilation. When the sense of association or consciousness of one group is merged with another, especially when a subgroup loses its identity to a national group.

Attel, Abe. (1884–1970) World featherweight boxing champion, holding title 1901 to 1912.

Aufbau. Literally, "reconstruction." A weekly German-language newspaper that flourished after World War II.

Baerwald, Paul. (1871–1961) Banker and philanthropist originally from Germany, he was chairman of the Lazard Frères banking firm in New York City. He took over the reigns of the JOINT DISTRIBUTION COMMITTEE in 1932; the School of Social Work at HEBREW UNIVERSITY is named in his honor.

Bamberger, Louis. (1855–1944) Leading Newark, New Jersey, department store merchant and philanthropist who funded, with his sister, the establishment of the Institute for Advanced Study at Princeton.

Bar Mitzvah Factory. Referring to synagogues whose educational programs and often catering halls are designed primarily for the function of providing a BAR/BAT MITZVAH, too often marking the conclusion of a child's Jewish education.

Baron, Salo Wittmayer. (1895–1990) Historian, born in Galicia, who studied in Vienna before coming to the United States in 1927 to teach at the Jewish Institute of Religion. He founded the JEWISH CULTURAL RECONSTRUCTION, which identified and reclaimed libraries and cultural artifacts following the HOLOCAUST. He is best known for his multivolume *A Social and Religious History of the Jews,* which emphasizes the social history of Jews rather than individual figures.

Baruch, Bernard M. (1870–1965) A stock analyst and Wall Street speculator who amassed a fortune by speculating on raw materials, he served as advisor to Presidents Woodrow Wilson and Franklin D. Roosevelt. Named chairman of the War Industries Board in 1918, he mobilized the American wartime economy. He was an advocate of the plan to establish UGANDA as a refuge for Jews and was the author of the first American policy on atomic energy.

Bayit. A communal-like living arrangement primarily popular during the 1960s around college campuses among college students.

Behrman House. Publishing firm, primarily of religious school textbooks, originally located in New York, now in New Jersey in its second generation.

Bellow, Saul. (1915–   ) American novelist raised in Canada and Chicago; best known for *Herzog,* whose hero is a professor caught between personal humanistic values and a dehumanized world.

Benderly, Samson. (1876–1944) Physician turned educator, influential especially as director of the first BUREAU OF JEWISH EDUCATION, which was part of the New York City KEHILLAH in the early twentieth century. He was active in the application of the educational principles of John Dewey to Jewish education; the many students he influenced came to be known as the "Benderly Boys."

Benjamin, Judah P. (1811–1884) Born in the West Indies, a resident of Louisiana, he served as chief counselor to Jefferson Davis as attorney general, secretary of war, and secretary of state of the Confederacy. An articulate advocate of slavery, he joined the exodus of southern statesmen from Washington and fled to England at the conclusion of the Civil War. There he produced the legal text *Benjamin on Sales.* He was one of the first Jews to be elected to the United States Senate and was considered its leading orator.

Benny, Jack. (1894–1974) Born Benjamin Kubelsky. Comedian, radio and t.v. entertainer.

Berg, (Moe) Morris. (1902–1972) Major league baseball player.

Berkowitz, Henry. (1857–1924) REFORM RABBI whose career was focused at Rodeph Shalom in Philadelphia. In 1893 he founded the JEWISH CHAUTAUQUA SOCIETY; he was also a member of the first graduating class of HEBREW UNION COLLEGE.

Berkowitz, Isaac Dov. (1885–1967) HEBREW and YIDDISH novelist, well-known as editor and translator of the works of SHOLOM ALEICHEM. He was a writer of short stories whose context was the social crisis that shook Eastern European Jews in his time.

Berle, Milton. (1908–   ) Formerly Berlinger. Comedian and actor known as "Uncle Miltie."

Berlin, Irving. (1888–1989) Originally Isadore Baline. Prolific composer of musical comedies and popular songs, including "God Bless America," whose proceeds he contributed to the Boy Scouts.

Berlin, Meyer. (1880–1949) Took the name Meir Bar-Ilan. An ORTHODOX RABBI, leader of AMERICAN MIZRAHI, who arrived from Germany in 1913, he actively represented the Orthodox Jewish community in the AMERICAN JEWISH COMMITTEE and the religious ZIONIST movements. He initiated the publishing of the *Talmudic Encyclopedia*. Bar Ilan University in Israel is named in his memory.

Bernstein, Leonard. (1918–1990) Composer and conductor, conductor of the New York Philharmonic Orchestra. He was active with the Israel Philharmonic Orchestra and is best known for his play, *West Side Story*.

Bernstein, Simon. (1884–1962) Journalist and HEBREW scholar, he was devoted to research, especially in the field of Hebrew poetry.

Bijur, Nathan. (1862–1930) A prominent lawyer who became a member of the New York State Supreme Court, he participated in the call to initiate the AMERICAN JEWISH COMMITTEE. Active in prison reform as well, his legal decisions helped extend legal doctrines to meet modern conditions, all based on the Constitution.

Binder, Abraham W. (1895–1966) Composer who exerted a great deal of influence on the work of the REFORM movement, especially by reintroducing biblical chant. He taught at the Jewish Institute of Religion and was musical director at the STEPHEN WISE Free Synagogue and the 92nd St. YMHA, both in New York City.

Bintel Brif. Advice and letters column in *The (Jewish Daily) Forward*.

Bitzaron. Literally, "citadel." A monthly Hebrew periodical issued mid-twentieth century, edited by CHAIM TCHERNOWITZ.

Blank, Samuel Leib. (1893–1962) Hebrew novelist and short story writer. Always focusing on a simple protagonist, he vividly depicted the Jewish worker of the soil amidst primitive surroundings.

Blaustein, David. (1866–1912) A social worker, he was among the delegates at the convention to found the JEWISH ALLIANCE OF AMERICA. He was superintendent of the EDUCATIONAL ALLIANCE in New York City, after establishing the first modern German–Hebrew School in the United States, located in Boston.

Bloch, Ernest. (1880–1959) Composer of orchestral works, best known for his *Sacred Service* for Sabbath morning.

Bloch Publishing Co. Founded in Cincinnati, Ohio, in 1854 by ISAAC M. WISE and Edward Bloch in order to publish books on Jewish subjects; located in New York since 1901.

Bloomgarten, Solomon Yehoash. (1872–1927) Using the pen name of Yehoash, he was a Bible translator and poet whose themes reflected Bible, TALMUD, and folklore. Creating his Bible translation from Hebrew to Yiddish and a major dictionary occupied most of his adult life.

Bloomingdale, Samuel J. (1873–1968) New York department store magnate and innovator of retailing techniques, he was also a philanthropist. He was a leader in the movement to set standards for accuracy in advertising.

Blue Laws. Laws that prevent commercial establishments to be open on Sundays; they adversely affect Sabbath–observant Jewish merchants.

B'nai B'rith, International Order of. Literally, "sons/children of the COVENANT." It was originally established in 1843 as the Independent Order of B'nai B'rith, a national fraternal order whose purpose was to provide mutual aid and insurance. It expanded by 1868 to include an extensive program in philanthropy and political action for the protection of Jewish rights here and abroad. It abandoned its secret ritual and mutual benefit program by 1890 and extended its program to include HILLEL FOUNDATIONS, and the ANTI-DEFAMATION LEAGUE. It organized its first foreign unit in 1889.

Board of Delegates of American Israelites. Lasting only from 1859 to 1878, when it surrendered its functions to the UNION OF AMERICAN HEBREW CONGREGATIONS and its name was changed to "Board of Delegates of Civil and Religious Rights," it was the first body representing a sizable segment of American Jewry.

Bogen, Boris. (1869–1929) Social worker and director-general of the AMERICAN JEWISH JOINT DISTRIBUTION COMMITTEE, he worked in various educational programs designed to help the children of immigrants.

Brandeis, Louis D. (1856–1941) Boston, Massachusetts lawyer, he was architect of the PROTOCOL OF PEACE. He came to be known as "the people's lawyer" and was a leader of the liberal forces in America, representing the common man against what he called "the curse of business." He was named associate justice of the Supreme Court by President Woodrow Wilson in 1919.

Brandeis University. Located in Waltham, Massachusetts, and named for LOUIS D. BRANDEIS, it was established in 1948 as the first secular and nonsectarian university in the United States under Jewish auspices.

Breira. Literally, "alternative." A short-lived organization, founded in 1973, established to give a critical voice to the then-current government policy in the State of Israel.

Brice, Fannie. (1891–1951) Originally Borach. Actress, comedienne, singer, and member of the Ziegfeld Follies.

Brith Abraham, Order. Established in 1859 as a fraternal and mutual benefit order. It split in 1887 when a secession group, called Independent Order Brith Abraham, formed, a result of inviting Jews of Russian and Polish origins to join its lodges. The original organization dissolved by 1927.

Brooks, Mel. (1926–   ) Born Melvin Kaminsky. Comedian, actor, and director, known for his use of Jewish themes in farce comedy.

Bund, The. Originally organized in 1897 in Lithuania, Poland, and Russia as the Jewish Workers Alliance *(Arbeiterbund)*. Influenced by radical socialism, it included a secular Jewish cultural program. Brought to America, it was especially influential in journalism, literature, and the labor movement.

Bureaus of Jewish Education (BJE). The first bureau was established in New York City as part of THE KEHILLAH. Serving as the central coordinating bodies for Jewish education in individual communities, they are sometimes referred to as the Board of Jewish Education. They are usually supported by the local JEWISH FEDERATION.

Cahan, Abraham. (1860–1951) Journalist, novelist, and labor leader who from 1902 until his death was editor-in-chief of THE (JEWISH DAILY) FORWARD.

Cantor, Eddie. (1892–1964) Born Isidor Iskowitch. Comedian and vaudeville performer who raised large sums for refugee relief following World War II, as well as for other Jewish and non-Jewish charities.

Cantorial Soloist. A late twentieth-century term usually used in the REFORM movement to refer to a singer, untrained as a CANTOR, serving in that general capacity; usually limited to the worship service itself.

Cardozo, Benjamin N. (1870–1938) In 1932, he joined LOUIS D. BRANDEIS as associate justice of the United States Supreme Court, having served the Supreme Court and Court of Appeals in New York; he was recognized as a great interpreter of the common law.

Castro, Henry. (1786–1861) Scion of a MARRANO family that had found refuge in France, he called himself Henri Comte de Castro. He encouraged some 5,000 German Jews to settle in Texas. Castro County and the town of Castroville, west of San Antonio, preserve his memory.

Centenary Perspective, The. Primarily authored by Eugene B. Borowitz, this document sought to consolidate and express the views of the Central Conference of American Rabbis on the 100th anniversary of the founding of Hebrew Union College.

Central Committee for the Relief of Jewish War Sufferers. A politically centrist organization, established in 1914 to provide immediate assistance and relief to Jews living in the war zone.

Central Conference of American Rabbis (CCAR). Established in 1889, it is the professional association of Reform rabbis around the world.

Chabad. The intellectual brand of Chasidism, the name is an acronym for the Hebrew words meaning wisdom, understanding, and knowledge. Referred to also as Lubavitch, led by the Schneersohn dynasty of rabbis.

Chipkin, Israel. (1891–1955) Educator, one of Samson Benderly's students, his major work was as director of the Jewish Education Association of New York and the American Association for Jewish Education. He created the Council of Jewish Education, a professional fellowship for educators.

Chosen, The. A novel written by Chaim Potok in 1967, it describes the relationship between a modern orthodox boy and his friend, who is the son of the local leader of Chasidism. It was later turned into a film.

Choynski, Joe. (1869–1943) Heavyweight boxing champion, who hung up his gloves in 1904 after a notable career of twenty years.

Churngin, Pinkhos. (1894–1957) Scholar, essayist, and religious Zionist leader who founded Ban-Ilan University in Israel; one of the moving spirits in the development of Yeshiva University.

Civil Judaism. Popular in the late twentieth century, a Jewish expression of the phenomenon of civil religion, primarily expressed through the Jewish Federation structure, analyzed through the scholarship of Jonathan Woocher.

Cleveland Conference. A national rabbinic meeting held in 1855 in order to (unsuccessfully) create a body with authority to speak and act for the entire American Jewish community.

Cohen, Alfred M. (1859–1949) Cincinnati, Ohio, lawyer, politician, and civic leader; a staunch advocate of rights for black Americans, he worked toward the goal of creating national Jewish unity in its struggle against Nazism.

Cohen, Benjamin Victor. (1894–1983) Lawyer, specializing in corporate reorganization and legal counseling to lawyers; he was an advisor to Franklin D. Roosevelt, providing ideas, facts, and statistics for many New Deal programs.

Cohen, Gerson B. (1924–1991) Historian, chancellor of THE JEWISH THEOLOGICAL SEMINARY OF AMERICA during the latter part of the twentieth century.

Cohen, Henry. (1863–1952) REFORM RABBI in Galveston, Texas; particularly active in prison reform, he gained national recognition for his work after the Galveston hurricane in 1900. He was active in the GALVESTON MOVEMENT.

Commentary. Right-wing, conservative periodical, published monthly by the AMERICAN JEWISH COMMITTEE.

Conference of Presidents of Major American Jewish Organizations. Founded in 1936 to represent the platforms and priorities of major Jewish organizations in America, this organization, founded with a revolving presidency, speaks for American Jewry on the national and international level.

Copland, Aaron. (1990–1991) Outstanding composer of uniquely American classical music.

Council for Jewish Education. National body primarily made up of the heads of BUREAUS OF JEWISH EDUCATION.

Council of Jewish Federations (CJF). Established in 1953, the national body coordinating the work of all of its member JEWISH FEDERATIONS.

Cutler, Colonel Harry. (1875–1920) Jewelry manufacturer, soldier, and prominent civic leader in Providence, Rhode Island.

Davidson, Israel. (1870–1939) Pathfinder and illuminator in the field of Medieval Hebrew Literature; taught at THE JEWISH THEOLOGICAL SEMINARY.

Day School. Refers to a school whose curriculum includes the study of Jewish and secular subjects, in contradistinction to a SUPPLEMENTARY SCHOOL.

de Haas, Jacob. (1872–1937) A man of bold and dynamic temperament, he came from England at THEODOR HERZL's request to become secretary of the FEDERATION OF AMERICAN ZIONISTS in 1902.

de Torres, Luis. (Fifteenth to sixteenth century) The first European to set foot on the first island that Christopher Columbus reached and called San Salvador; he was Columbus's interpreter and settled in Cuba after the expedition reached its second island stop.

Dearborn Independent, The. Henry Ford's widely circulated newspaper that published violent attacks against the Jews, beginning in 1920.

Deborah, Die. To promote his programs and projects, ISAAC MAYER WISE founded, edited, and published this German language periodical for women.

Dembitz, Lewis Naphtali. (1833–1907) Abolitionist who nominated Abraham Lincoln at the Republican Convention of 1860. A lawyer and civic leader in Louisville, Kentucky, he was the uncle of LOUIS BRANDEIS.

Deutsch, Gotthard. (1859–1921) The leading Jewish historian of his day in America, taught at HEBREW UNION COLLEGE in Cincinnati.

Dimont, Max. (1912–) Writer of popular Jewish history.

Doctorow, E.(dgar) L.(awrence). (1931–) Novelist, known for his *Book of Daniel,* a fictional account of the sons of JULIUS AND ETHEL ROSENBERG.

Dolitzki, Menachem Mendel. (1856–1931) A leading Hebrew poet in America; immigrated to the United States in 1892.

Downtown Jews. A reference to the Eastern European Jews who immigrated to the United States in the first quarter of the twentieth century and lived primarily in the LOWER EAST SIDE of New York City upon their arrival.

Drachman, Bernard. (1861–1945) ORTHODOX RABBI and scholar who launched the JEWISH SABBATH ALLIANCE OF AMERICA. He was first among the English-speaking and English-preaching Orthodox rabbis in America.

Dropsie College for Hebrew and Cognate Learning. Evolving into the Annenberg Institute in the 1980s, a post-graduate school of Jewish studies in Philadelphia; founded in 1907 with a large bequest left by Moses Aaron Dropsie.

Dual–Loyalty. Alternately, dual–allegiance. Usually used in a pejorative sense, refers to the conflict of the Jew living in the DIASPORA, yet supportive of the State of Israel.

Dubinsky, David. (1892–1982) One of the most distinguished leaders of Jewish labor, he began his career as a cloak cutter in 1911, rising to become the president of the International Ladies Garment Workers Union (ILGWU). He also became a potent force in politics. He helped found the American Labor Party, leaving it in 1944 when it fell to Communist influence, and helped launch the Liberal Party.

Dushkin, Alexander. (1890–1976) Educator, a disciple of SAMSON BENDERLY; moved back and forth between important educational posts in the United States, including the BOARD OF JEWISH EDUCATION in Chicago and HEBREW UNIVERSITY in JERUSALEM.

Dutch West India Company. Founded in Amsterdam in 1621, with a representative number of Jews as shareholders and directors; administrators under government charter of the first colony on Manhattan island overrode Governor Peter Stuyvesant's discrimination against the first Jewish settlers in 1654.

Dymov, Ossip. Pen name of Joseph Perelman. (1878–1959) A successful Russian playwright and novelist who began to write in YIDDISH when he arrived in New York in 1914; his best known play was *Bronx Express.*

Ecumenical Wedding. Usually refers to a wedding ceremony at which a RABBI and a non-Jewish clergyperson co-officiate.

Educational Alliance, The. Established in 1891, opened in 1891, the best-known AMERICANIZATION center in the country, located in New York. It now has a Greenwich Village branch called the Educational Alliance West.

Educators Assembly (EA). The professional association of educators affiliated with CONSERVATIVE JUDAISM.

Einhorn, David. (1809–1879) Abolitionist, RABBI at Har Sinai Congregation in Baltimore, Maryland, who was a militant advocate of REFORM JUDAISM. Forced to leave the city because of his stand against slavery, he eventually emerged as rabbi of Temple Beth El in New York City. He was a radical opponent to ISAAC MAYER WISE's more moderate reforms. Einhorn edited the monthly periodical *Sinai* and prepared a prayerbook, *Olath Tamid*.

Eisendrath, Maurice. (1902–1973) President of the UNION OF AMERICAN HEBREW CONGREGATIONS, particularly active in interfaith activities and social action.

Elzas, Barnet A. (1867–1939) REFORM RABBI and pioneer historian, especially of South Carolina Jewry. He later ministered to the Hebrew Congregation for the Deaf in New York City and was a prison chaplain.

Emanu-el Theological Seminary. (1874–1885) A short-lived attempt by Temple Emanu-El in New York City to establish its own seminary for the training of rabbis.

Encyclopaedia Judaica. The most recent full-scale English-language encyclopedia of Judaism that was intended to be all-encompassing; issued from Jerusalem in the 1970s.

Epstein, Abraham. (1880–1952) Literary critic, impressionistic rather than analytical in his approach.

Ezekiel, Moses. (1844–1917) A prominent figure among American sculptors who fought for the South during the Civil War; noted especially for his portrait busts.

Falcon Picnic, The. Annual social gathering of German–Jewish singles in Montgomery, Alabama, prior to World War II.

Farband. LABOR ZIONIST fraternal order, founded by Baruch Zuckerman, among others, in 1913.

Federation of American Zionists. Established in 1898 at a national conference of nearly 100 societies. It was short-lived, primarily due to the short lives of many of the member societies that gave the Federation meager support. It was replaced by the ZIONIST ORGANIZATION OF AMERICA in 1917.

Federation of Hungarian Jews of America. One of the many *landsmanshaftn* societies formed in the early years of the twentieth century to aid co-religionists in their countries of origin and to protect their rights.

Federbusch, Simon. (1892–1969) Orthodox rabbi and scholar who tried to clarify contemporary problems in the light of sacred literature. He was principal of the Yeshiva Rabbi Israel Salanter in the Bronx, New York and was active in American Mizrahi.

Fels, Mary. (1863–1953) Zionist teacher and philanthropist; following the death of her husband, she established the Joseph Fels Foundation in 1925 to improve living conditions through education and the exchange of ideas between the United States and Israel.

Felsenthal, Bernard. (1822–1908) Militant Reform rabbi who was an equally ardent abolitionist; he eventually rejected the mission of Israel as a basic tenet of Reform Judaism and helped to found the radical Chicago Sinai Congregation.

Ferber, Edna. (1887–1968) Writer who dealt with the general American and human scene; her central characters were usually women.

Fiedler, Leslie. (1917–) Author and critic, best known for his literary studies and critical essays; as his writing matured, the inclusion of Jewish themes grew as well.

Filene, Edward A. (1860–1937) Boston department store magnate, who believed in institutionalized social insurance, cooperative private enterprise, and higher "buying" wages. He was active in the world peace movement.

Finkelstein, Louis. (1895–1991) Scholar and administrator who was chancellor of The Jewish Theological Seminary of America, succeeding Cyrus Adler; generally considered an influential personality in supporting traditionalist elements within Conservative Judaism.

Fischel, Arnold. New York rabbi who approached President Abraham Lincoln on behalf of the Board of Delegates of American Israelites about a law passed in 1861 that required army chaplains to be "a regular ordained minister of some Christian denomination." As a result of his efforts, the law was changed the following year.

Fischel, Harry. (1865–1948) Businessman and philanthropist, especially known for granting both Saturdays and Sundays as days off for the Jewish builders who worked for him in his construction company. He worked toward the cause of the acceptance of Saturday in New York Sabbath laws.

Flexner, Abraham. (1866–1959) Physician educator who was responsible for a thorough reorganization of medical education in America.

Flexner, Bernard. (1865–1945) Lawyer and Zionist who had served as president of the Palestine Economic Corporation, concerned with social welfare and labor problems.

Flexner, Simon. (1863–1946) Scientist who made outstanding contributions to bacteriology.

Forward, The (Jewish Daily). Yiddish socialist newspaper originally edited by ABRAHAM CAHAN; it served as a powerful force of AMERICANIZATION and ACCULTURATION.

Frank, Leo M. (1884–1915) Factory manager in Atlanta, Georgia, wrongly accused of murder just before World War I and eventually lynched in 1915 by an angry mob. Frank was granted a posthumous pardon in 1985, after an 85-year-old eyewitness to the crime came forward.

Frankel, Lee K. (1867–1931) Economist and social worker who was a member of the Joint Palestine Survey Commission of the JEWISH AGENCY. His mission was to survey the economic resources in Palestine, reporting in 1928.

Frankfurter, Felix. (1882–1965) Jurist, professor at Harvard Law School, appointed to the United States Supreme Court in 1939, the year BENJAMIN NATHAN CARDOZO died and LOUIS D. BRANDEIS retired.

Franks, David. (1720–1794) A leading merchant in Philadelphia and supplier to George Washington in the French and Indian War. He signed a Non-Importation Resolution in 1765, urging the citizens of Philadelphia to boycott British goods "until after the repeal of the Stamp Act"; he was expelled from Philadelphia during the Revolution because of business dealings with the British.

Free Loan Society. A philanthropic organization, founded in 1847, that helped the needy toward self-support by advancing loans without interest.

Free Sons of Israel. A national fraternal and mutual benefit order established in 1849, eventually broadening its program of services to its members.

Free Synagogue, The. A number of cities boasted of these synagogues, which protected freedom of speech in the pulpit. The most notable was founded by STEPHEN S. WISE in New York City in the early twentieth century.

Freehof, Solomon B. (1892–1990) Long-time REFORM RABBI of Rodef Shalom Congregation in Pittsburgh, Pennsylvania, the foremost authority on Jewish RESPONSA and POSEK in the Reform movement in his generation.

Freiberg, Julius. (1823–1905) Cincinnati, Ohio, industrialist and civic leader, who served as president of the UNION OF AMERICAN HEBREW CONGREGATIONS from 1889 to 1903.

Freie Arbeiter Stimme. Weekly YIDDISH periodical, began in 1899 as a champion of anarchism, eventually championing the cause of democratic socialism.

Friedlaender, Israel. (1876–1920) Biblical scholar and essayist who taught at THE JEWISH THEOLOGICAL SEMINARY. The first president of YOUNG JUDEA, he met his death at the hands of thieves while engaged on a relief mission in Russia.

Galveston Movement. (1907–1914) An attempt through the BARON DE HIRSCH Fund's Jewish Agricultural and Industrial Aid Society "to relieve the prevailing conditions in our shelter" (which functioned until 1922), by diverting immigrants from the Atlantic seaboard by routing to the port of Galveston, Texas, and sending them on into the interior.

Gamoran, Emanuel. (1895–1962) Educator who, although a Hebraist and pro-ZIONIST, was the formative director of education at the UNION OF AMERICAN HEBREW CONGREGATIONS from 1923–1958.

Garment Center. Located in mid-Manhattan, New York City, the leading location for the production of ready-made garments from 1880 onward. Large numbers of Jews lived and worked there, organizing into labor unions, mainly under Jewish leadership.

General Order No. 11. In 1862, General Ulysses S. Grant, responsible for the Department of the Tennessee comprising parts of Kentucky, Tennessee and Mississippi, expelled all Jews from the area under his command. He alleged that Jews were involved in illegal trade. President Abraham Lincoln intervened and the order was revoked.

Gentlemen's Agreement. Classic 1950s novel by LAURA HOBSON about ANTI-SEMITISM in America. Made into a motion picture.

German Jews. Refers primarily to the tide of emigration from the Germanies between 1836 and 1860. German Jews are particularly known for their intellectualism and the creation of numerous American Jewish organizations and institutions.

Gershwin, George. (1898–1937) Composer whose work was rooted in jazz, with the influence of both black Southern and cantorial music.

Gilded Ghetto. Refers to wealthy post-World War II suburban Jewish neighborhoods.

Gimbel, Bernard. (1898–1966) Department store magnate, who played a large part in the New York World's Fairs of 1939 and 1964–65; philanthropist, especially in the work of the NATIONAL CONFERENCE OF CHRISTIANS AND JEWS.

Ginzberg, Louis. (1873–1953) Scholar of RABBINIC LITERATURE and teacher at THE JEWISH THEOLOGICAL SEMINARY whose work in the area of Jewish law and lore gained him a worldwide reputation.

Glueck, Nelson. (1900–1971) World-renowned biblical archaeologist who was president of HEBREW UNION COLLEGE and oversaw its merger with the Jewish Institute of Religion in 1950.

Gold, Michael. (1893–1967) Born Irwin Granich. Communist journalist and novelist who was best-known for his autobiographical work called *Jews without Money*.

Goldberg, Abraham. (1883–1942) Columnist and Zionist publicist, co-founder of POALE ZION; helped to form KEREN HAYESOD in 1921.

Goldeneh Medinah. Literally, "golden land." A reference to the United States as a country whose "streets are paved with gold."

Goldfaden, Abraham. (1840–1908) Founder of the YIDDISH theater, playwright, composer of Yiddish operas, poet, and journalist; best known for his song *"Rozhinkes mit Mandlen"* (RAISINS AND ALMONDS).

Goldfogle, Henry Mayer. (1856–1929) Congressman from New York City who was unsuccessful at attempts to pass legislation prohibiting the religious discrimination of American citizens in Russia.

Goldin, Judah. (1914–) Scholar and teacher who taught at Yale University, specialist in the rabbinic period.

Goldman, Solomon. (1893–1953) CONSERVATIVE RABBI who established a conservative synagogue in Cleveland, Ohio, and went on to serve Anshe Emet in Chicago; widely known as president of the ZIONIST ORGANIZATION OF AMERICA.

Goldstein, Herbert Samuel. (1890–1924) Teacher and organizer who was president of the RABBINICAL COUNCIL OF AMERICA.

Goldwyn, Samuel. (1882–1974) Originally Goldfish. Pioneer motion picture producer.

Gompers, Samuel. (1850–1924) Labor leader of the American Federation of Labor who served as president from its founding until his death in 1924; led the movement against free immigration.

Goodbye Columbus. Novel written in 1959 by PHILIP ROTH that depicts the conspicuous consumption of American Jews in the 1950s; made into a movie.

Goode, Alexander D. (1911–1943) Chaplain who went down with his three Christian colleagues on the Army transport DORCHESTER, which was torpedoed and sunk in the Atlantic in June 1943. They had given their life preservers to others.

Gordis, Robert. (1908–) Teacher at the JEWISH THEOLOGICAL SEMINARY, Bible scholar, author, and RABBI. His expertise is in WISDOM LITERATURE, rhetoric, biblical poetry, and the MASORETIC TEXT.

Gottheil, Gustav. (1827–1903) REFORM RABBI who served Temple Emanu-El in New York City; he was vice president in 1898 of the then newly formed FEDERATION OF AMERICAN ZIONISTS.

Gottheil, Richard. (1862–1936) Orientalist and professor of Semitic languages at Columbia University who served alongside his father, GUSTAV

GOTTHEIL, as president of the FEDERATION OF AMERICAN ZIONISTS from 1898 to 1904.

Gratz College. Founded in 1893 through an 1856 bequest of Hyman Gratz, in Philadelphia, one of the second generation members of the GRATZ FAMILY. A Hebrew college providing Judaic studies and teacher training for the community.

Gratz Family. A prominent family of merchants in Philadelphia, founded prior to the American Revolution by brothers and partners Bernard and Michael Gratz. Many of their children rose to distinction in commerce, government, education, and social service.

Gratz, Rebecca. (1781–1869) The best-known member of the GRATZ FAMILY, a pioneer in education and social service who, it has been said, was the model for her namesake, the heroine of Walter Scott's *Ivanhoe*.

Greenbaum, Samuel. (1854–1930) Justice of the New York State Supreme Court, he was part of the delegation that called for the establishment of the AMERICAN JEWISH COMMITTEE.

Greenberg, Chaim. (1889–1953) Exponent of labor ZIONISM, he wrote on questions of more general importance. He was a member of the JEWISH AGENCY executive from 1946 until his death.

Greenberg, Henry Benjamin (Hank). (1911–1986) Baseball player who in 1935 was voted "the most valuable player of the year" in the American League. Elected to the Baseball Hall of Fame in 1956.

Greenhorn. A newly arrived immigrant.

Guggenheim Foundation, John Simon. Established in memory of Meyer Guggenheim's first-born son, it has aided numerous artists, scholars, and scientists without regard to race, religion, or creed. The Guggenheim family, with Meyer at its head, started its financial success in the copper industry and later branched into other metals. It devoted much of its family fortune to philanthropy.

Habonim. Literally, "the builders." Zionist youth organization affiliated with the MAPAI party.

Hadassah. The Women's ZIONIST ORGANIZATION OF AMERICA, which began modestly in 1912 by federating a number of existing "Daughters of Zion" societies. It became the largest Zionist organization in the country, with the double aim of "promoting Jewish institutions and [especially health-related] enterprises in PALESTINE and fostering Zionist ideals in America."

Hadoar. Literally, "the post." Hebrew periodical published by the HISTADRUTH IVRIT beginning in 1921.

Halprin, Rose. (1896–1978) Early organizer and leader of HADASSAH.

Hammerstein, Oscar. (1847–1919) A successful cigar manufacturer, he was a builder of theaters and opera houses, composer, and producer of musical comedies and operas.

Hammerstein, Oscar II. (1895–1960) Musical comedy librettist, well-known for his collaboration with Richard Rogers.

Harby, Isaac. (1788–1828) Educator, journalist, and dramatist; took a leading part in the first movement for REFORM JUDAISM in America, which evolved into the REFORMED SOCIETY OF ISRAELITES.

Hatoren. Literally, "the mast." A literary monthly Hebrew periodical that lasted from 1913–1925, at one time edited by the essayist Reuben Brainin.

Hebrew Publishing Co. Commercial book publisher specializing in Jewish books.

Hebrew Sabbath School Union. Modeling itself after a Protestant organization, this organization, founded in 1886, attempted to coordinate curricula and instruction in congregational religious schools until replaced by the educational efforts of the UNION OF AMERICAN HEBREW CONGREGATIONS.

Hebrew Sheltering and Immigrant Aid Society (HIAS). An amalgamation (in 1909) of the HEBREW SHELTERING SOCIETY and the Hebrew Immigrant Aid Society; a philanthropic organization established to provide aid to Jewish immigrants in the United States and abroad.

Hebrew Sheltering Society. Popularly known by its tradition-laden Hebrew name of *Hakhnasas Orchim* (hospitality for wayfarers), a philanthropic organization established to provide immigrant aid, later merged into the HEBREW SHELTERING AND IMMIGRANT AID SOCIETY.

Hebrew Sunday School Society. Founded in 1838 in Philadelphia by Rev. ISAAC LEESER with REBECCA GRATZ as its first supervisor, to provide religious instruction for children, with lessons circulated to other communities. It later served children of those unaffiliated with congregations.

Hebrew Theological College. Located in Chicago, ORTHODOX rabbinical seminary established in 1923.

Hebrew Union College—Jewish Institute of Religion. The result of a 1948 merger of Hebrew Union College (established in 1875) and Jewish Institute of Religion (established in 1922) to train rabbis, cantors, educators, and communal executives under the auspices of the REFORM movement. It has campuses in New York, Cincinnati, Los Angeles, and Jerusalem.

Hecht, Ben. (1893–1964) Novelist, helped to rouse public opinion of America against the anti-Jewish policy of the British in PALESTINE.

Heifetz, Jascha. (1901–1989) Outstanding virtuoso violinist; he became the model for Jewish boys seeking to escape Czarist Russia through musical talent.

Heilprin, Michael. (1823–1888) Abolitionist immigrant from Hungary who wrote a reply to the pro-slavery position of MORRIS JACOB RAPHALL. He was an editor of *Appleton's New American Encyclopedia* and later helped to establish a farm settlement in Carmel, New Jersey.

Heller, Joseph. (1923–   ) Author, best known for his military satire, *Catch 22.*

Heller, Maximilian. (1860–1929) Prominent REFORM RABBI from Temple Sinai in New Orleans. A founding vice president of the ZIONIST ORGANIZATION OF AMERICA, he served as president of the CENTRAL CONFERENCE OF AMERICAN RABBIS in 1907.

Hellman, Lillian. (1909–1984) Playwright, well known for her work relevant to World War II.

Henry, Jacob. (1775–1847) Elected to the North Carolina state legislature in 1809, his right to a seat was challenged because he was a Jew. Following a remarkable presentation on liberty and equality that has become a classic, he was allowed to keep his seat.

Herberg, Will. (1909–1977) Theologian and social worker, best known for his sociological volume *Protestant–Catholic–Jew.* Herberg, raised as an atheist, saw Judaism as dependent on a COVENANTAL existence.

Hillel Foundations. Program of service and education on college campuses, established in 1923 under B'NAI B'RITH with the support of the local JEWISH FEDERATION.

Hillman, Sidney. (1887–1946) Labor leader and union organizer, advisor to Franklin D. Roosevelt; non-Zionist, sympathetic to the goals of the labor movement in PALESTINE.

Hirsch, Emil G. (1851–1923) RABBI at Chicago Sinai Congregation from 1880–1923, a champion of radical REFORM in the social, as well as the religious realm; one of the first to attempt to change the Jewish Sabbath to Sunday.

Hirsch, Samuel. (1815–1889) A radical proponent of REFORM JUDAISM who in 1866 succeeded DAVID EINHORN as the RABBI of Keneseth Israel in Philadelphia. One of the first rabbis to advocate supplementary services on Sunday, he hosted the important 1869 rabbinical conference of liberal rabbis in America.

Hirschbein, Peretz. (1880–1948) YIDDISH dramatist, author of *The Empty Tavern, The Blacksmith's Daughters, Green Fields,* and others. He is well known for his sympathetic travelogues; in his early work, he tried to achieve a synthesis of naturalism and symbolism and later became a neorealist.

Histadruth Ivrith, The. Literally, "the Federation for Hebrew Culture." Founded in 1916 by a group of Hebrew enthusiasts, mostly educators, to promote the speaking of Hebrew by American Jews.

Hobson, Laura. (1900–1986) Born Zametkin. Author best known for *A Gentleman's Agreement.* Her work tells of living as a Jew in a non-Jewish environment.

Honor, Leo. (1894–1956) Educator, was dean of the Chicago College of Jewish Studies and that city's Bureau of Jewish Education. He emphasized the principle of unity in diversity within the context of Jewish education and organized the national Council for Jewish Education.

Horovitz, Vladimir. (1904–1990) Virtuoso, Russian-born pianist whose interpretations were considered exemplary; he made a triumphant appearance in Moscow after an absence of sixty years.

Houdini, Harry. (1874–1926) Originally Eric Weisz. Magician and "escape artist."

Howe, Irving. (1920–   ) Literary critic, writer, and historian, who attempts to view literature in its social context; well known for *World of Our Fathers* and his interest in Yiddish literature.

Hurst, Fannie. (1889–1968) Novelist and short story writer who prepared for her characters by living in New York's slums, going to night courts, and working in sweatshops and department stores. She worked for social reform and the state of Israel, especially after World War II.

Husic, Isaac. (1876–1939) Scholar in the area of the history of Jewish philosophy; was professor at the University of Pennsylvania and editor at the Jewish Publication Society.

"Hymies." Anti-Semitic slur used to refer to Jews by Jesse Jackson during the 1988 presidential campaign; Jackson later apologized for the remark.

Hyphenated Americans. Refers to those who identify themselves from two perspectives, with adjectives such as in American–Jews.

Imber, Naphtali Herz. (1856–1909) Hebrew poet who won lasting fame as the author of Hatikvah, the Israeli national anthem.

Intercollegiate Menorah Association. Campus forerunner of the Hillel Foundation.

Interfaith. Refers to relationship or association between two religious communities or people, particularly Jews and non-Jews.

Intermarriage. While technically used by sociologists to refer to the marriage between a Jew and one who has converted to Judaism, the term has come to be used to refer to marriages between Jews and non-Jews; interchangeable with Mixed Marriage.

Isaacs, Samuel Myer. (1804–1878) Cantor at Congregation B'nai Jeshurun in New York, he was later Rabbi of the congregation Shaaray Tefilah in New York; he initiated the formation of the Board of Delegates of American Israelites and also spoke out boldly against slavery. He was a champion of traditional Judaism and editor of the *Jewish Messenger.*

It Can't Happen Here. Apologetic response to critics of America who maintain that the HOLOCAUST can happen again, even in America.

Jacobs, Rose. (1888–1975) Early leader and organizer of HADASSAH.

Jastrow, Marcus. (1829–1903) Early Zionist leader who was rabbi of Rodeph Shalom in Philadelphia, he helped to lay the foundation for CONSERVATIVE JUDAISM in America. He was the author of *A Dictionary of the Targumim, the Talmud . . . and Midrashim,* and the original editor of the JEWISH PUBLICATION SOCIETY's English translation of the Bible.

Javits, Jacob K. (1904–1986) Lawyer, New York congressman, and senator who gained fame in a 1933 bankruptcy case of Kreuger and Toll. An active ZIONIST who unsuccessfully positioned himself for a vice-presidential nomination in the Republican Party, he helped shape legislation in foreign affairs, social reform, urban redevelopment, and civil rights.

"Jew Bill," The (1826). Originating in Maryland, it removed, for the most part, the religious test from the Maryland Constitution that required a holder of public office to declare "his belief in a future state of rewards and punishment."

Jewish Alliance of America. An ambitious attempt in 1891, lasting only one year, to launch a permanent and representative body for American Jewry, regardless of individual religious orientation.

Jewish (Community) Center. Refers to the suburban evolution of the urban YM/YWHA, harkening back to the old world BET HAMIDRASH; it incorporates prayer, education, and assembly and also includes recreational, social, and cultural activities, along American lines. Also refers to the novel concept of combining a religious institution and social center, the influence of MORDECAI KAPLAN.

Jewish Chautauqua Society. Founded by HENRY BERKOWITZ in 1893 for "the dissemination of knowledge of the Jewish religion"; it now sponsors courses and Jewish library collections at universities throughout the country.

Jewish Encyclopedia, The. One of the most ambitious projects in the early twentieth century; the first encyclopedia of its kind in any language to be completed in twelve volumes by a corps of scholars; chiefly edited by Isidore Singer to "cast light upon the successive phases of Judaism, furnish precise information concerning the activities of the Jews in all branches of human endeavor, register their influence upon the manifold development of human intelligence, and describe their mutual relations to surrounding needs and peoples."

Jewish Federation, The. Also called Welfare Funds or Community Councils, it is a local oversight agency and fund-raising arm. It raises, allocates, and distributes funds for local, national, and overseas needs; affiliated with the COUNCIL OF JEWISH FEDERATION AND WELFARE FUNDS.

Jewish Hospitals. Various hospitals, including Mt. Sinai, Maimonides, and others, originally established to provide both for Jews in transit and Jewish physicians who could not practice elsewhere. They serve the entire community, and meet the needs of observant Jews as well.

Jewish Messenger. Edited by Samuel Myer Isaacs, it represented a traditional point of view.

Jewish Publication Society (JPS). A nonprofit community endeavor begun by Isaac Leeser in 1845, successfully revived in 1888 in Philadelphia by Joseph Krauskopf and Solomon Solis-Cohen. Its purpose is to publish books of Jewish interest for Jewish homes, primarily in history, biography, and religion with some fiction, especially for children; most significantly, it published two English translations of the Bible.

Jewish Sabbath Alliance of America. Launched in 1905 by Bernard Drachman to promote the traditional observance of the Sabbath, it found itself saddled with the responsibility of providing for the legal defense of transgressors of blue laws.

Jewish Socialist Federation. Organized by The Bund in 1912 as the Jewish section of the Socialist Party.

Jewish Theological Seminary of America, The. Rabbinical seminary and academic arm for Conservative Judaism. It was founded in 1887 by Sabato Morais and firmly established in 1902 under the presidency of Solomon Schechter, who gave it direction and impulse. Its headquarters are in New York, with a West Coast branch in Los Angeles. It also has a campus in Jerusalem.

Jewish Welfare Board. (JWB) Established in 1917 as the coordinating body for Jews serving in the military and later for Jewish Community Centers, it also has taken on the supervision of the Young Men's/Women's Hebrew Associations. It evolved from the Jewish Welfare Board to JWB to the Jewish Community Center Association (JCCA) as its role and mission changed.

Johnson Immigration Act, The (1924). Reduced the annual quota of immigrants from each country to two percent and changed the base of computation to the number of natives from any particular country living in the United States in 1890. It effectively reduced immigration and forced the development of an indigenous American–Jewish community. It was replaced in 1952 by the McCarran-Walter Immigration Act, which maintained a natural origins quota system.

Joint Distribution Committee, The American Jewish. Created in 1914, a joining of the Central Committee for the Relief of Jewish War Sufferers, the American Jewish Relief Committee, and eventually the People's Relief Committee. Its purpose was to raise money and dispense it for the relief of war victims: finding homes for refugees, providing medical aid, caring for orphan children, restoring educational and cultural institutions, and providing economic rehabilitation through free-loan societies, credit cooperatives, and farm settlements.

Jolson, Al. (1886–1950) Born Asa Yoelson, the son of a CANTOR. He was a singer, and a vaudeville and film star, best known for *The Jazz Singer,* the first full-length talking film in America, updated twice with other actor/singers.

Jonas, Joseph. (1792–1869) English-born jeweler, the first Jew to settle in Ohio. In 1824 he became president of Bene Israel Congregation in Cincinnati, the first Jewish congregation west of the Alleghenies. He served in the Ohio legislature from 1860–1861.

Joseph, Jacob. (1848–1902) Renowned preacher and talmudic teacher from Vilna who was to serve as the only chief RABBI of New York City, on the invitation of fifteen ORTHODOX congregations, a failed venture. He founded Bes Sefer Yeshiva (1900), which was eventually renamed in his memory.

Jung, Leo. (1892–1987) One of the leading spokesmen of NEO-ORTHODOXY in America, he was professor at YESHIVA UNIVERSITY and RABBI of the Jewish Center in New York.

Kadima. Activist ZIONIST organization of the REFORM movement in Canada.

Kallen, Horace M. (1882–1974) Philosopher and educator, a founder of the New School for Social Research in New York City. His philosophy has been characterized by Hebraism, aesthetic pragmatism, humanism, cultural pluralism, and cooperative individualism.

Kaplan, Kivie. (1904–1975) Businessman and philanthropist, particularly active as president of the National Association for the Advancement of Colored People (NAACP). He donated the social action center of the UNION OF AMERICAN HEBREW CONGREGATIONS in Washington, DC.

Kaplan, Nathan D. (b. 1877) An early member of the KNIGHTS OF ZION, he was among the first American Jews to settle in PALESTINE.

Kaye, Danny. (1913–1987) Actor and entertainer.

Kazin, Alfred. (1915–   ) Literary critic and author.

Kehillah, The. Literally, "the (Jewish) community." Founded in 1909 and modeled on the European community authority (KAHAL), it was a noble but unsuccessful experiment in establishing an all-encompassing community structure in New York City. It was led by JUDAH MAGNES and made strides in Jewish education in its BUREAU ON JEWISH EDUCATION under SAMSON BENDERLY. The active period of the Kehillah lasted about ten years, during which time it regulated religious aspects of marriage and divorce and the sale of kosher food through its Board of Rabbis; it established a court of Arbitration or BET DIN for religious disputes, a Bureau of Industry to arbitrate between Jewish employers and employees, a Welfare Committee to assist the local police in dealing with Jews involved in criminal litigation, and an Employment Bureau for the handicapped.

Kemelman, Harry. (1908–) Author of the Rabbi Small detective novel series.

"Kikes." Anti-Jewish ethnic slur.

Kirstein, Louis E. (1867–1942) Bostonian who was one of the foremost merchants and commercial leaders in New England.

Klutznick, Philip. (1907–) President of B'NAI B'RITH and chairman of UNITED JEWISH APPEAL, he was also a community planner, diplomat, and community leader.

Knights of Zion. A Zionist organization founded in Chicago in 1896 in response to THEODOR HERZL's call. Modeled on the Knights of Columbus, it was originally named the "Chicago Zionist Organization Number One." It became part of the FEDERATION OF AMERICAN ZIONISTS in 1913.

Kohs, Samuel C. (1890–1984) Prominent psychologist and social worker who documented the efforts of Jews in World War II by heading JEWISH WELFARE BOARD's Bureau of War Records.

Konvitz, Jacob. Middle twentieth century ORTHODOX RABBI in Newark, New Jersey, who exerted city-wide influence.

Koplik, Henry. (1858–1927) Pediatrician, known for his discovery (later named "Koplik's spots") in measles.

Kraus, Adolf. (1850–1928) Lawyer, staunch conservative, and president of B'NAI B'RITH, who was among the founders of the AMERICAN JEWISH COMMITTEE.

Krauskopf, Joseph. (1858–1923) REFORM RABBI who established the National Farm School (now National Agricultural College) in Doylestown, Pennsylvania. He helped to launch the JEWISH PUBLICATION SOCIETY.

Landsman. Plural, *landsleit.* Generally refers to those who hail from the same country. The term has grown in meaning to imply a certain sense of responsibility between newcomers and the immigrants who had preceded them.

Landsmanshaft. Plural, *landsmanshaftn.* Literally, "Hebrew Benevolent Society." Formed to look after the needs of fellow immigrants, determined by them from their family's country of origin.

Lasker, Albert. (1880–1916) Advertising executive who, after World War I, was named chairman of the United States Shipping Board by President Warren G. Harding. He reorganized the shipping industry and laid the foundation for the development of the American Merchant Marine.

Lazarus, Emma. (1849–1887) Poet whose immortal words, "Give me your tired, your poor, your huddled masses yearning to breathe free. . . ." are inscribed on the pedestal of the Statue of Liberty.

Leeser, Isaac. (1806–1868) Foremost champion of traditional Judaism, named preacher of Mikveh Israel in Philadelphia in 1829. He prepared the first English translation of the Bible and attempted unsuccessfully to create a national American Jewish body in 1841, following the DAMASCUS AFFAIR. In 1843 he launched *The Occident and Jewish Advocate* and was among the chief architects of the Jewish community in Philadelphia, including its JEWISH HOSPITAL, the first SUNDAY SCHOOL, the first JEWISH PUBLICATION SOCIETY, and MAIMONIDES COLLEGE.

Lehman Brothers (Arthur [1873–1936], Irving [1876–1945], and Herbert [1878–1963]). Irving rose to the highest judicial post in New York State. Herbert was New York governor (elected three times) and then United States senator from New York. Activists in the Jewish community, together they parlayed their fortunes into a financial firm that still exerts international influence on commerce and industry. Arthur was a partner in the family firm.

Leipziger, Henry M. (1853–1917) Educator and social worker involved in the establishment of the JEWISH ALLIANCE OF AMERICA and assistant superintendent of New York City Public Schools. He was responsible for its Free Lecture Series, which came to be known as the "People's University."

Leivick, H. (1886–1962) The pen name for Leivick Halper, who escaped to America after exile in Siberia. He was known for the profundity of his poetry as well as its mystic nuance. While some believe he was a social critic, he was really a lyricist who wrote with impassioned religious fervor.

Leonard, Benny. (1896–1947) World lightweight champion from 1917 to 1924; chairman of the World Maccabi Games in 1935.

Levenson, Sam(uel). (1914–1980) Comedian and educator, especially known for his stories about the LOWER EAST SIDE and his humorous writings on education.

Levi, Gerson B. (1878–1939) Among the early members of the KNIGHTS OF ZION. A Chicago RABBI, he succeeded his father-in-law, EMIL G. HIRSCH, as editor of *The Reform Advocate*.

Levi, Leo N. (1856–1904) Lawyer and communal worker, president of B'NAI B'RITH in 1900. In 1887, in an open letter, he asked the American rabbinate, "Tell Us: What is Judaism?" He was active in framing the petitions to the United States government following the KISHINEV POGROMS. A Hot Springs, Arkansas, hospital bears his name.

Levin, Meyer. (1905–1981) Novelist, he wrote about life on the KIBBUTZ and on a wide array of topics, from mysticism to the American–Jewish scene.

Levin, Shmarya. (1867–1935) Orator and potent force in American Zionism in the early years of the twentieth century.

Levinthal, Bernard Louis. (1865–1952) ORTHODOX RABBI, head of the United Orthodox Hebrew Congregations in Philadelphia. He was founder of many Orthodox institutions in Philadelphia and founder of the UNION OF ORTHODOX RABBIS.

Levy, Asser. (ca. 1628–1682) The first permanent Jewish resident in New York, he arrived in New Amsterdam in 1654. At that time, Jews were prohibited from serving in the military and were required to pay a tax instead. As a burgher, he demanded the right to stand guard duty rather than pay the tax. A butcher, he built New York's first slaughter house.

Levy, Moses. (ca. 1665–1728) Prominent merchant in colonial America, president of New York's congregation, who initiated building the first synagogue in North America.

Levy, Uriah P. (1792–1862) A career naval man who rose to the rank of Commodore after fighting ANTI-SEMITISM. He secured laws against corporal punishment in the Navy and purchased Thomas Jefferson's Monticello in order to preserve it.

Lewisohn, Ludwig. (1882–1955) Novelist who, in an eloquent style, urged the Jewish people to find strength found in their ancient faith.

Libin, Z. (1887–1925) Pseudonym for Israel Zalman Hurwitz, short story writer who wrote from the perspective of the sweatshop.

Lieberman, Saul. (1898–1983) Talmudic scholar who was eventually rector of THE JEWISH THEOLOGICAL SEMINARY OF AMERICA.

Lilienthal, Max (Menachem). (1815–1882) Reform rabbi who, after ten years as head of a private boys' school in New York, went to Cincinnati, Ohio, where he collaborated with ISAAC MAYER WISE.

Lippmann, Walter. (1889–1974) Critical author and journalist who was an assistant to the philosopher George Santayana. He was a founding editor of *The New Republic* and an editor of the *New York World;* he participated in the Paris Peace Conference.

Lipsky, Louis. (1876–1963) Outstanding figure in the early period of American ZIONISM, eventually attaining international leadership as well.

Literacy Tests. A means to limit the numbers of immigrants. People who were not able to read and write an acceptable language (which usually excluded YIDDISH), were not permitted to immigrate to America.

Littauer, Lucius. (1859–1944) Glove manufacturer and philanthropist who served a decade in the House of Representatives; he endowed a chair of Jewish literature in Harvard's Graduate School of Public Administration, provided support for The New School and to a newly established University in Exile for refugee scholars, and contributed heavily to many health causes.

Lookstein, Joseph. (1902–1979) RABBI who founded the Ramaz School in New York City and was its principal for over thirty years. He also served as chancellor and acting president of Bar-Ilan University.

Lopez, Aaron. (1731–1782) Leading merchant-shipper who renounced his Marrano past and embraced Judaism following his marriage. He was active in the slave trade and supported the revolutionary cause in Newport, Rhode Island.

Lower East Side. Section of Manhattan island in New York where thousands of Jewish immigrants lived upon arrival in the United States.

Maccabean, The. Edited by Louis Lipsky and established in 1901, this was the monthly organ of the Federation of American Zionists.

Mack, Julian W. (1866–1943) Chicago jurist and civic leader, active in American Zionism, and first president of the American Jewish Congress.

Magnes, Judah L. (1877–1948) Outspoken Zionist, Reform rabbi who headed The Kehillah and later became the first president of Hebrew University.

Mailer, Norman. (1923–   ) Novelist; a radical conservatist, whose novels speak in violent psychological and social terms.

Maimonides College. A short-lived, 1867 attempt by Isaac Leeser to establish in Philadelphia a seminary to train rabbis.

Malamud, Bernard. (1914–1986) Novelist, well known for *The Natural* and *The Fixer.*

Marcus, Jacob Rader. (1896–   ) Prolific American Jewish historian who founded the American Jewish Archives. He is credited with legitimizing the field of study of American Jewish history.

Margolis, Max L. (1866–1932) Bible scholar and linguist. He succeeded Marcus Jastrow as editor-in-chief of *The Holy Scriptures,* the first English translation of the Bible published by the Jewish Publication Society in 1917.

Marjorie Morningstar. A novel written by Herman Wouk in 1955, it is the story of a starstruck Jewish girl who makes it to the big stage.

Marshall, Louis. (1856–1929) One of the country's foremost constitutional lawyers, he played a significant leadership role in uniting American Jewry. As president of the American Jewish Committee, he led the struggle for unrestricted immigration and fought anti-Semitism.

Marx, Alexander. (1878–1953) Historian and bibliographer who taught at The Jewish Theological Seminary.

Marx Brothers (Chico [1891–1961], **Harpo** [1893–1964], **Groucho** [1895–1977], **and Zeppo** [1901–1979]). Motion picture comedy team.

Masliansky, Zevi Hirsch. (1856–1943) Zionist from Russia who was a master orator.

Maximon, S(halom) D(ov). (1881–1933) Born Maximowski. Essayist and educator, he edited *The Jewish Child* and founded *HaToren;* later he was registrar of HEBREW UNION COLLEGE.

Mayer, Louis B. (1885–1957) Motion picture producer.

McCarron–Walter Act, The. (1952) Replaced the JOHNSON ACT of 1924, which fixed maximum annual immigration from individual countries.

Melting Pot Theory. While SAMUEL GOLDENSON is claimed to have used it first, the term really became popular after ISRAEL ZANGWILL used it to refer to the amalgamation of cultures in the United States that would come, as a result of immigration quotas, to produce a uniquely American culture.

Menuhin, Yehudi. (1916–) A violinist; internationally acclaimed as a child prodigy; he became the first violinist to perform in Paris after its liberation after World War II.

Meyer, Eugene, Jr. (1875–1959) Financial expert who was active in American ZIONISM, he was manager of the War Finance Corporation and charged with the responsibility of financing businesses unable to join in the war effort.

Michelbacher, Maximilian. (1810–1868) The most prominent RABBI in the Confederate capital of Richmond, Virginia, he prepared and circulated prayers for Jewish soldiers in the Confederacy.

Mielziner, Moses. (1828–1903) Abolitionist Jewish scholar who wrote *Slavery Among the Ancient Hebrews,* he served as acting president of HEBREW UNION COLLEGE.

Miller, Arthur. (1915–) Playwright whose reputation was established through *Death of a Salesman;* he often dealt with the theme of ANTI-SEMITISM in such works as *Focus* and *Incident at Vichy.*

Minhag Amerika. An attempt by ISAAC M. WISE to create a uniform prayerbook for American Judaism.

Mirele Efros. YIDDISH play and film whose original subtitle was "The Jewish Queen Lear." Written in 1898 by Jacob Gordin.

Mitzvah Corps. Group of people, generally youth, banded together by the REFORM movement to do projects in urban ghettos, generally educational and basic home improvement.

Mixed Marriage. The marriage between people of different faiths, generally used to refer to Jews and non-Jews; used interchangeably with INTERMARRIAGE.

Mizrachi Veg (Way), Der. (1936–1980) YIDDISH periodical that spoke for religious ZIONISM.

Mogulesko, Sigmund (Zelig). (1858–1914) YIDDISH theater comic and composer, with ABRAHAM GOLDFADEN.

Monsky, Henry (Zevi). (1890–1947) ZIONIST president of B'NAI B'RITH from 1938–1947, he was a founder of the Omaha, Nebraska, Community Chest and Welfare Federation. In 1941, he planned the Office of Civilian Defense for President Franklin D. Roosevelt.

Morais, Sabato. (1823–1897) Active ZIONIST, RABBI of Philadelphia's Mikveh Israel Congregation and later president of THE JEWISH THEOLOGICAL SEMINARY; he helped to lay the framework for CONSERVATIVE JUDAISM.

Morgenstern, Julian. (1881–1976) Biblical scholar who served as president of HEBREW UNION COLLEGE and rescued a number of Europe's scholars during World War II.

Morgenthau, Henry, Jr. (1891–1967) Secretary of the Treasury from 1934 to 1945; in retirement he headed the UNITED JEWISH APPEAL and the campaign for the sale of ISRAEL BONDS.

Morgenthau, Henry, Sr. (1856–1946) United States ambassador to Turkey, appointed by President Woodrow Wilson in 1913.

Morning Journal, The. ORTHODOX daily newspaper published in YIDDISH beginning in 1901; dignified, sedate, and Republican, it was founded by Jacob Saphirstein and edited by Peter Wiernik.

National Association of Temple Educators (NATE). Professional association of REFORM Jewish educators, founded in 1955.

National Community Relations Advisory Council (NCRAC). National community defense agency that promotes intercommunity relations and monitors anti-Jewish feelings and acts; a coordinating body set up in 1944, originally designed to include the AMERICAN JEWISH COMMITTEE, B'NAI B'RITH (both of which refused to participate), AMERICAN JEWISH CONGRESS, Jewish Labor Committee, Jewish War Veterans, UNION OF AMERICAN HEBREW CONGREGATIONS, UNITED SYNAGOGUE OF AMERICA, and the UNION OF ORTHODOX JEWISH CONGREGATIONS.

National Conference of Christians and Jews. Established in 1928 "to moderate—and finally eliminate—a system of prejudices which disfigures and distorts our business, social and political relations."

National Conference of Synagogue Youth (NCSY). Youth groups affiliated with the ORTHODOX movement.

National Council of Jewish Women (NCJW). Founded in 1893 by Hannah Greenebaum Solomon, it undertakes a wide range of activities including SUNDAY SCHOOLS for poverty-stricken children, vocational and industrial classes and urban redevelopment programs of various kinds, as well as libraries, employment bureaus, kindergartens and nurseries, and summer camping programs. In Israel it has been active in teacher education.

National Desertion Bureau. Founded in 1905 in order to help in cases of desertion or other forms of marital breakdown; later called the Family Location Service.

National Federation of Temple Brotherhoods (NFTB). Synagogue brotherhoods affiliated with the REFORM movement and the UNION OF AMERICAN HEBREW CONGREGATIONS. It absorbed the JEWISH CHATAUQUA SOCIETY and its programs.

National Federation of Temple Sisterhoods (NFTS). Synagogue sisterhoods affiliated with the REFORM movement and the UNION OF AMERICAN HEBREW CONGREGATIONS.

National Foundation for Jewish Culture. Established in 1959 by the COUNCIL OF JEWISH FEDERATIONS in order to support programs and provide information on Jewish culture.

Ner Israel Rabbinical College. ORTHODOX rabbinical seminary located in Baltimore, Maryland; founded in 1933 by Rabbi Jacob I. Ruderman. There is a second branch in Toronto, Canada.

Neumann, Emanuel. (1893–1980) ZIONIST leader who served as education director of the ZIONIST ORGANIZATION OF AMERICA (1918–1920); chairman of the United Palestine Appeal (1925–1928), as well as a member of the JEWISH AGENCY.

Neumark, David. (1866–1924) Scholar and philosopher of REFORM JUDAISM who taught at HEBREW UNION COLLEGE from 1907–1924. He articulated the mainstream position of the period, calling Judaism an evolving religion whose main element is ETHICAL MONOTHEISM.

Neusner, Jacob. (1932–   ) Formerly of Brown University, scholar and historian who focuses on the rabbinic period and rabbinic literature. Now at the University of South Florida.

New Amsterdam. New-world settlement on the tip of the island of Manhattan in what is now New York City.

"New Colossus." Poem written by EMMA LAZURUS; its verses are engraved on the base of the Statue of Liberty.

Niger, Samuel. (1883–1955) Pseudonym of Samuel Charney, YIDDISH literary critic who emphasized the importance of bilingualism in Jewish tradition.

Noah, Mordecai Manuel. (1785–1851) Editor, playwright, and politician, probably the best known Jew of the Jacksonian period. He was clerk in the United States Treasury, and attempted to create a proto-ZIONIST Jewish colony in New York State, called ARARAT.

Nones, Major Benjamin. (1757–1826) Patriot and soldier during the American Revolution.

North American Federation of Temple Youth (NFTY). Originally established as the National Federation of Temple Youth, this organization is affiliated with the REFORM movement through the UNION OF AMERICAN HEBREW CONGREGATIONS.

Occident, The. Launched in 1843 as *The Occident and Jewish Advocate* by **Isaac Leeser,** a monthly journal that defended traditional Judaism and advocated Leeser's programs and projects.

Ochs, Adolph S. (1858–1935) Publisher of the *New York Times.* At the height of rampant "yellow journalism," he coined the phrase "All the News That's Fit to Print" and raised the standards of writing, printing, and advertising.

Odets, Clifford. (1906–1963) Playwright who expressed the hardships of the 1930s and portrayed American Jews on the stage.

Olson, Tillie. (1912–) Born Tillie Lerner. Novelist and short story writer. While not generally a writer on Jewish issues, her well-known "Tell Me a Riddle" won the O. Henry Award for the best short story in 1961 and includes an old Jewish couple among the central characters.

Oppenheimer, J. Robert. (1904–1967) Physicist who was responsible for the construction of the first atomic bomb.

Orlinsky, Harry. (1908–) Biblical scholar and translator, especially known for his work on the Protestant *Revised Standard Version* and the new translation of the **Pentateuch** in 1962 for the **Jewish Publication Society;** teaches at **Hebrew Union College—Jewish Institute of Religion.**

Ornitz, Samuel. (1890–1957) Literary author, especially active in the left-wing "Proletarian" literary movement, who depicted the Jewish immigrant generation.

Our Crowd. Anecdotal history by author Stephen Birmingham that refers to the interrelated German–Jewish banking families of the late nineteenth and early twentieth century.

Outreach. Term coined by the **Reform** movement in the last quarter of the twentieth century in an effort to "reach out" to non-Jews married to Jews, whether converted or not.

Ozick, Cynthia. (1928–) Author. It is said that her first published novel, *Trust,* ended her career as an American novelist and initiated her into the world of Jewish novels. Her work is infused with various disciplines, including psychology and philosophy. Her characters are torn between what Ozick refers to as a struggle between the pagan and the sacred, evidenced most succinctly in the *The Pagan Rabbi and Other Stories.*

Paley, Grace. (1922–) Author who has taught at various institutions of higher learning. She is currently at Sarah Lawrence College. Among her best known stories is "The Loudest Voice," about a Jewish girl's participation in a Christmas pageant. In all her work, Paley characterizes her Jews as spiritual underdogs.

Parnas. In Europe in larger communities in the later Middle Ages and early modern times it referred to the head of the community; in modern times, the term is used for the president of the **Spanish and Portuguese Synagogue.**

Peixotto, Benjamin. (1834–1890) Lawyer, diplomat, and community leader, he was the first United States consul in Bucharest, where he pressed for Jewish emancipation.

People's Relief Committee. Left-wing organization established in 1915 that raised money and dispensed it for relief of war victims.

Persky, Daniel. (1887–1962). Advocate of Hebraism and frequent contributor to HADOAR. He taught at the Herzliah Hebrew Teachers College.

Petuchowski, Jakob. (1925–1991) Scholar and theologian who has blended the concepts of REFORM JUDAISM and traditional theology.

Philadelphia Conference. In 1869, a group of German-born REFORM rabbis met in Philadelphia in an effort to continue the German Rabbinical Conferences of the 1840s, but could reach no lasting agreement.

Philipson, David. (1862–1949) Among the first class of 1885 to receive ordination at HEBREW UNION COLLEGE. A representative of classical REFORM JUDAISM, he wrote the first history of Reform Judaism.

Pi Tau Pi. A national social and philanthropic fraternity of German Jews, founded in the mid-1920s, noted for its annual Mother's Day services.

Pinner, Moritz. (1828–1909) Abolitionist activist who helped form the local Republican Party in Missouri.

Pinski, David. (1872–1959) YIDDISH dramatist and novelist and an active Zionist. He edited various periodicals, especially literary journals and those that promoted LABOR ZIONISM. The subject matter of his plays ranged throughout Jewish history; he began as a realist and grew into symbolism and romanticism as his writing matured.

Pioneer Women. Worldwide LABOR Zionist women's organization founded in New York City in 1925. Its mission has been to provide social services for citizens of PALESTINE (Israel), especially new immigrants. It also encourages American Jewish women to take an active role in affairs in the American Jewish community.

Pittsburgh Platform. The guiding principles of REFORM JUDAISM as promulgated in 1885 by fifteen RABBIS at the Pittsburgh Rabbinical Conference defined what came to be known as "classical Reform" until they were abrogated in 1937.

Po'ale Zion. Literally, "workers of Zion." A movement that tried to reconcile ZIONISM and socialism in the 1890s. It began in the United States in 1903, as a result of its Russian roots.

Podhoretz, Norman. (1930–) Author and editor, particularly of COMMENTARY.

Portnoy's Complaint. Novel by PHILIP ROTH; representative of Jewish self-hatred and stereotyping of Jewish mothers.

Potok, Chaim. (1929–) Novelist, best known for *THE CHOSEN,* the story of a relationship between a traditional Jewish boy and his modern

ORTHODOX friend; was formerly editor of *Conservative Judaism,* a quarterly journal, and of the JEWISH PUBLICATION SOCIETY.

Poznanski, Gustavus. (1809–1879) REFORM RABBI. When the REFORMED SOCIETY OF ISRAELITES rejoined Congregation Beth Elohim in Charleston, South Carolina, he introduced a growing number of reforms.

Protocol of Peace. Agreement negotiated by LOUIS D. BRANDEIS that reconciled union demands for "closed shops" and the Employers Association that opposed them. It basically set up a "preferential shop" and a Board of Arbitration to deal with infractions and the like.

Pulitzer, Joseph. (1847–1911) Editor and publisher, who built a newspaper empire based on promotion, sensationalism, sympathy for labor and the underdog, and innovations in typography and illustrations. He endowed the Pulitzer School of Journalism at Columbia University and the well-known Pulitzer Prizes.

Purim Ball. A favorite method of congregational fund-raising among late nineteenth- and early twentieth-century congregations, usually organized by women.

Quota System. Refers to a limit on jobs, admissions, and immigrations determined by religion and country of origin.

Rabbi Isaac Elchanan Theological Seminary (RIETS). ORTHODOX rabbinical school, the initial unit of YESHIVA UNIVERSITY.

Rabbinical Assembly of America. Founded in 1901 by the graduates of the JEWISH THEOLOGICAL SEMINARY to serve as the professional association of CONSERVATIVE RABBIS.

Rabbinical Council of America (RCA). Rabbinical authority of the UNION OF ORTHODOX JEWISH CONGREGATIONS, founded in 1923 and merged with the Rabbinical Association of the RABBI ISAAC ELCHANAN THEOLOGICAL SEMINARY in 1935.

Race Theory. While anthropologists today agree that differences in races are limited to physical features, former generations contended that there were differences in regard to intelligence and virtue. This theory was taken to the extreme as the pivotal point of Nazism.

Ramah. Literally, "high places." Various geographic locations in the Bible; camping movement of CONSERVATIVE JUDAISM.

Raphall, Morris Jacob. (1798–1868) RABBI at B'nai Jeshurun, New York, who articulated a proslavery position based on the Bible.

Rayner, Isidore. (1850–1912) Lawyer and politician who was a vigorous opponent of black disenfranchisement laws and Jim Crow.

Reconstructionist Rabbinical College (RRC). Rabbinical school, established in Philadelphia for the training of RABBIS to serve RECONSTRUCTIONIST synagogues and CHAVUROT.

Reformed Society of Israelites. Group that separated in 1824 from Congregation Beth Elohim in Charleston, South Carolina, in order to establish a congregation of its own (with reforms); they returned in 1841, introducing reforms with the help of Gustavus Poznanski.

Reisen, Abraham. (1876–1953) Yiddish poet and short-story writer. He was primarily concerned with the individual but expressed the feelings of the exploited Jew and the Jewish community.

Religious Tests. Another means of restricting immigration, determined by the religion of the potential immigrant.

Revel, Bernard. (1885–1940) Educator and scholar who reorganized the Rabbi Isaac Elchanan Theological Seminary and founded Yeshiva College, which later developed into Yeshiva University.

Reznikoff, Charles. (1894–1976) Poet and lawyer who was associated with a group of poets known as objectivists. He is perhaps best known for *By the Waters of Manhattan.*

Ribalow, Menachem. (1895–1953) Hebrew editor and essayist from Russia who immigrated to the United States in 1921. Editor of Hadoar, he wrote under the pseudonym M. Shoshani.

Ribicoff, Abraham. (1910–   ) Politician, active in the Democratic Party, first in the United States House of Representatives, then as governor of Connecticut. He often spoke out on issues of special concern to Jews.

Rickover, Admiral Hyman G. (1900–1986) Naval officer who is considered the father of the atomic-powered submarine. He was active in education and issues related to nuclear power.

Rivkin, Ellis. (1918–   ) Historian, professor at Hebrew Union College. He analyzed the relationships of Jewish life and the surrounding culture, especially in applications to new methodologies to solve the problems of Jewish historiography.

Rodgers, Richard. (1902–1979) Prolific composer of popular music for musical comedies. He worked chiefly with Moss Hart and Oscar Hammerstein II.

Rose, Ernestine. (1810–1892) Feminist and social activist who was influenced by the English social reformer Robert Owen. Together with Susan Anthony, she led the radical wing of the women's suffrage movement.

Rosen, Al(bert). (1924–   ) Big league baseball player. American League homerun champion in 1950 and 1951, named the League's Most Valuable Player in 1953.

Rosenberg, Israel. (1875–1956) Orthodox rabbi who was first vice president and acting dean of the Rabbi Isaac Elchanan Theological Seminary. He was also the founder/director of the Joint Distribution Committee and a leader of Yiddish-speaking Orthodox Jewry.

Rosenberg, Julius and Ethel. (1918–1953 and 1920–1953, respectively) Charged and convicted of espionage for delivering United States atomic bomb secrets to Russia in 1951. They were eventually executed. The case remains extremely controversial.

Rosenfeld, Isaac. (1918–1956) Novelist whose stories are Kafkayesque. While his legacy of writings is small, he enjoys a significant reputation, especially for "King Solomon," the last of his writings.

Rosenfeld, Morris. (1862–1923) Yɪᴅᴅɪsʜ poetry pioneer, author of twenty published volumes. His pioneering efforts and innovations in style gave rise to a Yiddish renaissance among later writers.

Rosenthal, Herman. (1843–1917) Although he was a writer, he was best known for his attempts to build Jewish settlements in the United States, such as Sicily Island, near New Orleans, Louisiana, in 1882, Crémieux in Dakota, as well as Woodbine, New Jersey, in 1891.

Rosenwald, Julius. (1862–1932) Merchant and philanthropist who built the Sears, Roebuck and Company into a major mail-order and retail sales merchandiser. He was especially opposed to Zɪᴏɴɪsᴍ. His son, Lessing Julius Rosenwald, was president of the Aᴍᴇʀɪᴄᴀɴ Cᴏᴜɴᴄɪʟ ғᴏʀ Jᴜᴅᴀɪsᴍ.

Ross, Barney. (1909–1967) Born Barret David Rosofsky. A boxing champion, he simultaneously held the world lightweight and welterweight titles.

Roth, Henry. (1906–) Novelist, best known for his only novel, *Call It Sleep,* which deals with immigrant life on New York's Lower East Side (ca. 1912). It is considered one of the most important contributions to American–Jewish literature.

Roth, Philip. (1933–) Novelist who has a bent for portraying middle-class American Jews in a sarcastic, biting style.

Russian Treaty Affair, The. Refers to the Treaty of Commerce and Navigation of 1832 between the United States and Russia, whose aim was to compel the government to protect their equality as citizens in each other's country. Because Russia did not fulfill its obligations to Jews, even under protest from American Jews and the United States Government, the United States abrogated the Treaty in 1911.

Sachar, Abram. (1899–) Educator and historian who was the founding president of Bʀᴀɴᴅᴇɪs Uɴɪᴠᴇʀsɪᴛʏ and an early director of B'ɴᴀɪ B'ʀɪᴛʜ Hɪʟʟᴇʟ Fᴏᴜɴᴅᴀᴛɪᴏɴs.

Sachar, Howard M. (1928–) Historian, founding director of Bʀᴀɴᴅᴇɪs Uɴɪᴠᴇʀsɪᴛʏ's Jacob Hiatt Institute in Israel.

Salomon, Haym. (1740–1785) Financier who posthumously became famous for his services to the American Revolution. In 1776, he was arrested by the British and sentenced to death as a spy, but escaped to Philadelphia.

Salute to Israel Parade. Annual spring parade held near Israeli Independence Day in New York City in support of Israel.

Samuel, Maurice. (1895–1972) Author and translator who attempted to reconcile Anglo and Jewish cultures but, in the end, determined that they were antithetical. A popular exponent of messianic ZIONISM, he believed that the objective of classical Zionism included rebuilding world Jewry with Israel at its core.

Sarna, Nahum. (1923–   ) Biblical scholar who taught at BRANDEIS UNIVERSITY.

Sarnoff, David. (1891–1971) Pioneer in electronics who eventually became president of the Radio Corporation of America (RCA). He was active in Jewish affairs as well.

Scattered Nation, The. First delivered in 1868, Senator Zebulon B. Vance of North Carolina frequently delivered this notable address in defense of Jews against their detractors.

Scharfstein, Zevi. (1884–1972) Hebrew educator, journalist, and publisher who was a contributor to HADOAR.

Schechter, Solomon. (Shneur Zalman, 1847–1925) Scholar and president of THE JEWISH THEOLOGICAL SEMINARY OF AMERICA who led it to become an important center of learning and Jewish intellectual revival. Considered to be the chief architect of CONSERVATIVE JUDAISM in America.

Schiff, Jacob H. (1847–1920) Philanthropist and financier who was eventually head of Kuhn, Loeb and Co., one of the two most powerful and prominent investment banking houses in the United States. He used his great wealth and influence on behalf of Jews everywhere.

Schlossberg, Joseph. (1875–1971) Union leader and journalist who helped found the Amalgamated Clothing Workers of America and served as its secretary–treasurer for twenty-five years. In 1940, he devoted his time to the American National Committee for LABOR Israel, hoping to bring socialism to Israel, having failed in America.

Schneersohn, Joseph Isaac. (1880–1950) The LUBAVITCHER Rabbi who built the CHABAD community in the Williamsburg section of Brooklyn and established a network of elementary and higher schools.

Schneersohn, Menachem M. (1902–   ) Son-in-law and successor to JOSEPH ISAAC SCHNEERSOHN. He continued to build the CHABAD community worldwide.

Schneur, Zalman. Sometimes spelled Shneour. (1887–1959) YIDDISH and HEBREW litterateur; considered a father of modern Jewish literature, he wrote numerous volumes in both languages.

Schocken Books. Originally established by Zalman Schocken in Berlin in 1929 for the publication of medieval Hebrew poetry and the collection of previously unknown manuscripts of that era. The company was eventually established in New York and Tel Aviv as a general publisher of Judaica.

Schoolman, Albert. (1894–1980) Educator who headed the Central Jewish Institute in New York, the first American Jewish community center with an educational focus.

Schwartz, Delmore. (1913–1966) Poet, author, and critic, known for his pessimistic perspective on Jewish life.

Second Generation, The. Refers to the generation of children (now adults) born to survivors of the HOLOCAUST.

Seixas, Gershom Mendes. (1746–1816) The first native-born Jewish "minister" in the United States; served Congregation SHEARITH ISRAEL in New York and Congregation Mikveh Israel in Philadelphia. Many of his family members became prominent communal leaders.

Seligman, Joseph. (1819–1880) Banker and financier of the North during the Civil War. He gained notoriety after he was refused permission as a Jew to register at the Grand Union Hotel in Saratoga, New York, in 1877.

Shahn, Ben. (1898–1969) Painter, calligrapher, and social critic who often dealt with Jewish themes.

Shaw, Irwin. (1913–1984) Novelist and playwright, whose keen insight into everyday life was seen early in *Bury the Dead,* an antiwar drama, and in *The Gentle People,* about a community that turns on a gangster.

Sheftall, Mordecai. (1735–1797) His BAR MITZVAH was the first recorded in the United States. He served in the Revolution as commissary general for South Carolina and Georgia, the highest rank achieved by a Jew.

Shulman, Max. (1919–1988) Leader of the KNIGHTS OF ZION. Author and humorist, especially popular among college students in the 1950s and 1960s.

Siegel, Seymour. (1937–1988) Theologian who taught at THE JEWISH THEOLOGICAL SEMINARY OF AMERICA.

Silver, Abba Hillel. (1893–1963) Cleveland, Ohio, REFORM RABBI and outspoken Zionist leader, particularly active as an early organizer of anti-Nazi boycott and chairman of the UNITED PALESTINE APPEAL. As president of the American section of the JEWISH AGENCY, he presented the case for a Jewish state before the United Nations in 1947.

Silver, Eliezer. (1882–1968) Chief rabbi of Cincinnati, Ohio, leading spokesman for ORTHODOX JUDAISM. He was president of the UNION OF ORTHODOX RABBIS (1923) and founded the United States Branch of AGUDAT ISRAEL in 1939, serving as its first president.

Silverman, Joseph. (1860–1930) Prominent REFORM RABBI who occupied the pulpit of Temple Emanu-El, New York City, from 1902–1922 and succeeded Isaac M. Wise as president of the Central Conference of American Rabbis.

Singer, Isaac Bashevis. (1904–1991) Yiddish writer, winner of the Nobel Prize for literature in 1978, who used several pseudonyms including "Tse," "Isaac Bashevis," "Y. Varshavski," and "D. Segal." His early stories were serialized in The Forward. He directed his writings to two distinct audiences: the sophisticated public who read him in translation and the Yiddish readers who were less sophisticated but had wider Jewish knowledge.

Singer, Israel Joshua. (1893–1944) Yiddish novelist, playwright, and journalist, older brother of Isaac Bashevis Singer. He often wrote under the name G. Kuper. He was known as the master of the family novel—what has evolved into the three-generation saga in popular fiction; his best-known work was *The Brothers Ashkenazi*.

Sisterhood. Synagogue women's groups.

Sklare, Marshall. (1921–   ) Sociologist, specialist in the sociology and demographics of American Jewry. He was study director for the American Jewish Committee.

Social Clubs. Introduced by German Jews in each established American Jewish community. New York's Harmonie Club pioneered in 1847, and eastern Europeans followed suit. Anti-Jewish discrimination produced country clubs in the twentieth century.

Solis-Cohen, Solomon da Silva. (1857–1948) Physician and poet, active in Jewish affairs, who served as a non-Zionist member of the Jewish Agency.

Sonneborn, Rudolph G. (1898–1986) Zionist leader and businessman who worked secretly with the Haganah to secure and transport arms to the Jews who settled in Palestine after World War II.

Sons of Zion, Order. Centrist or general Zionist organization established in 1907. It aimed to bring the individual into a more intimate relationship with Zionist ideology than possible in fraternal societies, while working toward the fulfillment of the Basel Program.

Spanish and Portuguese Synagogue (Shearith Israel). Located in New York City and dating back to at least 1654. The oldest congregation in the United States.

Spiegel, Sholom. (1899–1984) Scholar and teacher, primarily in the area of medieval Hebrew literature, he was professor at The Jewish Theological Seminary of America.

Spivak, Charles D. (1861–1926) Physician and communal leader active in the establishment of the Jewish Alliance of America. He collaborated with Yehoash on a Yiddish dictionary.

St. Charles, The. Or *Ste. Catherine.* In 1654 this ship brought twenty-three Jewish refugees from the Portuguese conquest of Dutch Brazil to New Amsterdam.

Steinberg, Milton. (1903–1950) CONSERVATIVE RABBI who concerned himself with a philosophical approach to Judaism. Later a critic of RECONSTRUCTIONISM, he was one of the founders of its house organ.

Stern, Isaac. (1920–   ) Concert violinist who is active in the America–Israel Cultural Foundation.

Stone, Irving. (1903–1984) Biographer and novelist who became well-known for his biographies of Vincent Van Gogh, Michelangelo, Abraham Lincoln, and Sigmund Freud.

Straus, Oscar S. (1850–1926) Statesman, diplomat, and scholar who wrote in his *Origin of the Republican Form of Government in the United States* that "in the spirit and essence of our Constitution, the influence of the Hebrew Commonwealth was paramount." He was appointed by President Grover Cleveland in 1887 as envoy to Turkey. This appointment was a rebuke to Austria–Hungary, which had previously refused to accept an envoy because his wife was Jewish. Straus succeeded so significantly that he aided three succeeding presidents with difficult missions to Turkey.

Sulzberger, Mayer. (1843–1923) Jurist and communal leader who helped to organize, and was the first president of the AMERICAN JEWISH COMMITTEE, as well as founder and first president of the YOUNG MEN'S HEBREW ASSOCIATION in Philadelphia. Although not a ZIONIST, he believed that Israel should be a place of refuge for the Jews. Sulzberger helped in the reorganization of the JEWISH THEOLOGICAL SEMINARY and was secretary of the Board of Trustees of MAIMONIDES COLLEGE, as well as one of the original members of the AMERICAN JEWISH HISTORICAL SOCIETY.

Sunday Laws. Also called BLUE LAWS; they restrict or prohibit the opening of some or all retail establishments on Sundays.

Sunday Sabbath Movement. A movement in the late nineteenth and early twentieth century, primarily among radical members of the REFORM movement, who sought to transfer the Jewish Sabbath to a uniform day of rest on Sunday.

Sunday School. A reference to supplementary religious schools often or usually held on Sundays.

Swiss Affair, The. In 1850, the American Minister to Switzerland signed a general treaty with the Swiss Confederation establishing the rights of the citizens of each country to travel and reside in the other, but gave the right to the ruling cantons in Switzerland to restrict Jews. President Millard Fillmore objected to the treaty related to "Christians alone." A new treaty was signed and ratified a short time later that removed the word "Christians" but did not change the intent.

Synagogue Center. Community structure envisioned by MORDECAI KAPLAN to include a synagogue for worship, a school for study, and a social center for social and recreational activities.

Synagogue Council of America. Established in 1926 at the suggestion of Abram Simon, then president of the CENTRAL CONFERENCE OF AMERICAN RABBIS, in order to create a congregational/rabbinic body that would represent the major Jewish religious movements in American.

Syrkin, Marie. (1899–1988) Author, translator, and editor who has written about the American public school system (*Your School, Your Children,* 1944), Jewish resistance under the Nazis (**BLESSED IS THE MATCH,** 1947), and a biography of GOLDA MEIR (*Way of Valor,* 1955). She also edited the LABOR ZIONIST monthly *Jewish Frontier* and taught at BRANDEIS UNIVERSITY. She was married to CHARLES REZNIKOFF.

Szold, Benjamin. (1829–1902) A RABBI and scholar, he led Congregation Oheb Shalom in Baltimore, Maryland, which was on the verge of becoming REFORM, toward more traditional practices but not beliefs.

Szold, Henrietta. (1860–1945) Ardent ZIONIST and philanthropist, she wrote for the *Jewish Messenger,* signing the name "Sulamith." She took on the majority of writing for the first AMERICAN JEWISH YEAR BOOK and collaborated in compiling the JEWISH ENCYCLOPEDIA. In 1912 she organized the Hadassah chapter of the Daughters of Zion, later changed to just HADASSAH, and was long-time paid secretary of the board of the JEWISH PUBLICATION SOCIETY. In 1918, Szold was responsible for the dispatch of the American Zionist Medical Units to Palestine, and in 1927, she became the first woman to become a member of the Zionist Executive. After the Nazi rise to power, she became the active leader of YOUTH ALIYAH.

Tageblatt (Jewish Daily News). The first YIDDISH daily in the world, launched in 1885 by Kasriel Sarasohn, when he thought that the influx of immigration from Eastern Europe required another newspaper. It was ORTHODOX and ZIONIST, with conservative social and political views. It lasted until 1928, when it merged with the MORNING JOURNAL, which merged with *The Day* in 1953.

Talmud Torah. Community elementary schools, taken from the general Hebrew term for Jewish education or learning, or more specifically, the study of TORAH.

Tchernowitz, Chaim. (1871–1949) Pseudonym of Rav Zair, talmudic scholar and Hebrew author who taught at the Jewish Institute of Religion and had founded his own YESHIVAH in Odessa. He attempted to apply the methods of modern research to traditional study in order to revive Jewish learning.

Teitelbaum, Aaron. (1890–) RABBI, active in the JOINT DISTRIBUTION COMMITTEE, who carried out overseas missions.

Teller, Edward. (1908–) Physicist who invented the hydrogen bomb.

Thomashefsky, Boris. (1868–1939) Actor and director, one of the pioneers of YIDDISH theater in the United States. Since there was a shortage of women on stage, he often played female roles. He also adapted Shakespeare for presentation on the Yiddish theater stage.

Torah Corp. A venue for intensive study, especially in camps and during camp-like retreats by youth of the REFORM movement.

Torah Umesorah (National Society for Hebrew Day Schools). Founded in 1944, this is the largest body that serves ORTHODOX DAY SCHOOLS in the United States and Canada.

Touro, Judah. (1775–1854) Merchant and philanthropist whose last will and testament was a model of generosity that included almost every established Jewish institution.

Touro Synagogue. The oldest synagogue building in the United States still standing is Jeshuat Israel (Salvation of Israel) in Newport, Rhode Island. It was erected in 1763 and preserved by the bequests of JUDAH TOURO and his brother Abraham, sons of Isaac Touro, first CANTOR of the SYNAGOGUE.

Touroff, Nissan. (1877–1953) Educator who was one of the founders of Hebrew (Teachers) College in Boston. He was also editor for a brief period of two educational journals, *Ha-Hinnukh* and the daily *Haaretz,* and founder of the educational periodical *Shevilei ha-Hinnukh* in 1925. His major education themes were ZIONISM and Hebraism, and he employed psychological techniques to the discipline of education.

Trefa Banquet. When HEBREW UNION COLLEGE was established, it was originally intended to be a seminary for all of American Judaism. The differences of ideological opinion that ISAAC M. WISE had struggled to keep in balance were disrupted at a celebratory banquet at which seafood was served, which took place after the first ordination. This incident occurred in 1883.

Triangle Shirtwaist Factory Fire. In 1911, 146 workers of the Triangle Shirtwaist Company of New York were killed in a fire due to unsafe sweatshop conditions, which prevented their escape. This brought public attention to the cause of safety in labor.

Trilling, Lionel. (1905–1970) Author and critic who taught at Columbia University but generally avoided Jewish subjects.

Tucker, Sophie. (1884–1966) Flamboyant actress who entertained in English and YIDDISH. Her best known song was *My Yiddishe Momma.*

Twersky, Yohanan. (1900–1967) Hebrew novelist who taught at Hebrew College in Boston before settling in Israel in 1947. He produced novels with Jewish and non-Jewish heroes; of special interest is his work on CHASIDISM.

Union of American Hebrew Congregations (UAHC). Established in 1873 as the first national body of synagogues, it provided the framework to found HEBREW UNION COLLEGE and remains the structural organization for REFORM JUDAISM in North America.

Union of Orthodox Jewish Congregations (UOJCA). Founded in 1899, it is the largest organization of ORTHODOX synagogues in the United States. It was originally oriented toward English, rather than YIDDISH speaking congregations.

Union of Orthodox Rabbis (Agudas Harabonim). The oldest organization of ORTHODOX RABBIS, founded in 1902. It was responsible for establishing most of the DAY SCHOOLS in the early twentieth century.

United Hebrew Trades. Established in 1888 to promote union activity among Jewish immigrants to New York City and its surrounding communities.

United Jewish Appeal (UJA). Founded in 1939 as a project of the AMERICAN JEWISH JOINT DISTRIBUTION COMMITTEE and the United Palestine Appeal to coordinate fundraising campaigns; was preceded by campaigns in 1934 and 1935 for KEREN HAYESOD. Since that time, it has been the primary means for providing financial support for Jews overseas and resettlement in Israel and elsewhere. The UJA has enabled the JEWISH AGENCY to assist over one million Jews to immigrate and settle in Israel.

United Synagogues of America. Founded by SOLOMON SCHECTER in 1913, this is the association of CONSERVATIVE SYNAGOGUES in America.

Universal Jewish Encyclopedia. Published in 1941, under the direction of Isaac Landman; the first major undertaking of its kind since the JEWISH ENCYCLOPEDIA, with special emphasis on American Jewish life. It lacked the authoritative scholarship of its predecessor.

Untermeyer, Louis. (1885–1977) Poet, author, and translator who left a lucrative family-owned jewelry business in order to devote himself to literature.

Uptown Jews. Usually refers to those who have moved up economically (from New York's LOWER EAST SIDE); a general reference to the German Jews who had immigrated earlier than the Eastern European Jews and, therefore, had a generation to move ahead before the arrival of the immigrants from Eastern Europe.

Uris, Leon. (1924–   ) Novelist who gained particular acclaim for EXODUS and *Mila 18,* which dealt with the two momentous events in Jewish history of the generation, the HOLOCAUST and the establishment of the State of Israel.

Vidrevitz, Chaim Jacob. Known as the "Moscover Rov," influential New York City ORTHODOX RABBI.

Wallenrod, Reuben. (1899–1966) Frequent contributor to Hebrew periodicals, he was known for his Hebrew writings on American Jewish life.

Warburg, Felix M. (1871–1937) Banker and philanthropist who was married to JACOB SCHIFF's daughter and became a partner in Kuhn, Loeb and Co. He was an early supporter of the EDUCATIONAL ALLIANCE and the Henry Street Settlement, both organizations created to assist immigrants in the process of **AMERICANIZATION**. His philanthropic interests included art and culture, as well as educational institutions. He chaired the **AMERICAN JEWISH JOINT DISTRIBUTION COMMITTEE** (1914–1932) and was involved in the American Society for Jewish Farm Settlement in Russia. Although not a **ZIONIST**, he worked with **LOUIS MARSHALL** and **CHAIM WEIZMAN** to expand the **JEWISH AGENCY** to include non-Zionists.

Warheit, Die. Yiddish newspaper established in 1905 by Louis E. Miller to compete with **ABRAHAM CAHAN'S FORWARD**.

Waves of Immigration. Refers to the groups of immigrants who came in large numbers at different periods of time, such as the mass immigration from the Germanies (1836–1860) and Eastern Europe (1881–1914).

Waxman, Meyer. (1887–1969) Literary critic and historian; his major work was *History of Jewish Literature* (4 vols.); he taught at the **HEBREW THEOLOGICAL COLLEGE** in Chicago.

Weidman, Jerome. (1913–   ) Novelist who has received negative attention because of his less-than-positive characterization of Jews. He used his own experience for the substance of his novels. For example, he worked in the garment trade before writing *I Can Get It For You Wholesale,* 1937, and told of his own experiences between Jews and non-Jews in *The Enemy Camp.*

Weill, Kurt. (1900–1950) Composer who came indirectly to the United States after the Nazis seized power in Germany. He produced several successful musical comedies, especially in the area of *gebrauchsmusik* (literally, utilitarian music), readily accessible to the masses.

Weiss-Halivni, David. (1927–   ) Talmudic scholar who employs a source–critical method. He led the traditional group at the **JEWISH THEOLOGICAL SEMINARY** before he left (following the acceptance of women) in order to teach at Columbia University. He helped found the Institute for Traditional **CONSERVATIVE JUDAISM** in order to train **RABBIS**.

West, Nathaniel. (1903–1940) Pseudonym of Nathan Wallenstein (Weinstein), novelist who wrote about human corruption but was mostly known for his self-hatred in his portrayals of Jews and Judaism.

Willowski, Jacob David. (1845–1913) Talmudist known as the Ridbaz, he was brought to the United States in 1903 to become the chief rabbi of Chicago, as well as the elder rabbi of the **UNION OF ORTHODOX RABBIS**. He left for Israel after a short period because of what he felt was a lack of religious life in the United States. He is especially renowned for his work on the **JERUSALEM TALMUD** and his disputes with **RABBI ABRAHAM ISAAC KOOK**.

Wise, Isaac Mayer. (1819–1900) Considered to be the father of **REFORM JUDAISM** in the United States, he came to this country in 1846 from Bohemia. He set out to create an American Judaism that reconciled freedom and Judaism and began introducing reforms, such as mixed pews, choral singing, and **CONFIRMATION**. In order to champion his reform, he created **THE AMERICAN ISRAELITE** and **DIE DEBORAH,** and later built the

UNION OF AMERICAN HEBREW CONGREGATIONS, HEBREW UNION COLLEGE, and the CENTRAL CONFERENCE OF AMERICAN RABBIS. Wise really never intended to create a faction within American Judaism. Instead, he aimed to have the organizations he created as all-embracing.

Wise, Jonah B. (1881–1959) Son of ISAAC MAYER WISE, founder of *The Scribe,* a weekly in Portland, Oregon. As rabbi of New York's Central Synagogue, he created the "Message of Israel" in 1939, a pioneer inspirational radio broadcast that is still in production today (under the auspices of HEBREW UNION COLLEGE—JEWISH INSTITUTE OF RELIGION). While not a ZIONIST, he was active as chairman of the AMERICAN JEWISH JOINT DISTRIBUTION COMMITTEE and the UNITED JEWISH APPEAL.

Wise, Stephen S. (1874–1949) REFORM RABBI and ZIONIST leader who was active in areas of social welfare. He founded the FREE SYNAGOGUE in New York City to exercise the freedom of the pulpit in which he believed, as well as the Jewish Institute of Religion (which merged with HEBREW UNION COLLEGE in 1948) for a traditionalist, Zionist approach for the training of rabbis for all these movements. He was an intermediary for President Woodrow Wilson and an advisor to President Franklin D. Roosevelt, especially as he sounded the warnings of Nazi terror. He launched the WORLD JEWISH CONGRESS in 1936 and was president of the ZIONIST ORGANIZATION OF AMERICA, as well as a co-founder of the NAACP.

Wolf, Simon. (1836–1923) Lawyer and lobbyist, he defended President Ulysses S. Grant against charges of ANTI-SEMITISM, a result of Grant's GENERAL ORDER No. 11. He was a skillful community leader who served as president of B'NAI B'RITH and worked on behalf of Jews in various areas of civil and community service, writing *The American Jew as Patriot, Soldier and Citizen* to answer the canard that Jews did not fight in America's wars.

Wolfson, Harry A. (1887–1974) Historian of philosophy, he became the first Jew appointed professor at Harvard University. He was author of numerous important works, including books on BARUCH SPINOZA and PHILO OF ALEXANDRIA.

World of Our Fathers, The. IRVING HOWE's nonfiction account of the immigrants from Eastern Europe and their lives on the LOWER EAST SIDE in New York City.

Wouk, Herman. (1915–   ) Novelist and playwright. He is best known for MARJORIE MORNINGSTAR, 1955, the story of starstruck Jewish girl who makes it to the big stage, *This is My God,* 1959, a personal affirmation of traditional Judaism, and *War and Remembrance,* a story of World War II.

Wynn, Ed. (1886–1966) Born Edward Leopold. Comedic actor in vaudeville, on Broadway, on radio, and in films; he occasionally wrote and produced his own shows.

Yahudim. Literally, "Jews." Refers to the downtown (or Eastern European) Jews—the masses.

Yekke. Refers to the German Jews and their stereotypical intellectualism, decorous, punctual ways.

Yerushalmi, Yosef. (1932–   ) Jewish historian who teaches at Columbia University.

Yeshiva University. While this school may be traced back to 1886 when an elementary school (Yeshivat Etz Chaim) merged with the rabbinical school, this institution of higher education located in New York City was founded around the work of the Rabbi Isaac Elchanan Theological Seminary (founded in 1897) and admitted its first student in 1928. The institution grew under the presidency of Bernard Revel and today includes a full-scale program of studies. Although the school has non-Jewish and Jewish faculty and students, it is committed to Orthodox Judaism.

Yezierska, Anzia. (1885–1970) Novelist whose writings form a social criticism of immigrant life in the early part of this century, especially in New York's Lower East Side.

Yiddishe Volk, Das. Yiddish periodical, an advocate for Zionism.

Yiddisher Kemper, Der. Yiddish weekly, founded in 1906 as the organ of the Poale Zion Party; it has had an irregular pattern of issuance, moving from weekly to biweekly; has also been called Yiddisher Arbeter.

Yinglish. A slang term referring both to the infiltration of Yiddish words into everyday English, as well as the patterns of speech of immigrants that included English and Yiddish.

Young Leadership. Refers to a division of the United Jewish Appeal of those people under 40 years of age who are being trained to be future leaders and donors.

Young Men's/Young Women's Hebrew Association (YM/YWHA). Beginning as a venture in adult Jewish education, the first association for men was established in Baltimore, Maryland, in 1854, but the movement did not take hold until Y's were founded in New York in 1874 and in Philadelphia in 1875. In 1902, a separate women's association was established in New York. Not distinguished for the Jewish content of its program, this is primarily a secular institution that provides young members with recreational opportunities and cultural pursuits.

Yulee, David Levy. (1810–1866) Born David Levy, taking a new ancestral surname, he was the first Jew ever elected to the United States Senate (from Florida). He was a supporter of slavery and opposed the abolition of flogging as naval punishment. He was a member of the Confederate Congress.

Zeitlin, Aaron. (1898–1973) Hebrew and Yiddish writer, whose early poetry is lyrical but whose later poetry is expressive of an attempt to employ mystical religious insight in rhythmic verse.

Zhitlowsky, Chaim. (1865–1943) Yiddish writer and philosopher who may be considered the pre-eminent theorist of nationalism and Yiddishism in the DIASPORA.

Zion College. An unsuccessful attempt in 1854 by ISAAC M. WISE to establish an institution of higher Jewish learning that combined Hebrew and secular studies.

Zionist Organization of America (ZOA). Evolved from the FEDERATION OF AMERICAN ZIONISTS, YOUNG JUDEA, and HADASSAH in 1918. Founded as an organization of General Zionists, the ZOA shifted from a political enterprise to fund-raising and public relations after the state of Israel was founded.

CHAPTER 6

Israel

The Land of Israel is the birthplace of the Jewish people. Here the spiritual, political, and religious identity of the people was shaped. Ancient Israel also created the cultural values of national and universal significance that gave rise to the Bible. Few countries have as many special attractions per square mile as Israel. When one adds the depth of feeling for the country shared by Jews around the world, its unique appeal becomes more obvious.

Over the centuries, the Land of Israel has been known by many names: Eretz Yisrael (Land of Israel), Zion, Palestine, the Promised Land, and the Holy Land. To most Israelis, however, the country is simply called *HaAretz*—the Land.

For the Jews of the Diaspora, the Land of Israel was always the focus of their religious attention. The yearning to return one day to Jerusalem has been an integral and vibrant part of Jewish literature and liturgy.

The ingathering of the exiles, the return of the Jewish people to the land of their ancestors from the countries of their dispersion, is one of the fundamental principles on which the State of Israel was founded. Prior to the establishment of the State of Israel in 1948, the majority of settlers came from Europe. Immediately following independence, Israel's population doubled with the arrival of Jews from Arab lands and Holocaust survivors. In recent years thousands of newcomers have arrived from the ancient Jewish community of Ethiopia. In the wake of the recent major political changes in Eastern Europe, a new wave of Jewish immigrants began arriving from the Soviet Union.

"Next Year in Jerusalem"—more than a prayer, more than a yearning, more than a geographical statement—this unadorned one-line imperative helps inaugurate the festival of Passover and closes the Day of Atonement. It symbolizes the eternal longing of the Jewish people to visit Israel and its ancient capital, the City of David, the Holy City of Jerusalem.

All countries differ from one another in their culture, traditions, laws, language, and political structure. Israel seems especially unlike the others. Its unique blend of various elements has made it a land of modern miracles and a spiritual center for people throughout the world.

This chapter presents those essential concepts related to Israel's geography, history, people, and government institutions.

Absorption. The process of acculturating new immigrants to Israel. In modern times this especially refers to Ethiopian and Russian Jews who, when immigrating to Israel, need assistance with the HEBREW language, housing, and job placement.

Agnon, S.Y. (1888–1970) Hebrew novelist and Nobel Prize winner for literature, Agnon is regarded as the great epic writer of modern HEBREW literature. His works are highly symbolic and skillfully blend elements from the Bible and talmudic literature.

Agudat Israel. Hebrew for "Union of Israel." World organization of ORTHODOX Jews, founded in 1912 by Polish, German, and Ukranian Jews in order to solve problems concerning Jewry. Until the emergence of the State of Israel it was anti-ZIONIST, but today it has representation in Israel's KNESSET.

Akko. Formerly known as Acre. Israel town located at the northern extremity of HAIFA bay, it was the most important seaport in Israel from ancient times until the nineteenth century. Since 800 B.C.E. it has served as a Greek and Roman port, a Crusaders' fortress, and a French trading center. Since 1948 a large Jewish residential area has developed outside the Old City of Acre.

Al–Fatah. Arab terrorist movement founded in 1965 to carry on the struggle for the "liberation of PALESTINE."

Aliyah. Hebrew for "ascent." Immigration of Jews to Israel since the onset of modern Zionism. The FIRST ALIYAH (1882–1903) commenced under the shadow of the Russian pogroms and was led by the LOVERS OF ZION. It is estimated that 25,000 Jews immigrated during the First Aliyah, establishing agricultural settlements as they arrived. The SECOND ALIYAH (1904–1914) also derived chiefly from Russia, and some 35,000–40,000 Jews entered during this period. The BALFOUR DECLARATION gave the impetus for a THIRD ALIYAH (1919–1923), in which a youthful element dominated. Annual immigration figures for 1920–1923 averaged 8,000. The FOURTH ALIYAH (1924–1928) consisted of mostly Polish Jews who came to escape persecution. The FIFTH ALIYAH (1933–1939) consisted of German newcomers.

Allenby, Edmund. (1861–1936) British military leader who won a decisive victory over the Turks near MEGIDDO, ending Turkish resistance.

Allon, Yigal. (1918–1980) Israel military commander. He was one of the founders of the PALMACH, commanding Israel armies on various fronts during the War of Independence in 1948. In 1961 he became Minister of Labor.

Aquaba, Gulf of. Gulf at the northeastern end of the RED SEA, which in ancient times provided a port for SOLOMON's ships. Today it provides JORDAN's only harbor. Israel's strike on June 5, 1967 was a response to Egypt's threatened attack, when it announced a blockade of the Gulf of Aquaba, thus cutting off the Israeli port of EILAT.

Arab League. Political organization founded in 1945 by EGYPT, Syria, LEBANON, Iraq, JORDAN, Saudi Arabia, and Yemen. The main issue uniting the Arab League is common enmity toward the State of Israel.

Arabic Language. Semitic language borrowing many Jewish–ARAMAIC words. It is spoken by many of Israel's Jews and is recognized as an official language of the Arab minority.

Arabs. Semitic people who trace their origin to ISHMAEL. They live in EGYPT, Saudi Arabia, Yemen, Syria, Iraq, JORDAN, LEBANON, and Israel.

Arabs, Palestinian. Refers to the Arabs living in Israel before statehood. Israel was previously called PALESTINE, and its Arab population was called Palestinian Arabs.

Arad. NEGEV town mentioned in the Bible as captured by JOSHUA. Many archaeological treasures have been discovered in the modern era. The modern town of Arad (founded in 1961) is located 32 miles east of BEERSHEBA. It is the first Israel development town to be planned by a group of architects and engineers living on the site.

Arafat, Yassir. Leader of the PALESTINIAN LIBERATION ORGANIZATION (PLO), a terrorist group whose aim is to eradicate the State of Israel. By 1975, the PLO was officially accepted by more than 100 governments.

ARZA. The REFORM movement's official party in the World Zionist Organization. Its English acronym stands for Association of Reform Zionists of America. In Hebrew ARZA means "to the land" (onward).

Ashdod. One of the chief PHILISTINE cities in ancient PALESTINE. In 1948 the Egyptian advance along the coast was stopped here. Today, modern Ashdod is an Israel immigrants' town located twenty-four miles south of TEL AVIV. It is a port of call visited by a steadily increasing number of cruise liners.

Ashkelon. Ancient Mediterranean seaport and one of the chief PHILISTINE cities. Today, modern Ashkelon lies thirty-five miles south of TEL AVIV along the Mediterranean Sea. Its extensive bathing beach makes it very popular with visitors.

Ashkenazim. Members of a biblical people since the ninth century C.E. The term is applied to German Jews and their descendants, in contrast to the SEPHARDIM. They came to Israel in the sixteenth century and took the lead in starting some of the first agricultural settlements.

Avdat. Ancient NABATEAN city, dating back to the third century B.C.E. The ruins of the city of Avdat lie forty miles south of BEERSHEBA and have been partially reconstructed. They are among the most important monuments from the Nabataean, Roman, and Byzantine periods in the NEGEV.

Balfour, Arthur James. (1848–1930) British philosopher and statesman, he headed the government with which Theodor Herzl negotiated in 1902. As foreign secretary in 1917 he issued the BALFOUR DECLARATION, and in 1925 he opened the HEBREW UNIVERSITY.

Balfour Declaration. Official statement issued on November 2, 1917, by the British foreign secretary ARTHUR JAMES BALFOUR, declaring that the British government favors "the establishment in Palestine of a national home for the Jewish people . . ." The document was approved by the Allied Governments in 1922.

Bank Leumi. Bank established in 1903 by the Jewish Colonial Trust as the Anglo Palestine Company, it soon became the central bank of Palestinian Jewry. From 1948–1954 it acted as banker to the Israel government.

Banyas. Located in the GOLAN region of Israel on a tributary of the JORDAN RIVER, Banyas is set in a beautiful landscape. The area has been occupied by Israel since 1967 and is a favorite tourist attraction for both Israelis and foreigners.

Bedouins. Nomadic Arabs, the majority of whom still live in tents. Their main occupation is breeding sheep, goats, and camels in the NEGEV.

Beersheba. Originally a biblical town serving as the southernmost administrative and religious center of PALESTINE. Today Beersheba is a thriving modern city, whose important sights include Ben Gurion University and the Desert Research Institute, which investigates the special conditions of life in the Negev.

Begin, Menachem. (1913–) Orator, writer, and militant Zionist, Begin became the commander-in-chief of the Israeli underground forces, the IRGUN, and led the fight against the British mandatory government. In 1948 he formed the CHERUT PARTY and became its president. In 1977 he became Prime Minister of Israel. Today he lives in seclusion in the city of JERUSALEM.

Beit Alpha. Israel communal settlement in the VALLEY OF JEZREEL, founded in 1922. A mosaic floor of a sixth-century synagogue unearthed on the site (and depicting the wheel of the zodiac) has become a popular tourist attraction.

Beit Shearim. Israel smallholders' settlement in the VALLEY OF JEZREEL, founded in 1936. The ancient town of Beit Shearim became a spiritual center in 170 C.E. when JUDAH THE PRINCE transferred his academy and SANHEDRIN there. Archaeological excavations have revealed a synagogue and many rock tombs of the second through the fourth centuries, which have become a major tourist attraction.

Ben Gurion, David. (1886–1973) Pioneer builder of the Jewish State and its first prime minister, he played a decisive role in the struggle for the establishment of the State of Israel. As prime minister and minister of defense during the formative years of the state, he may be credited with many of its achievements.

Ben Yehudah, Eliezer. (1858–1922) "Father of spoken Hebrew" in modern times. His monumental life work was *The Dictionary of the Hebrew Language, Old and New.* He coined numerous words for daily use and published many newspapers and textbooks in his lifetime.

Berit Trumpeldor. Youth organization of the Zionist Revisionist Movement, originally a scouting movement. Its principles are nonsocialist ZIONISM, the building of Israel on a national basis, and militarism. Members of Berit Trumpeldor (also known as "Betar") also played prominent roles in the IRGUN underground movement.

Bethel. Ancient Israelite city north of JERUSALEM, formerly called "Luz." ABRAHAM erected an altar there, and the ancient tabernacle and ark were housed there during the period of the JUDGES. Because its name in English means "House of God," many synagogues are named Beth El.

Bethlehem. Name of an ancient PALESTINIAN town south of JERUSALEM, Bethlehem is the birthplace of DAVID. Christians ascribe special sanctity to Bethlehem as the scene of Jesus's birth. Today Bethlehem is primarily an Arab town located in the so-called WEST BANK of Israel. Its Church of Nativity is a popular tourist site.

Bialik, Chaim Nachman. (1873–1934) One of the greatest HEBREW poets of modern times. One of his most famous poems, "The City of Slaughter," written after the KISHINEV POGRAM of 1903, roused the younger generation to take up arms in self-defense. The Bialik home in TEL AVIV has been preserved as a cultural center, and Bialik prizes for outstanding contributions to Hebrew literature are symbolic monuments to his memory.

Bnai Brak. Originally an ancient Palestinian city northeast of JAFFA, Bnai Brak became an important Jewish center in the first and second centuries C.E., including the home to RABBI AKIVA's academy. In 1924 it was founded as an agricultural colony by religious Polish Jews, and today it is home to a large number of YESHIVOT and HASSIDIC sects.

British Mandate. In July 1922, the League of Nations formally entrusted

Britain with a mandate that incorporated the BALFOUR DECLARATION, recognized the historical connection between the Jewish people and the land, and called upon Britain to smooth the way for the creation of the national home. This mandate extended over both banks of the JORDAN RIVER. Several months later Britain partitioned the area of the Mandate, establishing an autonomous Arab emirate in eastern PALESTINE called Transjordan.

Cabinet. The Cabinet, headed by the prime minister, is the main policy-making body of the State of Israel. Once the Cabinet gains the confidence of the KNESSET and majority support, it may decide foreign, defense, internal, and economic policies. The Cabinet initiates the bulk of the legislation.

Caesarea. Originally an ancient Mediterranean coastal town that provided a flourishing port in the Hellenic period. When Judea became a Roman province, Caesarea was its capital. Today its excavated Roman amphitheater has been reconstructed and is again used for outdoor concerts. The Israel government's Fisheries Research Station is in Caesarea, as is Israel's only golf course.

Camp David Accord. Agreement signed in 1988 at Camp David (United States presidential retreat) between MENACHEM BEGIN, Prime Minister of Israel, ANWAR SADAT, President of Egypt, and President Jimmy Carter. In this agreement Israel agreed to leave the SINAI Desert and return it to Egypt. Egypt agreed to open the SUEZ CANAL and the Straits of Tiran. Israel also agreed to allow the Arabs of the WEST BANK and GAZA to be autonomous (that is, govern themselves).

Capernaum. Ancient town on the northwest shore of the SEA OF GALILEE. Jesus visited the place and preached in its SYNAGOGUE. In 1894 Franciscan monks built a monastery there and restored part of the synagogue, which today is a major tourist attraction.

Carmel, Mount. Mountain range in Israel, between the VALLEY OF JEZREEL, the HAIFA coastal plain, and the Mediterranean Sea. Haifa's modern suburbs extend up its slopes. Israel's only subway, called the "Carmelite," travels up and down its slopes.

Chagall Windows. Stained glass windows in the HADASSAH Medical Center in JERUSALEM depicting the twelve tribes of Israel. Created by Marc Chagall, they are an important tourist attraction.

Chalutzim. Hebrew for "pioneers." The Chalutzim made up the bulk of the THIRD ALIYAH to PALESTINE from 1918–1924. They undertook the difficult tasks of building roads, draining the insect-infested swamps, and establishing colonies. The first World Conference of the Hechalutz movement took place in 1921, and the movement thereafter began to establish training farms in many countries, to help prepare the pioneers for agricultural life in Palestine.

Chanaton. Name for the first CONSERVATIVE movement KIBBUTZ to be established in Israel. Established in 1984 by twenty-five American and Israeli settlers, it is located on the site of the biblical Chanaton, in the Lower GALILEE. Its goal is to build a modern traditional community that combines dynamic observance with social equality and pioneer living.

Cherut Party. Israeli political party founded in 1948 by veterans of the IRGUN and members of the REVISIONIST ZIONISM party and BERIT TRUMPELDOR movement. MENACHEM BEGIN, former prime minister of Israel, was once the leader of the Cherut Party, whose movement objectives include unselective ingathering of the exiles and liberalism in internal and economic policies. Cherut means freedom in Hebrew.

Chief Rabbinate. The chief rabbinate is Israel's final religious authority. An ASHKENAZI and SEPHARDI Chief RABBI preside over it jointly. Its departments control such religious functions as dietary laws, marriages, and the regulation of SCRIBES.

Coalition Government. The ruling party in Israel at any given time must retain a majority or at least a parity of seats in the CABINET, so as to be able to outvote all the minor parties. This has often necessitated the formation of a coalition government, whereby the ruling power invites other parties to join its ranks in order to retain a majority.

Damascus. Capital of Syria, its Jewish associations date back to the reign of King DAVID. In King Herod's time the city had a large Jewish population.

Dan, Kibbutz. Situated five miles east of Kiryat Shemona, it was founded in 1939, taking its name from the Tel of the ancient city of Dan. The Dan River, one of the three headwaters of the JORDAN RIVER, rises at the foot of the Tel. The Dan Nature Reserve and Trail has become a popular tourist stop.

Davar. A labor newspaper founded by Berl Katzenelson in the early twentieth century. One of a number of Israeli daily newspapers, it also publishes a children's weekly.

Dayan, Moshe. (1915–1981) Founder of the PALMACH, he lost an eye in 1941 while serving in the British army on Lebanese territory. From 1953–1958 he was chief of general staff of the Israel army and in 1956 he was responsible for the SINAI CAMPAIGN. In 1967 he became minister of defense and played an important role in administering the newly occupied areas after the SIX DAY WAR of 1967.

Dead Sea. The southernmost and largest of Israel's lakes, the Dead Sea is the lowest point on earth (1,300 feet below sea level). Although there are no living creatures that can survive its salty waters, the Dead Sea is rich in saline and provides potash and bromine compounds for export.

Dead Sea Scrolls. Ancient biblical manuscripts discovered in 1947 by Arab BEDOUINS in the QUMRAN caves on the northwest shore of the DEAD SEA. Among the scrolls that were discovered was the Book of ISAIAH in its entirety. The Dead Sea Scrolls (generally believed to date back to the first century B.C.E.) have advanced the study of the HEBREW text of the Bible.

Declaration of Independence, Israeli. Official document read by Prime Minister BEN GURION on May 14, 1948, proclaiming official statehood of Israel.

Deganyah. First established Israeli KIBBUTZ (1908) immediately south of the SEA OF GALILEE. It became a prototype for other communal settlements to follow.

Diaspora Yeshiva. Traditional Judaic school of higher learning located in Jerusalem for foreign students with little or no background in Judaica.

Dome of the Rock. Also known as the Mosque of Omar, this Moslem mosque was built in the center of the TEMPLE area in JERUSALEM ca. 738 C.E. It is situated on the traditional site of MOUNT MORIAH, the mountain where ABRAHAM was told to offer his son ISAAC as a sacrifice.

Druzes. Followers of a religious sect that split from Islam in the eleventh century. Living in villages throughout the GALILEE and on MOUNT CARMEL, the Druzes have the status of a self-governing religious community, with their own spiritual leadership and religious courts of law. The Druze serve in the Israel Defense Forces.

Eban, Abba. (1915–) Former chief of Israel's delegation to the United Nations and ambassador to Washington. One of the most eloquent spokespersons on the international scene, he presents a variety of subjects with sharp clarity. His book *My People,* a history of the Jews, has become a classic.

Eilat. Southernmost town in Israel, situated on the northern end of the RED SEA. With its dry, hot climate, Eilat attracts tourists from all over Israel and abroad.

Ein Gedi. Israeli communal settlement, founded in 1953 near an oasis on the west shore of the DEAD SEA. It was a desert town at the time of JOSHUA, and DAVID hid there from SAUL. Its vineyards are described in the SONG OF SONGS.

El Al. Israel airline established in 1949. It now runs services to four continents, including regular flights to Europe and New York.

Entebbe. In 1976, Palestinian terrorists highjacked a plane on its way from Israel to Greece and flew the plane to UGANDA. There, Idi Amin, ruler of Uganda, and the terrorists announced that they would kill all hostages unless Israel released more terrorists from prison. The daring rescue of the hostages by the Israelis, known as "Operation Entebbe," showed the world that it was possible to defeat terrorism without giving in to terrorist demands.

Ephraim. Younger son of JOSEPH, the name of an Israelite tribe, and a term applied to the more northern of the two Israelite kingdoms, the other being Judah (Judea). The prophets later spoke of the Houses of Judah (Judea) and Ephraim as representing the two branches of the Jewish people.

Eshkol, Levi. (1895–1969) Statesman and third prime minister of Israel. His portfolios over the years included executive director of the Jewish Agency, minister of finance, and minister of agriculture. During the time he was prime minister, diplomatic relations were established with West Germany, and the various labor parties united to form the Israel Labor Party. Eshkol is noted for his abilities in holding together disparate elements in his government.

Ethiopian Jews. Black Jews from Ethiopia, formerly called Falasha, meaning stranger. They trace their ancestry to Menelik, who is claimed to be the son of King Solomon and the Queen of Sheba.

Fatah Organization. Founded in 1965, one year after the founding of the PLO, to carry on the struggle for the so called "liberation of Palestine."

Fedayin. Terrorist raiders in the Arab refugee camps of Gaza and Sinai that were trained by Egyptians and sent into Israel to murder. From 1950–1955, almost 1,000 Israelis were wounded or killed by these terrorists.

Felafel. Ground chick peas, shaped into balls and fried, often served with salad in a Middle Eastern sandwich on pita bread.

Gadna. Israel movement for preliminary army training of youth between the ages of 14 and 18. Set up by the Haganah as an underground organization in 1939, it passed under Israel government sponsorship in 1949. Today Gadna operates pioneer farms and occupational training projects.

Galilee. Northern district of Israel, originally occupied by the tribes of Naphtali and Asher. Jesus was bred in the Galilee and began his preaching there. The first kibbutz in Israel, Deganyah, was established in the Galilee. Safed, once a great seat of Jewish learning, is one of the oldest towns in the Upper Galilee. The most important town in the Lower Galilee is the Arab town of Nazareth, famed for its Christian shrines.

Garin. Literally, "kernel." Refers to incipient groups of individuals who band together and prepare for the development of a kibbutz.

Gaza. Ancient Palestinian city on the south coastal plain of Israel. In the twelfth century b.c.e. it was captured by the Philistines and remained the most important of their five coastal cities. Gaza was captured in 1956 by Israel forces, who remained there until 1957. It again passed under Israel rule during the 1967 Six Day War.

Gaza Strip. Tongue of land including the town of Gaza, along the Israel coast for twenty-two miles.

Gerizim, Mount. Mountain in northern Israel. When the Israelites entered Canaan, a ceremony was held at which the people assembled on Mount Gerizim blessed all who observed the law. Mount Gerizim came to be especially important to the Samaritans, whose entire religious life was bound up with what they called the "Chosen Mount." They still perform their paschal SACRIFICE atop Mount Gerizim.

Gezer. Originally a CANAANITE center in the third and second millennia B.C.E. The Egyptian PHARAOH gave the town to SOLOMON as a dowry for his daughter. In 1945 a KIBBUTZ was established in Gezer by the YOUTH ALIYAH graduates from Central Europe. The tel of Gezer is an interesting place to visit for those interested in archaeology.

Gilboah, Mount. Ridge of mountains southwest of Beit Shean. It was the site of the PHILISTINE victory over the Israelites when SAUL and three of his sons were killed.

Golan Heights. Strategic hills located north of the Upper GALILEE, it was often used by the Syrians to bombard the KIBBUTZIM along the upper JORDAN. It was captured by the Israelis in the SIX DAY WAR of 1967 and has become a very important part of Israel's defense from the north.

Good Fence. Established as a point of exchange between LEBANON and Israel, it has become somewhat of an anachronism since civil war has destroyed Lebanon and the Israeli military controls the southern part of the country.

Habimah Theatre. Israel's national theater since 1958. Located in TEL AVIV, Habimah's repertoire includes original Israeli and Jewish works as well as translations both of classics and modern successes.

Hadassah. WOMEN'S ZIONIST ORGANIZATION OF AMERICA, founded in 1912 by HENRIETTA SZOLD. Today Hadassah provides Israel with a network of medical services as well as various forms of agricultural and vocational education. In 1949 Hadassah opened Israel's first medical school, jointly operated with HEBREW UNIVERSITY. Its hospital in Ein Karem is an important tourist attraction, since its synagogue boasts of the famous CHAGALL WINDOWS.

Haganah. Clandestine organization for Jewish self-defense in PALESTINE before the establishment of the Jewish State. After World War II the Haganah established an illegal underground immigration system through which European Jews streamed to Palestine. After the Palestine partition by the United Nations in 1947, the Arabs embarked on an all-out campaign to destroy Israel. The Haganah was instantly transformed into the Army of Israel.

Haifa. Israel's chief seaport, located below the northern slopes of MOUNT CARMEL. The city is an important staging post for the export of agricultural produce and an industrial center; it also has a university and a technical high school. It is also the home of a Bahai Temple.

HaShomer. Organization of Jewish workers in PALESTINE founded in 1909. It performed the dual function of defense of Jewish settlements and struggle for the employment of Jewish workers.

HaShomer HaZa'ir. Zionist youth organization and former Palestinian political party. In 1946 it formally became a political party and in 1948 participated in the formation of Mapam, United LABOR PARTY.

Hatikvah. Hymn of the Zionist movement and now the national anthem of the State of Israel. The words, composed by NAPHTALI HERZ IMBER in 1886, express the hope of Jewish redemption and a return to Zion.

Hatzofim. Israeli scouting organization; its graduates have founded several KIBBUTZIM.

Havlagah. The official policy of the JEWISH AGENCY and the HAGANAH during the Arab revolt in the late 1930s in PALESTINE. This policy of self-restraint was based on a belief in self-defense without retaliation or attacks on Arabs not known to be implicated in the outbreaks.

Hazor. In the course of excavations it has been established that there were twenty-one different settlements on this site, located in the northeastern GALILEE. It was once the site of a battle between Jonathan the MACCABEE and Demetrius of Syria. Many archaeological findings from the Tel Hazor are now housed in the museum in the nearby KIBBUTZ of Ayelet ha-Shachar.

Hebrew Language. Hebrew, together with Moabite and Phoenician, belongs to the CANAANITE branch of Semitic languages. Hebrew, along with ARABIC, is one of the official languages of Israel.

Hebrew University. A teaching and research institution, one of the finest in the Middle East, opening in 1925 on MOUNT SCOPUS. Of particular interest are its studies of contemporary Judaism, Asian and African studies, and its outstanding Department of Bible. A second campus is located in the Givat Ram section of Jerusalem.

Hebron. Ancient city of JUDAH, eighteen miles south of JERUSALEM. The modern city of Hebron is one of Israel's four sacred cities. It was there that ABRAHAM purchased a burial plot for his wife SARAH. In 1948 Hebron was incorporated into the kingdom of JORDAN, and in 1967 it was captured by the Israeli army.

Hermon, Mount. Mountain range in LEBANON, since 1967 under Israeli rule. The highest point is always snowcapped and provides a popular ski resort attraction for tourists.

Herzl, Theodor. (1860–1904) Founder of modern political ZIONISM. His solution to the problem of ANTI-SEMITISM was the creation of a Jewish State, which he describes in his book *Judenstaat.* He presided over five ZIONIST CONGRESSES, and later wrote a novel entitled *Altneuland,* a utopian vision of the Zionist state. He is well known for his famous phrase of optimism, "If you will it, it will be no legend."

Herzliah. Israel municipality in the PLAIN OF SHARON, founded in 1924 by sons of settlers from established MOSHAVOT. It is a leading holiday resort and the site of film studios.

Herzog, Chaim. (1918–   ) Head of the Israel military intelligence from 1948–1950 and again from 1959–1962. From the eve of the 1967 SIX DAY

War, he became the leading military commentator for the Israel Broadcasting Services.

Hess, Moses. (1812–1875) Political leader, writer, and forerunner of modern Zionism. In his book *Rome and Jerusalem,* which he published in 1862, he wrote that the only solution to the Jewish question is the colonization of Palestine. The ideas in his book came to be a basic part of Zionist thinking.

Histadrut. Israeli labor federation, founded in 1920. It acts today for the working class in all national bargaining on wages and conditions.

Horah. Israeli folk dance, it has remained the country's most popular. Many Israeli composers have composed songs in the horah rhythm.

Intifada. Referring to an Arab uprising, it literally means "shaking off."

Irgun. Palestinian Jewish underground organization, founded in 1937. Its original aim was retaliation against Arab attacks, but later its target became the British authorities in Palestine. In 1943 the Irgun was headed by Menachem Begin, later to become prime minister of Israel.

Israel, Kingdom of. Northern of the two kingdoms into which Palestine was divided after the revolt led by Jeroboam in 933 b.c.e. It is sometimes called Samaria after the city that became its capital ca. 890.

Israel Bonds. Chief source of investment capital for Israel's economic infrastructure. The Israel Bond Organization was founded in 1951. Since then it has channelled billions of dollars to help build roads, communications, transport, and many other facilities.

Israel Defense Forces (I.D.F.). Established in 1948, the Israel Defense Forces has three main elements: a regular army of officers, national servicemen (all citizens from their eighteenth year), and a reserve of men (up to the age of 55) and women (up to age 34). An integrated command oversees the Air Force, Infantry, Tank Corps, Navy, Intelligence, and Regional and Civil Defense Systems.

Jabotinsky, Vladimir. (1880–1940) Writer, orator, and Zionist leader, he organized the first Jewish defense in Jerusalem in 1920. In 1925 he formed the World Union of Zionist Revisionists.

Jaffa. Israel's oldest seaport. The King of Hiram floated the cedars of Lebanon down to Jaffa for the building of Solomon's Temple. Its modern Jewish community dates to the nineteenth century. Jaffa remained an Arab town until 1948 when it was incorporated into Tel Aviv. The Jaffa orange, developed in the coastal area of Israel, is internationally famous.

Jericho. City in the south Jordan valley, one of the oldest in the world. It was inhabited through Canaanite times until destroyed by Joshua. Destroyed and rebuilt many times, modern Jericho is inhabited mostly by Arab villagers.

Jerusalem. Capital of Israel since David established his throne there about

1000 b.c.e. Situated in the JUDEAN hills, more than 2,000 feet high, it is a holy city for Jews, Christians, and Moslems. Among its many famous sites and tourist attractions are the WESTERN WALL, HEBREW UNIVERSITY, the KNESSET, and the DOME OF THE ROCK.

Jerusalem Post. Israeli English newspaper, founded as the PALESTINE Post by Gershon Agron in 1932. It played a significant role as the mouthpiece of the official Jewish agencies under the BRITISH MANDATE. Its overseas weekly edition is read around the world.

Jewish Agency. Prior to the establishment of the State of Israel, the WORLD ZIONIST ORGANIZATION was designated as the Jewish Agency for the purpose of advising and cooperating with the Administration of Palestine in matters concerning the establishing of the Jewish national home. Today the Jewish Agency maintains headquarters in Jerusalem and New York, and its activities are carried out through many departments whose purpose includes settling new immigrants in Israel, training immigrants for agriculture, establishing Israel institutions outside Israel, encouraging capital investment by foreigners, and providing Zionist educational materials.

Jewish Brigade. Infantry brigade group formed as part of the British army in 1944, in answer to the insistent demand of the JEWISH AGENCY for the establishment of a separate Jewish fighting force. The Brigade went into action in 1945 in Italy. Later the Brigade was moved to the Italian–Austrian border, where it was able to make the first contact with Jewish survivors of the CONCENTRATION CAMPS. The Brigade disbanded in 1946 after returning to PALESTINE.

Jewish National Fund (JNF). Institution of the WORLD ZIONIST ORGANIZATION for the acquisition, development, and afforestation of land in PALESTINE. In the early days the Jewish National Fund was the Zionist colonizing agency as well as its land-buying arm. As part of its afforestation program, the JNF has planted millions of trees in forests and has lined many roads with shade trees. Its gifts, solicited by numerous volunteer workers, take various forms, including tree certificates and the blue and white coin boxes.

Jezreel, Valley of. Plain and valley of northern Israel dividing the mountains of SAMARIA and CARMEL from those of the Lower GALILEE. It is the main communication route from the maritime plain to JORDAN and has always been of major strategic importance and the scene of many battles. Today the valley is inhabited and farmed by people living in collective and cooperative villages.

Jordan, Kingdom of. Formally known as TRANSJORDAN (land across the JORDAN RIVER), because it included only the land east of the JORDAN RIVER, it was established as a principality by the British in 1923. It 1946 it became independent and adopted the current name of Jordan. Amman is Jordan's capital and largest city. The city of JERUSALEM was divided between Jordan and Israel after the Arab–Israeli WAR OF INDEPENDENCE in

1948, with Jordan occupying the eastern part. After the Arab–Israeli War of 1967, Israel took over all of Jerusalem.

Jordan River. Israel's largest river and main source of Israel's water supply. It figures prominently in biblical history, from the time it was crossed by Joshua. It is revered by Christendom—Jesus is said to have been baptized in its waters.

Judah, Kingdom of. Name of the southern kingdom, which included the territory belonging to the tribes of Judah, Simeon, and part of Benjamin. The word "Jew" is derived from the Hebrew for Judah, *Yehudah,* meaning praiseworthy.

Keren Hayesod. Financial arm of the Zionist Organization. Until 1948, Keren Hayesod financed all of the Jewish Agency's activities in Palestine, including settlement, security, and education. After 1948 Keren Hayesod concentrated its resources on financing immigration and absorption.

Kibbutz. Israel collective village, established by the early pioneers on the principle of complete equality. The members of each settlement own its property in common. Deganyah, the first kibbutz in Israel, was established in 1909 and was the birthplace of Moshe Dayan.

King David Hotel. Exclusive luxury hotel located in Jerusalem. During World War II and after, it was used as administrative headquarters by the British troops, which is why the Irgun blew up one wing in 1946.

Knesset. Israel's parliament, created in 1949. It has 120 seats, which are filled by proportional representation based on the total vote of the country. The Knesset building is located in Jerusalem.

Kol Yisrael. "Voice of Israel," it is Israel's official radio station, broadcasting the news of the day.

Kook, Abraham Isaac. (1865–1935) Religious thinker and first Chief Rabbi of Palestine. He identified himself with the pioneers and exerted a great influence on the younger generation.

Labor Party. Political party formed in 1968 by the union of three earlier parties: Mapai (established in 1930), Achdut Ha'Avoda–Poalei Zion (1944), and Rafi-Israel Labor List (1968). Mapam is the United Labor Party, and its main strength lies in the Shomer HaZa'ir and its communal settlements. It is the most radical among the labor Zionist parties.

Lavon, Pinchas. (1904–1976) Israel labor leader, he was secretary-general of the Histadrut (1949–1951 and 1956–1961), minister of agriculture (1950–1951), and minister of defense (1954–1955).

League of Nations. International political organization set up after World War I, theoretically exercising supervision over the Palestine Mandate. Founded in 1920, it formally ceased to exist in 1946.

Lebanon. Middle Eastern republic, whose capital is Beirut. It is made up of both Arab Moslems and Arab Christians. In 1975, when Palestinian terrorists upset the balance of power in the government, a civil war broke out. The country fell into the hands of terrorists, who opened up camps along the Israel–Lebanon border and raided Israel.

Likud Party. Major political party in Israel's KNESSET, it is made up of the CHERUT PARTY, the Israel Liberal Party, and several smaller parties. This group is to the right of the LABOR PARTY.

Lochame Cherut Yisrael. Known as "Lechi," or by its opponents as the "STERN GANG," after its founder Avraham Stern, this revolutionary Jewish organization split in 1940 from the IRGUN, maintaining that Britain must be fought notwithstanding the war effort against the Germans. Among the acts attributed to them were the murders of the British minister Lord Moyne in 1944 and Count Bernadotte in 1948.

Lod. Previously known as Lydda. Israel town southeast of Tel Aviv, on the road to the Judean hills. It served as an important commercial center between DAMASCUS and EGYPT. It was conquered by the Israel Army during the WAR OF INDEPENDENCE in 1948, and today Israel's largest airport, BEN GURION, is located near the town.

Lotan. One of two KIBBUTZIM established by the REFORM movement in Israel. The other is YAHEL.

Lovers of Zion. In Hebrew, *Choveve Zion.* An East European nineteenth-century organization for the settlement of Jews in PALESTINE, it derived its strongest impulse from the 1881 POGROMS. It proved to be of great importance to later developments in the creation of the State of Israel.

Ma'abarot. Temporary villages erected in Israel during the period of immigration in 1948. These transition camps were located near towns and villages. Their residents found work in the neighborhood and remained in the ma'abarot until permanent housing was provided.

Ma'ariv. Israel afternoon mass-circulation newspaper founded in 1948 by Azriel Carlebach.

Maccabiah. International Jewish sports festival under the auspices of the Maccabi World Union. It draws participants from an international field and has been held in different places, including Czechoslovakia, Belgium, and Israel.

Marcus, David. (1902–1948) American soldier, military advisor to the HAGANAH in 1948, he was killed in action in JERUSALEM during the WAR OF INDEPENDENCE. He was the subject of the novel by I. Berkman, *Cast a Giant Shadow,* which was made into a film in 1965. A village in JUDEA, Mishmar David, is named after him.

Masada. Stronghold located west of the DEAD SEA, situated on a high, isolated rock. In 40 B.C.E. it served as a refuge for HEROD's family, where he built a palace. Masada became a zealot fortress until 73 C.E., when all of the Jews atop Masada committed suicide in order to avoid capture by the Romans. In 1965 Masada underwent archaeological excavations, and today many of the sights have been reconstructed, including the site of the earliest known SYNAGOGUE.

Masoreti Movement. Name for the movement of CONSERVATIVE JUDAISM in Israel.

Mea Shearim. Stronghold of Jewish ORTHODOXY, Mea Shearim was established in 1875 in JERUSALEM. Today it boasts of many YESHIVOT and SYNAGOGUES, while its inhabitants have retained the mode of life practiced and the garments worn in the GHETTOS of Europe.

Megiddo. Ancient PALESTINIAN city in the VALLEY OF JEZREEL, strategically located on the ancient highway linking Egypt to the south of Israel to Syria in the north. During World War I the British defeated the Turks near this spot. The tel, or mound, which is all that remains of Megiddo, has been the subject of archaeological diggings. Excavations have revealed twenty-one different civilizations, the earliest probably dating back to 3,500 B.C.E. The museum at Megiddo is a popular tourist stop. Megiddo is also the inspiration for James Michener's book *The Source.*

Meir, Golda. (1898–1978) Labor Zionist leader, foreign minister of Israel, and former prime minister of Israel. Among her main achievements in foreign relations was extension of Israeli aid to the emergent African nations and the establishment of friendly relations with them.

Mercaz. Movement to reaffirm CONSERVATIVE ZIONISM. A member of the WORLD ZIONIST ORGANIZATION, Mercaz is the ZIONIST action organization of the CONSERVATIVE MOVEMENT.

Mikveh Yisrael. Israel agricultural school near TEL AVIV, founded in 1870. It was the first modern Jewish agricultural undertaking in the country, and today it is one of the foremost agricultural institutions in all of Israel.

Miluim. Refers to reserve duty in the army. After serving a regular term in the Israeli army, Israelis become part of the "citizen" army. They can be called up again to serve at any time, and must fulfill a period of "miluim" as reserve army people each year, currently up to three months per year for men until age fifty-five.

Mizrachi. Religious Zionist movement. It first made its appearance as a political party in 1902 with the convening of the Mizrachi conference in Vilna. The Mizrachi rallied many religious Jews to its banner and worked to fight secularism. Its network of religious schools eventually became part of the government's religious school system. Mizrachi of America built and sponsored Bar-Ilan University, the first religious institution of higher academic learning in Israel.

Mizrachi Hapo'el. A political party, a labor movement, and a trade union. It cooperates with other labor parties, has a construction company, a banking institution, and a well-established youth organization in Israel. It has been a member of the Israel government since 1948, and today is a part of the National Religious Party of Israel.

Modi'in. Ancient Israelite town, southeast of Lod (Lydda). It was the home of the Hasmoneans and the scene of Mattathias' first rebellion against the officials of Antiochus. In modern times a burning torch is carried from Modi'in to Jerusalem each Chanukah by relay runners.

Moriah, Mount. Mountain in Jerusalem identified as the place where Abraham prepared to offer his son Isaac as a sacrifice. Later the Jerusalem Temple was erected there. Today it is the location of the Dome of the Rock.

Moshav. An agricultural village in which farming is conducted on individualist lines on privately owned land. The moshav originated during the First Aliyah, and its earliest examples are Petach Tikvah and Rishon Le-Zion.

Museum of the Diaspora. One of Israel's newest museums, it is located on the campus of Tel Aviv University. Using the latest audio visual and other modern techniques of exhibition and presentation, the museum traces the history of the Jewish people from their dispersal after the Roman conquest to the present day.

Nabateans. People of Arab extraction who occupied Edom in the sixth century b.c.e. After developing agricultural techniques they established a chain of agricultural settlements across the Negev. In 1948 the ancient Nabatean irrigation system was reconstructed by archaeologists, and a number of experimental farms were created, growing crops that were cultivated by Nabateans years ago.

Nablus. Ancient Canaanite town originally situated between Mount Gerizim and Mount Ebal. From 1948–1967 it was in Jordanian territory and since then has been controlled by Israel. The present town, twenty-six miles northeast of Tel Aviv, is the hub of Arab nationalism. Nablus also has a community of Samaritans.

Nachal. Branch of the Israel Defense Forces training cadres for agricultural settlements. Members are recruited from youth movements, pioneer youth organizations abroad, and the army.

National Water Carrier. Completed in 1964, it brings water from the Sea of Galilee through eighty-one miles of giant pipes, aqueducts, open canals, artificial reservoirs, tunnels, and dams.

Naturei Karta. Orthodox Jewish zealots, they oppose political Zionism and refuse to recognize the State of Israel. Originally part of Agudat Israel, they seceded in 1937.

Navon, Itzhak. (1921–   ) In 1978 he became the fifth president of the State of Israel.

Nazareth. Israel town in Lower Galilee, twenty-four miles east of Haifa. It is mentioned several times in the New Testament as the home of the family of Joseph and the place where Jesus was raised. Today Nazareth is the largest town in the Arab part of Israel. Its inhabitants are mostly Christian.

Negev. The southern dry land of Israel, extending over an expanse of almost 5,200 square miles. For many centuries the Negev was a forsaken wasteland. In modern Israel there are many new settlements to which immigrants are being directed. BEERSHEBA is the largest city in the Negev.

Netanyah. Israel coastal town founded in 1929. It developed as a seaside resort, and from World War II it became a center of the diamond polishing industry. Modern day Netanyah is located twenty miles north of TEL AVIV on the Mediterranean, and owes its popularity as a holiday and seaside resort to its pleasant climate and fine sandy beach.

No Confidence Vote. If the KNESSET does not like the government or the actions of the government, it can vote for "no confidence" in the government. If this vote passes, the entire cabinet must resign and the president must start anew, searching for a new prime minister.

Occupied Territories. Referring to the territories of GAZA, JUDEA, and SAMARIA, which Israel captured during the SIX DAY WAR.

Old City of Jerusalem. In the sixteenth century the Ottoman sultan SULEIMAN constructed massive gates and walls around the city of JERUSALEM. Until about one hundred years ago, the enclosed section formed the city's total inhabited area. Today the Old City remains divided into four quarters: Moslem (northeast), Christian (northwest), Jewish (southeast), and Armenian (southwest). The WESTERN WALL and the DOME OF THE ROCK are just two of many tourist attractions that are located in the Old City.

Olives, Mount of. Mountain extending east of JERUSALEM, beyond the Kidron Valley. It has three summits, one occupied by the et-Tur village, the second by the Victoria Hospice, and the third by the original buildings of HEBREW UNIVERSITY. Various incidents described in the New Testament are said to have occurred on the Mount of Olives; it is the place where Jesus wept over Jerusalem.

Operation Magic Carpet. Name of the Israeli airlift in 1950 that transported YEMENITE Jews out of Yemen.

Oriental Jews. Oriental Jewish communities originated from various Moslem and ARABIC speaking countries, including Yemen, Iraq, Kurdistan (in northern Iraq), Persia (Iran), Afghanistan, and Cochin (in Southern India). All of these Oriental Jews have established communities throughout Israel.

Ottoman Empire. Four centuries of Ottoman rule began when Selim I conquered Syria and Egypt. His son, SULEIMAN THE MAGNIFICENT, divided the land of Israel into four districts: JERUSALEM, GAZA, NABLUS, and SAFED, and attached it to the Province of DAMASCUS. At the outset of the Ottoman era (1500s), there may have been 1,000 Jewish families in the country.

Palestine. Denotes the land of the PHILISTINES. It is probable that the name Palestine was imposed by the Romans on the former Judea in order to minimize the Jewish association of the country. Palestine was originally known in Hebrew as CANAAN.

Palestine Liberation Organization (PLO). A terrorist organization whose convenant called for the world to accept the rights of Palestinians and for the destruction of the State of Israel. The Arab nations declared this organization the sole representative of the Palestinian people and Yassir Arafat became its leader. Since its inception the PLO has carried out numerous raids and countless numbers of persons have been either wounded or killed.

Palestinian State. The Arabs have used the word Palestinian to refer to those Arabs who left Israel when the state was created, confident that the Arabs would destroy it. When Israel survived, the Arabs who had left to help in the nation's destruction were homeless. These Arabs today desire their own homeland within Israel and refer to such a homeland as the Palestinian State.

Palmach. The striking arm of the Haganah founded in 1941. It was maintained underground until 1948, when it became an organic part of the Israel Defense Forces. During the War of Independence the Palmach assumed a foremost role in the military operations.

Partition Plan. Term applied to the division of Palestine into autonomous areas proposed at various times before the establishment of the State of Israel. The United Nations Special Committee on Palestine recommended that Palestine be divided into an Arab and a Jewish state, with Jerusalem placed under international control. The U.N. accepted this recommendation in 1947. The plan was never adopted because soon thereafter Arab forces attacked Israel in the hopes of preventing it from gaining statehood.

Peres, Shimon. (1923–   ) Israel politician, he served in the Ministry of Defense from 1948–1959. In 1967 he became secretary of the Rafi Party and initiated negotiations that led to the formation of the united Israel Labor Party. In 1970 he was appointed minister of transportation and communications.

Petach Tikvah. A plantation colony founded in 1883 by Lovers of Zion. Petach Tikvah is located on Israel's coastal plain, a few miles east of Tel Aviv. It is both an industrial and an agricultural town.

Pinsker, Leon. (1821–1891) Russian physician, writer, and Zionist leader. In 1882 he published his famous pamphlet, *Auto-Emancipation,* in which he diagnosed anti-Semitism as an incurable disease caused by fear of the landless Jew. He prescribed the creation of a Jewish nation as the cure. In 1884 he became president of the Lovers of Zion and served the Zionist movement with distinction until his death.

Pita. A Middle Eastern sandwich bread whose pocket is generally stuffed with salad, felafel, or various kinds of meat.

Po'ale Zion. Socialist Zionist party, originating at the close of the nineteenth century. The Jewish socialists saw the solution of the Jewish problem in a utopian world that socialism aimed to create for all peoples.

In 1903 Nachman Syrkin founded the first Po'ale Zion group in London. The Labor Zionists came to PALESTINE as the famous pioneering SECOND ALIYAH, which established agricultural cooperatives and organized the self-defense that protected Jewish colonies from attack. Before World War II the Labor Zionists were divided into the parties of Po'ale Zion and Hapo'el HaZair. In 1929 these two parties merged to form the Workers Party of Israel (Mapai).

Popular Front for the Liberation of Palestine. An extreme terrorist group that emerged in the late 1960s. They hijacked regular airplane flights and attacked EL AL offices and Israeli government offices in foreign countries.

Rabbi, Chief. The Chief Rabbinical Council is the final religious authority. In Israel, an ASHKENAZI and a SEPHARDI Chief RABBI preside over it jointly. Its departments control dietary supervision, the regulation of SCRIBES, the approval of registrars of marriages, the sanction of rabbinical ordination, and others. The Chief Rabbis preside over the Supreme Rabbinical Court, which hears appeals from decisions of District Rabbinical Courts.

Rabin, Yitzchak. (1922–   ) Israeli soldier and politician, he served in the PALMACH and in the WAR OF INDEPENDENCE commanded the brigade that helped to raise the siege of JERUSALEM. In 1964 he became head of the ISRAEL DEFENSE FORCES, and in 1968 was appointed Israeli ambassador to the United States.

Rachel, Tomb of. According to GENESIS 35:19, RACHEL died on the way to Ephrat and was buried in BETHLEHEM. From the Byzantine Period onward her tomb was shown five miles south of JERUSALEM. An eighteenth-century domed building in Bethlehem stands on the traditional site where Jews used to pray. It is still a popular place for prayer and a usual tourist stop.

Rafi Party. Political party that broke away from the Mapai Labor Party in 1965 under the leadership of DAVID BEN GURION. In 1968 it merged with Mapai and Achdut Avodah to form the Israel LABOR PARTY.

Ramleh. Israel town, founded by Arabs in 716 C.E. It soon became the capital of PALESTINE. Ramleh is located twelve miles southeast of TEL AVIV. Its population is primarily Arab.

Red Sea. A branch of the Indian Ocean extending from the Strait of Aden and forking to Suez and EILAT. Early on it was identified with the "Reed Sea" crossed by the Israelites during their EXODUS from Egypt. It now forms Israel's southern outlet to the Indian Ocean by way of Eilat.

Refugees, Palestinian. Arabs who left Israel when the state was created, confident that the Arab armies would destroy it. When Israel survived, the Arabs who had left to help in the nation's destruction were homeless. These are the Palestinian refugees of today.

Rehovot. Israel town founded in 1890 by the BILU pioneers. CHAIM WEIZMANN, Israel's first president, made his permanent home there. To-day's modern Rehovot is located thirteen miles southeast of TEL AVIV on the coastal plain. It is the center for orange cultivation and has pharmaceutical and glass industries. It also has become particularly well known as the location of the Weizmann Institute of Sciences.

Return, Law of. A law passed by the KNESSET stating that any Jew can become a citizen of the State of Israel just by arriving in Israel and stating the intention to stay. This law was passed in 1950 and is one of the earliest and most significant of the basic laws of the State of Israel.

Revisionist Zionism. A ZIONIST party organized in 1925 by VLADIMIR JABOTINSKY. It called itself "Revisionist" because it felt the need for revision of the official Zionist policy toward Great Britain as the mandatory government of PALESTINE. The program of Revisionism included the creation of a Jewish majority on both sides of the JORDAN RIVER, unrestricted mass immigration of Jews into Palestine, and the outlawing of strikes.

Rishon Le-Zion. Israel town in the JUDEAN coastal plain, founded in 1882 by Russian BILU pioneers. Vineyards became the mainstay of the village, and today Rishon Le-Zion is home to the Carmel wine cellars. Interestingly, Rishon Le-Zion boasts a number of "firsts" in modern Israel, including the country's first Jewish kindergarten and elementary school.

Rosh Pina. Israel village in Upper GALILEE, and the first PALESTINIAN Jewish agricultural settlement in the modern period. Rosh Pina is located sixteen miles north of TIBERIAS and owes its present importance to its airport for domestic flights.

Rothschild, Edmond de. (1845–1934) Noted philanthropist, the first ZIONIST pioneers in PALESTINE appealed to him in the early 1880s to save them from financial collapse. He readily answered and continued to support Palestinian colonization.

Sabra. Native of Israel. The term refers metaphorically to their alleged characteristic of the prickly pear fruit grown in Israel, which has a tough exterior and soft interior.

Sadat, Anwar. (1918–1981) President of Egypt in 1970, succeeding Gamal Nasser. In 1977 he made a historic visit to Israel, the first such visit by an Arab leader. In 1978 he shared the Nobel Peace Prize with MENACHEM BEGIN for their efforts toward peace between Egypt and Israel. He was assassinated in 1981.

Samaria. Capital of the NORTHERN KINGDOM of Israel. Today it is part of the so-called WEST BANK, along with JUDEA.

Samaritan. Smallest religious sect in the world. Most of its members live in NABLUS, an Arab city northeast of TEL AVIV. They strictly obey the FIVE BOOKS OF MOSES but have rejected the books of the PROPHETS.

Scharansky, Anatoly. (1948–) Famous Soviet REFUSENIK who now resides in Israel. He now calls himself Natan Scharansky.

Scopus, Mount. Mountain in the vicinity of JERUSALEM, it is the home of HEBREW UNIVERSITY.

Sde Boker. Israeli KIBBUTZ in the NEGEV, twenty-five miles south of BEERSHEBA, founded in 1952. Its most famous member was DAVID BEN GURION, former prime minister of Israel. Today one can visit Ben Gurion's grave along with his archives, housed in a small museum located on the kibbutz.

Senesh, Hannah. (1921–1944) A gifted poet born in Budapest. In 1943 she joined parachutists from PALESTINE who jumped into Nazi-occupied Europe on rescue missions. She was the first to cross into Hungary from Yugoslavia, where she landed and fought with the partisans. At age twenty-three she was captured and executed. Her famous poem, "BLESSED IS THE MATCH," has been set to music.

Sephardim. Descendants of the Jews of Spain, the Sephardim arrived in PALESTINE in the fifteenth century after their expulsion from Spain. They brought with them the Spanish dialect LADINO, a mixture of Spanish and HEBREW written in Hebrew characters. Until the nineteenth century, the bulk of the Jewish population of Palestine was Sephardi. There are thousands of Sephardi Jews living in modern Israel today. They have their own religious customs and a CHIEF RABBI who renders judgment related to Sephardi custom and law.

Sephorris. Ancient city in GALILEE and its capital during Second TEMPLE times. It was once the seat of the patriarchate in the time of JUDAH THE PRINCE. In 1949 a MOSHAV was established at Sephorris, four miles northwest of NAZARETH.

Shamir, Yitzchak. (1915–) Leader of the LOCHAME CHERUT YISRAEL, along with AVRAHAM STERN. Elected to the KNESSET in 1973, he became foreign minister in 1980. He became prime minister in 1986.

Sharett, Moshe. (1844–1965) Statesman and Israeli socialist, he led the campaign against the BRITISH WHITE PAPER policy in 1939. From 1953–1955 he served as foreign minister as well as prime minister. Noted for his moderation, he resigned from the cabinet in 1956 as a result of differences with BEN GURION.

Sharm-el-Sheikh. Located on the southern tip of the SINAI peninsula, its strategic position allowed it control of the Straits of Tiran. It was a prime target for the Israel army in the SINAI CAMPAIGN of 1956 and the 1967 SIX DAY WAR, having on each occasion been fortified by the Egyptians in order to block ships sailing from EILAT.

Sharon, Arik. (1928–) General of the Israeli army and minister of defense during the war in LEBANON. When the Israeli army allowed a group of Christian Lebanese to enter the refugee camps near Beirut, resulting in the massacre of PALESTINIAN civilians, Sharon and two army generals were forced to resign.

Sharon, Plain of. Large coastal plain that stretches thirty-seven miles from Mount Carmel to the Yarkon River in Tel Aviv and from the Mediterranean to the hills of Samaria. Today the Plain of Sharon is densely populated and subject to intensive agriculture, especially the cultivation of citrus fruits.

Shazar, Zalman. (1889–1974) Third president of Israel in 1963, and re-elected in 1968. He has written extensively on political, historical, and literary topics.

Sheba, Queen of. Ruler of southern Arabian kingdom who visited King Solomon. The Ethiopian royal family claims descent from a legendary union of the queen and Solomon.

Shekel. A silver unit of weight, and later a permanent accepted coin among Jews. The shekel and its derivatives are still used today as currency in modern Israel.

Sherut. Shared taxi service in Israel.

Sinai Campaign. Israeli military operation directed against Egypt in 1956. Among its objectives was to destroy Egyptian armaments and to eliminate marauder bases in the Gaza strip. Within several days Israel conquered the entire Sinai peninsula. The Sinai campaign resulted in the opening of the Gulf of Eilat to Israeli shipping.

Six Day War. War between Israel and Egypt, Jordan, and Syria in 1967. Within six days Israel destroyed all of the armies on her frontiers, reunited Jerusalem, and was in complete control of Sinai, Judea, Samaria, and the Golan Heights.

Suez Canal. Waterway linking the Mediterranean with the Gulf of Suez and the Red Sea. Following the Six Day War the canal became the scene of prolonged hostilities between the Egyptians on the West Bank and the Israelis on the east.

Suleiman the Magnificent. Ottoman ruler who set laborers to work for six years from 1536–1542 to build the huge wall that still encircles the Old City of Jerusalem.

Tabor, Mount. Mountain in Lower Galilee, serving as a boundary point for several of the Tribes of Israel. According to Christian tradition, Jesus was transfigured on Tabor. In 1873 the Franciscans established themselves on Tabor by the side of a Greek Orthodox Church.

Tali Schools. Referring to the network of schools now being established in Israel for children of the Masoreti (Conservative) Movement.

Technion. Israel Institute of Technology established in Haifa in 1924. It is the most outstanding technological institute in all of the Middle East.

Tel Aviv. Israeli city, founded in 1909 as a suburb of Jaffa. Today it is Israel's largest city as well as the hub of the country's commerce. Its principal buildings include the Shalom skyscraper, the HABIMAH Theatre, Tel Aviv University, and headquarters of the HISTADRUT.

Tel Chai. Settlement founded in 1917 in the Upper GALILEE, it was attacked by Arabs revolting against the French mandatory authorities. YOSEF TRUMPELDOR and others fell in the defense of Tel Chai in 1921. Today it has an interesting museum, and annual pilgrimages by youth groups take place here in commemoration of its inspiring defense.

Tiberias. City on the Sea of GALILEE, famous for its healing hot springs. The SANHEDRIN was once located in Tiberias, and during the following centuries many pilgrims came to it as one of the four Holy Cities of Israel. Today, Tiberias is the economic center of the Lower Galilee and one of Israel's principal health resorts.

Timna. Located north of EILAT, Timna is the area of the ancient copper mines that were in operation until the twentieth century. Over the years erosion has shaped the rocks into the form of columns, and the archaeologist Nelson Glueck gave them the name of "SOLOMON's Pillars." Timna is an interesting attraction for tourists who enjoy their climb through the strangely shaped rocks.

Transjordan. Name once applied to the area east of the JORDAN RIVER. Today it is simply called Jordan.

Trumpeldor, Yosef. (1880–1921) ZIONIST leader, he worked with JABOTINSKY for the establishment of a Jewish unit to fight with the British against the Turks in PALESTINE. In 1919 he lead a pioneer group and later organized volunteers to protect exposed Jewish settlements in the Upper GALILEE. He was killed in the defense of TEL CHAI.

Tsfat (Safed). Town in the Upper Galilee, twenty-two miles from TIBERIAS. It has been a holy town for Jews since the sixteenth century, when it became a center of KABBALISTIC MYSTICISM. Several SYNAGOGUES in the town, including the JOSEPH CARO synagogue, are reminders of this. The quarter where Arabs lived until 1948 is now an artists' colony and a popular tourist attraction.

Uganda. Country in Africa, once offered by British colonial secretary Joseph Chamberlain to THEODOR HERZL as an area for Jewish settlement. Known as the "Uganda Scheme," the proposal was rejected by the Seventh Congress in 1905.

Ulpan. An intensive HEBREW language study experience whose goal is to immerse the student with spoken language in a short period of time; oral Hebrew is used in the classroom even for beginners.

Via Dolorosa. Located in the OLD CITY OF JERUSALEM, it is the painful route that Jesus took on his walk to crucifixion. Points along the way where he stopped or some memorable event occurred have been marked as the fourteen Stations of the Cross. Franciscans lead groups in prayer along the Via Dolorosa every Friday afternoon.

Wailing Wall. Alternately Western Wall. Together with the southwestern wall, it comprises the only remains of the enclosures of the Second Temple. Since Jerusalem was reunited after the Six Day War it has continued as an open air synagogue. The adjacent plaza is a forum for dancing and singing.

War of Attrition. In the period between April 1969 and August 1970, more than 9,000 armed incidents were reported from the Egyptian front, and 263 Israelis were killed. Israel's response forced the evacuation of three-quarters of a million inhabitants from the Suez Canal towns. Simultaneously there were clashes with Jordan and increased terrorist activity.

War of Independence. This war began with a series of Arab attacks on the Jewish community. In 1948 the regular armies of Egypt, Transjordan, Iraq, Syria, and Lebanon invaded, killing 6,000 Israelis. The fighting was long and bloody, but Israel finally triumphed.

Weizmann, Chaim. (1874–1952) Zionist leader and first president of the State of Israel. He was also president of the World Zionist Organization in 1920. In 1933 he planned an institute of science, which formally opened as the Weizmann Institute of Science in 1946. Among its research activities are optics, isotopes, organic chemistry, and plant genetics.

West Bank. Area west of the Jordan captured by Israel during the Six Day War in 1967. Israel refers to this area as Samaria and Judea.

White Papers, British. British government statement of Palestine policy (1939), declaring the British intention of setting up after ten years an independent Palestinian state in which Jews and Arabs would participate in the government proportionately to their numbers. The document was vehemently opposed by the Zionist movement but guided British policy in the ensuing years.

"Who is a Jew?" The Law of Return states that any Jew who wishes to claim Israeli citizenship can do so immediately upon arrival in Israel. To put this law into practice, it became necessary for the Israelis to define the word "Jew," and the question of "Who is a Jew?" became a burning question in Israel. The Orthodox political parties claim that only a person born of a Jewish mother or one converted to Judaism under Orthodox supervision is truly a Jew. But Reform Judaism also includes as Jewish those born to a Jewish father and raised as Jew, and both Conservative and Reform believe that people converted according to their practices are authentic Jews. Cases continue to arise that challenge the Orthodox definition of a Jew, but the Law of Return has basically remained the same.

World Zionist Organization. Founded at the First Zionist Congress convened by Theodor Herzl in 1897, its aim was the establishment of a legally secured, internationally recognized Jewish state in the Land of Israel. Today it works mainly in the diaspora to promote Zionism.

Yadin, Yigal. (1917–1984) Israel soldier and scholar, noted today for his archaeological research. Starting in 1952, he lectured in archaeology at HEBREW UNIVERSITY; he also did extensive research on the famous DEAD SEA SCROLLS.

Yad Mordechai. Named for MORDECAI ANILEWICZ, this Israeli KIBBUTZ was founded in 1943 by a group in Poland. In 1948 it was captured by the Egyptians and rebuilt after its liberation. The battle area has been faithfully reproduced, and tourists today can visit an audiovisual program that describes the bloody battle with the Egyptians.

Yad Vashem. Israel official authority for the commemoration of the massacre of the Jews during the period known as the HOLOCAUST. Its seat is on Memorial Hill adjoining Mount HERZL, JERUSALEM. Its museum contains an array of artifacts from the Holocaust.

Yahel. One of two KIBBUTZIM established in Israel by the REFORM movement. The other is LOTAN.

Yamit. Israeli town built in the SINAI after Israel conquered the Sinai and took it from the Egyptians. As part of the CAMP DAVID ACCORD, the Israelis were required to leave the town.

Yarkon River. Israel river flowing into the Mediterranean north of TEL AVIV. Since 1955 its waters have been partly directed to the NEGEV for purposes of irrigation.

Yemenite. An ORIENTAL JEW from Yemen, a Moslem state in Arabia. The first Yemenites arrived in PALESTINE in the sixteenth century. With the beginning of the ZIONIST movement many more came to PALESTINE. After Israel became a state the entire community of forty thousand Yemenite Jews was transported within approximately one year in an airlift operation called MAGIC CARPET.

Yemin Moshe. A small suburb in JERUSALEM, named for Sir MOSES MONTEFIORE. Today Yemin Moshe houses an artists' colony and is a favorite attraction among tourists.

Yishuv. A settlement or population group. More specifically, it refers to the Jewish community of Palestine before the establishment of the state.

Yom Kippur War. Beginning on YOM KIPPUR in 1973, this war took Israel by surprise and kept the ISRAEL DEFENSE FORCES off balance for the first three days. Egypt succeeded in crossing the SUEZ CANAL, and Syria advanced into the GOLAN HEIGHTS. By the time the fighting ceased eighteen days later, Israeli forces had counterattacked across the Suez Canal, and held a substantial piece of Egyptian territory. This war is one of Israel's greatest military victories because of the fact that its forces were caught so unprepared.

Youth Aliyah. Organization for transferring young persons to Israel and educating them there. In 1933 it was headed by HENRIETTA SZOLD, the founder of HADASSAH. Youth Aliyah brought out of Nazi Europe nearly thirty thousand young people, helped them to reach Israel, and placed them in villages and KIBBUTZIM across the country.

Zin Desert. One of the four wildernesses of the Sɪɴᴀɪ peninsula, it is situated southwest of the Dᴇᴀᴅ Sᴇᴀ. In the Book of Nᴜᴍʙᴇʀs, the spies sent by Mᴏsᴇs visited Zin.

Zion, Mount. The biblical prophets called Jᴇʀᴜsᴀʟᴇᴍ "Zion" when they wanted to stress its spirituality. In Mᴀᴄᴄᴀʙᴇᴀɴ times, Mount Zion was identified with the Tᴇᴍᴘʟᴇ Mount and the City of Dᴀᴠɪᴅ together. Since the crusader period, the Tomb of David on Mount Zion became an established Jewish tradition.

Zionist Congresses. Regular conferences of representatives of the Zionist movement, instituted by Tʜᴇᴏᴅᴏʀ Hᴇʀᴢʟ in 1897. The Zionist Congress constitutes the supreme legislative body of the Zionist Organization. Some of its functions include the fixing of the budget and the determination of the policy of the executive institutions.

CHAPTER 7

Philosophy and Theology

W hile the foundational ideology of the Jew finds its roots in the Bible, there are various concepts that developed throughout Jewish history that extend and transcend these basic ideas essential to Judaism. This chapter presents the reader with brief, concise explanations of the basic, the sublimely sophisticated, and even the most complicated beliefs of Judaism (both mainstream and fringe) as well as biographical sketches of those who have articulated such statements of faith and understanding.

Each generation has added to the layers of Jewish thinking its own nuances to ideas central to Judaism. At times, these new understandings developed into full-scale systems that eventually led the way away from Judaism. Yet, these too are indispensable to the understanding of the tapestry of Jewish thoughts and thinkers and are therefore included. Thus, the terms contained in this chapter do not present *the* theology or *the* theologian; instead, the reader is challenged by a panoply of ideas by those many thinkers who have contributed in some way to the rich philosophical culture of Judaism.

Abrabanel, Isaac. (1437–1509) The last of the great Jewish statesmen in Spain, he moved to Italy following the expulsion of the Jews. His encyclopedic knowledge included Christian literature. Although he wrote a commentary on the GUIDE FOR THE PERPLEXED, he moved toward dogmatism. Utilizing a traditional posture, he argued that Judaism cannot be reduced to a creed since every line in the TORAH is to be given unconditional credence; his best argument evolved around the idea of creation.

Abrabanel, Judah. (ca. 1460–1523) Known among Christians as Leone Ebreo, he was the son of ISAAC ABRABANEL (1437–1508). Influenced by Italian Platonism, he wrote in Latin, indicating a desire to write for the world, not merely for Jews as had his father's generation. He even wrote about pagan myths utilizing a philosophic interpretation, the first one to do this in Jewish philosophy. Abrabanel's philosophy can best be categorized as giving emphasis to the esthetic direction of the Platonic form of thought, making the beauty of bodies dependent on the ideas they embody, with God the source of all beauty. The world is categorized by him as a living unity, animated and given its vitality by the supreme power of love. Abrabanel's central doctrine is that love streams from God to His creatures and creations.

Abraham b. Moses b. Maimon. (1186–1237) The only son of MAIMONIDES. While his philosophy was similar to that of his father, his religious spirit was different. He believed that our destiny is completely within the hands of God and that the realization of our ideals depends at every moment on God's will. He accepted the importance of reason, but was far removed from his father's rationalism.

Abulafia, R. Meir b. Todras. (ca. 1170–1244) Probably the most renowned RABBI of Spanish Jewry in the first half of the thirteenth century. His work focused on HALAKHAH, MASORAH, MAIMONIDES's interpretation of RESURRECTION, and HEBREW poetry.

Adam Kadmon. Primordial man, a concept from KABBALAH inferred from GENESIS 1:26, "Let us make man in our image," that the first human was made in the image of a spiritual being also called Adam. The concept is sometimes referred to in earlier literature as *Adam Elyon* (supreme man), and sometimes refers to the totality of the divine emanation in the ten SEFIROT or in one of several of them.

After Auschwitz. A book by RICHARD RUBENSTEIN that focuses on the controversies that developed in the 1960s regarding the existence of God in the light of the HOLOCAUST. Its influence shaped the form these controversies took and became the fabric for the philosophic consideration of God in the modern era tainted by the death of six million Jews.

Ahad Ha'Am. (1856–1927) Literally, "one of the people," the pen name of Asher Ginzberg. He thought that science had refuted religion and substituted a high-level appreciation for humanity and the notion of nationhood for God and revelation. Considered to be the foremost proponent of CULTURAL or SPIRITUAL ZIONISM, he believed that the Jewish people had an unusual genius for high culture centered on ethics and that the revised Jewish state was to be the spiritual center of Judaism. Before World War I, he lived in England and played an important role in the events leading up to the BALFOUR DECLARATION.

Albalag, Isaac. Thirteenth-century philosopher of southern France/ northern Spain, he was the first (and for many the only) Jewish philosopher to maintain the doctrine of the double truth. He claimed that philosophic knowledge does not have to conform to the teaching of REVELATION; contradictions may be answered from the perspective of facts and not from the perspective of philosophy without harming either knowledge or revelation.

Albo, Joseph. (Fifteenth century) A student of HASDAI CRESCAS, he is best known for his book SEFER HAIKKARIM (Basic Principles), which was devoted to a discussion of dogma. For Albo, the basic principles of Judaism are God, REVELATION, and REWARD AND PUNISHMENT.

Anan ben David. Eighth-century Ascetic sage in BABYLONIA, considered by the KARAITES to be their founder; founder also of a sect called Ananites.

Ani Ma'amin. Literally, "I believe" . . . with perfect faith. A formulaic statement of MAIMONIDES' principle regarding the coming of the MESSIAH. It became a badge of courage for the Jews of Europe as they marched into the gas chambers chanting, "I believe with perfect faith in the coming of the Messiah and, though he may tarry, nonetheless, I still believe."

Anshei Emunah. Literally, "men of belief." One of many terms referring to adherents of the KABBALAH.

Anti-Maimunists. Those who rejected the rationalistic transformation of Jewish religion by MAIMONIDES.

Aristobolus of Paneas. A Jewish HELLENISTIC philosopher who lived in the first half of the second century B.C.E. He utilized allegory to interpret the

Bible, believing that scripture should be interpreted in a manner befitting God.

Articles of Faith, Thirteen. Articulated by MAIMONIDES as the minimum of Jewish philosophical knowledge in his *Commentary on the Mishnah.* These truths of religion that must be acknowledged by each individual Jew are: (1) the existence of God, (2) God's unity, (3) God's incorporeality, (4) God's eternity, (5) the obligation to worship only God, (6) there is prophecy, (7) MOSES is the greatest of all prophets, (8) the Torah, delivered by Moses, is of divine origin, (9) the eternal validity of the TORAH, (10) God knows all the deeds of human beings, (11) God metes out rewards and punishment accordingly, (12) God will send a messianic redeemer, and (13) God will resurrect the dead.

Artscroll Publications. A contemporary right-wing ORTHODOX series of publications, primarily translations and commentaries of biblical and classic rabbinic texts.

Atchalta D'geulah. The beginning of the redemption, often related to the establishment of the State of Israel, where the foundations have been laid by human hands under divine guidance.

Atonement. Reconciliation with God through a process of repentance.

Azriel of Gerona. (Early thirteenth century) One of the earliest and most profound thinkers of KABBALISTIC mysticism.

Ba'alei Hasod. Literally, "masters of the mystery." A term used to refer to the adherents of KABBALAH.

Ba'alei HaYediah. Literally, "the masters of knowledge." A term used to refer to the adherents of KABBALAH.

Baal Shem Tov. Literally, "master of the good name," also called the *Besht.* Baal Shem is a name given in literature and especially in KABBALAH to the one who possesses secret knowledge of the TETRAGRAMMATON and other names of God. The name Baal Shem Tov was used by the founder of CHASIDISM, Israel Ben Eliezer (1700–1760), a charismatic leader who became known through the oral tradition of his students who handed down tales of his travels and good works.

Baeck, Leo. (1873–1956) A liberal theologian, he won recognition after the publication of the ESSENCE OF JUDAISM. He had a unique nonphilosophic approach to human piety and believed that ethics without religious certainty is reduced to mere moralism. He spoke more about what God does rather than who God is. The only modern Jewish theologian who endured and survived Nazi death camps, he contended that evil was the misuse of human freedom.

Bahya ben Joseph ibn Pakuda. A moral philosopher who lived in Spain in the latter half of the eleventh century. His best known work, translated into Hebrew *(Duties of the Heart),* focuses on the obligation of the individual regarding his inner life, rather than his actions.

Basic Judaism. Refers to a book by Conservative rabbi Milton Steinberg, and the name of a general introductory course in Judaism; often used to indicate the mode of instruction for potential converts to Judaism.

Berdichevski, Micah Joseph. (1865–1921) Critic of the galut who felt that it was detrimental to the true Jewish spirit, he was influenced by Fredrich Nietzche in his call for radical human change, which he referred to as a "transvaluation of all values." He stressed the value of physical development and military strength, felt that universalism (rather than particularism) was the cause of what he considered the galut mentality, and felt that Judaism should be dissolved in order for nationalism to grow.

Berkovits, Eliezer. (1900–) Orthodox rabbi whose real contribution lies in his understanding of the Holocaust, although he also has shed light on the rabbinic period. Berkovits maintains that those who were not in Nazi death camps do not have the right to say whether God was there or not. He contends that those who believe that God was not in the concentration camps extrapolated from the few disillusioned survivors who denied God's presence. Instead, Berkovits gains strength of faith from those who were there and whose belief in God grew stronger as a result.

Bernays, Isaac. (1792–1849) Chief rabbi of Hamburg whose name is associated with the *Biblical Orient* (although it was published anonymously). This volume, published in 1821, attempts to interpret the historical development of the spirit in a philosophical way.

Binah. Insight and understanding, intelligence; the third sefirah in the kabbalistic understanding of the world.

Bleich, J. David. (1936–) Orthodox rabbi and attorney who is a leading authority on the complex issues surrounding bioethics.

Borowitz, Eugene B. (1924–) Reform rabbi and leading liberal theologian whose work focuses on an exploration of autonomy in decision making and a Covenant Theology in explaining the relationship between God and the individual.

Breaking of the Vessels, the. Also referred to as the death of the Kings. According to Isaac Luria, at creation the vessels holding the upper three sefirot kept the divine light that flowed into them. The light that struck the next six, however, was too strong and broke and scattered the vessels and the light that they held.

Brenner, Yosef Hayyim. (1881–1921) Probably considered the foremost exponent of Shelilat HaGalut, he saw nothing positive about the Jewish experience outside of Israel. He considered galut without value because, by definition, it places the Jewish people in a subordinate position; only Zionism could transform the Jewish people.

Buber, Martin. (1878–1965) A religious existentialist influenced by Chasidism, most remembered for his dialogic I and Thou approach to the relationships with God and between people.

Catholic Israel. A term coined by SOLOMON SCHECHTER to refer to the entire community of Israel, similar or synonymous to KLAL YISRAEL.

Chasidism. A traditional religious movement, devoted to strict observance of Jewish ritual and tradition, founded by the BAAL SHEM TOV in the eighteenth century. It is dominated by a unique communal structure that focuses on ecstacy and mass enthusiasm. It is close-knit community with a RABBI (REBBE) as charismatic leader.

Chokhmah. Wisdom, also the second level of the KABBALAH notion of SEFIROT.

Chosen People. Often referred to as the election of Israel. Although interpreted differently, it refers to the selection of the Jewish people by God for the REVELATION of TORAH.

Choshen Mishpat. The fourth major section in the CODE OF JEWISH LAW SCHULCHAN ARUKH, dealing with civil and criminal laws. Also the full name for the breastplate (usually referred to by its shortened name, CHOSHEN).

Chutzpah Klappei Shamaya. Or *chutzpah klappei malkhut.* Refers to a posture of confrontation or criticism toward God, associated with LEVI YITZCHAK OF BERDITCHEV, among others.

Cohen, Hermann. (1842–1918) Originally unrelated to Jewish philosophy as a neo-Kantian, later he best exemplified a synthesis of Jewish philosophy and German idealism, which grew out of his concern for ethics. He extended Kant's rational views of ethics, in which universal ethics must be social and take the concerns of all humankind into consideration; this ethical thinking led Cohen to a rational argument for God as well.

Coming of the Messiah. A belief that has kept the Jewish people optimistic throughout its history, a belief that the MESSIAH will come to save the Jewish people.

Commandments of Obedience. A notion of SA'ADIA that distinguishes between rational commandments that REVELATION reiterates and the commandments of obedience that are exclusive to revelation and include the cultic and ceremonial laws of the Bible.

Conservative Judaism. The organized, institutionalized system of Judaism that follows the HISTORICAL SCHOOL. It maintains a traditional view on law, which holds that contemporary decisions should be fixed by a body of rabbinical experts and interpreted by local RABBIS. Conservative Judaism holds that the religious legal tradition must be held in reverence, but that the need for changes and adjustments must be recognized and addressed when they become pressing.

Costa, Uriel da. (1585–1640) Also called Acosta. Philosopher. Born into a MARRANO family in Portugal, he lived in Amsterdam to avoid the Inquisition. After his book *Examen dos Tradiçoens Phariseas Conferidas* was burned, he criticized the rabbinic community for being too rigid and ritualistic. In particular, he believed that the doctrine of IMMORTALITY OF THE SOUL was questionable and not derived from the Bible. After seeking reconciliation, he was excommunicated, and was required to be trod over by the entire congregation. He was a hero in the fight against religious intolerance and is said to have inspired BARUCH SPINOZA. He later committed suicide.

Covenant Theology. A theological system based on the fundamental relationship in which the individual Jew stands, namely, the COVENANT. This covenant was made and also maintained in the context of the community where the individual Jew's relationship with God was established. Thus, the individual's (and the people's) relationship to God is of primary importance to Judaism and the Jewish people.

Creatio ex Nihilo. Creation from nothing; the theological notion that God created the world out of nothing.

Crescas, Hasdai. (ca.1340–1410) As chief RABBI of the Aragonian Jewish communities, he was one of the most influential leaders of Spanish Jewry, working hard toward its reconstruction following the terrible persecution of 1391. He wrote little and his intended work on the TALMUD was never realized. His magnum opus, *The Light of the Lord (Or Adonai),* is a collection of dogmas listed in order of their dogmatic importance.

Cultural Zionism. Best articulated by AHAD HA'AM, it was a program of revived Jewish folk life rather than religion. ZIONISM could re-energize latent national tendencies that had been subordinated by unbelievable and unrealistic approaches to God's commands or a Jewish mission and would allow for a restructured Jewish culture.

Da'at. Knowledge; in the KABBALAH, a harmonizing between the SEFIROT of CHOKHMAH and BINAH.

Da'at Elohim. Knowledge of God.

Dati. Literally, "religious." Used to refer to Israeli ORTHODOX, although the term is debated by LIBERAL JEWS who also consider themselves religious.

Day of Judgment. At the END OF DAYS everyone will come before God for a final judgment regarding how each individual lived his or her life in preparation for the world to come.

Devekut. Literally, "the clinging or cleaving (of one to God)." A mystical concept.

Din Ve'cheshbon. A judgment and accounting of the individual by God.

Disciples of Aaron. A reference to the PRIESTHOOD.

Divine Attributes. Characteristics or behaviors of God.

(Divine) Revelation. Usually associated with the giving of TORAH by God to MOSES on SINAI. Anytime God directly communicates with humankind, or the Jewish people in particular, en masse.

Dogma(s of Judaism). Although it has been debated throughout Jewish history as to whether, in fact, Judaism has dogmas at all, philosophers and theologians have attempted to set down these statements as essential principles of Jewish belief. Examples include JOSEPH ALBO's *Ikkarim (Basic Principles)* and MAIMONIDES' *Thirteen Articles of Faith.*

Ein Sof. Literally, "without end or infinitesimal." The name for God in KABBALAH.

Emet. Literally, "truth." *Emes* in ASHKENAZIC HEBREW as well as in YIDDISH; also, one of the levels of the SEFIROT in KABBALAH.

Empowerment. Buzzword of the 1990s, referring to the power to control one's destiny, in this case ritual and learning, moving from the traditionally accepted authority to the individual.

Emunah. Faith. One of the levels of the SEFIROT, according to the KABBALAH.

End of Days. An obscure concept regarding which there is little mainstream agreement; generally refers to the period in which time will no longer be reckoned as we know it, following the coming of the MESSIAH.

Enlightenment. Also called the *Haskalah.* In Eastern Europe it refers to the middle of the eighteenth century and beyond when, for the first time, the major streams of European thought came into contact with and influenced the world of Judaism, both socially and spiritually. This contact had a significant impact on Jewish philosophy; perhaps the first representative philosophy of this type was that of MOSES MENDLESSOHN.

Epikoros. Also spelled *apikoros.* Rabbinic term for nonbeliever or skeptic. Technically refers to a heretic but is generally used to refer to a disbeliever or one who questions the authority of tradition.

Essence of Judaism, The. LEO BAECK's first book, which gained him an almost instant reputation. It was modeled after Adolf von Harnack's book, *Essence of Christianity,* published in 1900. It may even have been penned as a response to it. It represents Baeck's conclusion that ETHICAL MONOTHEISM is the essence of Judaism, but his exposition of it extends beyond the ethical into the realm of religious consciousness as well.

Eternal Thou. In MARTIN BUBER's view of the world, the potential relationship one has with God is the model for all relationships. In this way, God is called the Eternal Thou.

Ethical Culture. Although critics argue that this is the logical extension of REFORM JUDAISM's notion of ETHICAL MONOTHEISM, this approach was originated by FELIX ADLER, son of REFORM RABBI Samuel Adler. Based on humanist ideology, it was institutionalized into The Society for Ethical Culture in 1876. While the New York Society for Ethical Culture was largely an offshoot of upwardly mobile German Reform Jews, the suburban societies have become popular for MIXED MARRIAGE couples.

Ethical Monotheism. The notion that this is the essential element of

Judaism once all ritual and ceremony is stripped away; the belief in one God who is the standard for ethics in the world.

Even HaEzer. Literally, "stone of help"; the work of Eliezer Ben Nathan of Mainz, known as RaBaN (ca. 1090–1170). It is the first complete extant book that emanated from German Jewry. Following the order of the Talmud, it contains responsa, as well as a variety of rulings on halakhah, with commentaries on customs, liturgy, midrashim, and then contemporary rabbinic authorities. Also the name of the third section of the Shulchan Arukh, which deals with marriage, divorce, and related topics.

Everything is Foreseen, Yet Permission is Given. The classic statement of Rabbi Akiba from Pirke Avot, which expresses the reconciliation between God's omniscience and the notion of free will; the individual is free to do what is chosen but God knows ahead of time what the choice will be.

Everything is in the Hands of Heaven. The classic statement that expresses utter abandon to God, who is in control of everything in the world.

Exile. A traditional notion that God punished the Jewish people, destroyed the Temple, and dispersed them through the world as punishment for not fulfilling their part of the covenant. Referred to as galut (or galus), it represents a state of mind as well, reflecting the feeling of the Jewish people historically for not returning to the land of Israel.

Fackenheim, Emil. (1916–) Reform Jewish theologian/philosopher, most significant for his discussion of themes related to the Holocaust. He has been a leader of the existential rejection of the rational approach of liberal Jewish theology since the 1940s, he arguing that Judaism did not have to be a religion of reason but is based on the revelation of Torah. He felt that God was absent in the Holocaust. He argues that the Holocaust marked a new level of human evil and the Jewish response to it is a new revelation—the absolute commitment of the Jewish people is a response to the absolute end of the Nazis.

Feinstein, Moshe. (1895–1989) Twentieth-century Orthodox rabbi and posek, leader of Orthodox Jewry. Head of Metivta Tiferet Jerusalem in New York, Feinstein became the leading halakhic authority of his time.

Feldman, David. (1929–) Conservative rabbi and authority on bioethics and medical ethics.

Fisch, Harold. (1923–) Author of *The Zionist Revolution,* this British-born Israeli immigrant focuses on Israel's special suffering. He argues that the Israelis' insistence on doing their duty is a response to a transcendent reality that has laid claim on them. For him, Zionism is not secular nationalism; it is an act of faith. He also argues from an Orthodox point of view that God gave Eretz Yisrael to the Jews absolutely and the Arabs have no claim to any part of it.

Formstecher, Solomon. (1808–1889) Author of *Die Religion des Geistes*

(The Religion of the Spirit), an attempt to provide a philosophical basis for Judaism. His concept of religion flows from metaphysical presuppositions borrowed from Schelling; he is considered to be the individual whose philosophic approach to ritual and ceremony (and the discard of their particularistic elements) laid the foundation for REFORM JUDAISM.

Free Will, Doctrine of. A philosophical notion that allows for the individual to select a course of action from a number of choices and is the cause of the action that results from his choice.

Gabirol, Solomon ben Judah ibn. (ca. 1020–1057) Poet and philosopher who lived in Spain. His writings reflect mystical tendencies and scientific knowledge, especially of astronomy. His major philosophical work is called *Mekor Chaim,* primarily devoted to the issues of matter and form, written in the style of a dialogue between student and teacher.

Gematria. A HERMENEUTIC for interpreting the TORAH, it involves the explanation of a word or group of words through the assignment of a numerical value to the letters.

Gershon, Levi ben. (1288–1344) Also known as Gersonides, or the RaLBaG, he was well known for his work as a mathematician, astronomer, and philosophical commentator for the BIBLE. He also authored *Wars of the Lord,* a commentary on the TORAH. As a commentator, he extracted the ethical, religious, and philosophical teachings from the text, calling them *to'alot* or *to'aliyyot.* He attempted in his large commentary to reconstruct the HALAKHAH based on nine principles of logic, which he substituted for HERMENEUTICS. His proof for the existence of God is based on the orderliness of the world rather than on God as a prime mover, which was favored by the followers of Aristotle.

Gnosticism. Reflecting a dualism or schism in the world between light (good) and darkness (evil), it is a mystical system, based on *gnosis* (knowledge) of God. Primarily a Christian movement, Judaism influenced it through the Bible, as well as through the use of names, concepts, and descriptions taken from the HEBREW or ARAMAIC. Although this is contrary to the Jewish notion of the unity of God, there were groups of Jews who shared these general attitudes.

God–Torah–Israel. The threefold foundation for Judaism where each element is indispensable to Jewish survival and continuity.

Gordon, Aharon David. (1856–1922) Considered to be the spiritual mentor of LABOR ZIONISM, he emphasized self-realization of the Jewish people only through settlement on the land and a return (out of the cities) to the soil.

Greenberg, Blu. (1936–   ) Wife of IRVING GREENBERG and author of *How to Run a Jewish Household,* she represents the modern ORTHODOX woman.

Greenberg, Irving "Yitz." (1933–   ) Leader of CLAL, the Center for Learning and Leadership, Greenberg is a modern ORTHODOX RABBI who has worked toward Jewish renewal through KLAL YISRAEL.

Guide for the Perplexed. Originally written in Arabic; in HEBREW, *Moreh Nevukhim*. The philosophic magnum opus of MAIMONIDES in which he reveals the hidden philosophic truths inherent in the Bible. His argument presupposes the intentioned use of equivocal language by MOSES.

Ha'atakah. Kabbalistic concept, referring to transference, often found as *gilgul*.

Halevi, Judah. (1085–1141) Poet and philosopher who was born in Toledo, and eventually settled in southern Spain, probably in Cordoba. He belonged to no one philosophical school; he considered philosophy arbitrary. He is best known for his book, THE KUZARI. Legend has it that he died upon his arrival in Palestine.

Halutziyut. The ideology of labor as articulated in the LABOR ZIONIST ideal.

HaMakom. Literally, "the place." A name for God.

Heikhalot. A genre of literature that provides the literary source for the mystic focus on emotional and ecstatic experiences.

Heschel, Abraham Joshua. (1907–1972) Philosopher who attempted to illumine the relationship between God and people. This relationship provides the foundation for religion. In addition to his work on the classic sources, Heschel also articulated a contemporary theology that is the result of the application of the insights he garnered from traditional sources, which shed light on contemporary problems and conflicts. He argued that religion has faded in the modern world because we have not attempted to recover the dimension of reality in which a divine encounter might take place.

Hirsch, Samson Raphael. (1808–1888) Probably the foremost spokesperson for ORTHODOX JUDAISM in the nineteenth century in Germany. He is best known for the focus of his philosophy, quoting from Pirke AVOT 2:2, "The study of the Torah is excellent together with DEREKH ERETZ [worldly occupation/secular education]." He coined the term *Jissroelmensch* (Israel–man) for an enlightened Jew who also observed the precepts of Judaism. He was also an ardent opponent of REFORM JUDAISM.

Historical School. The basic approach of CONSERVATIVE JUDAISM, and synonym for the movement in Europe, it was an alternative religious response to EMANCIPATION and the position Jews found themselves in as a result.

Hochschule fuer die Wissenschaft des Judenthums. Center for the Scientific Study of Judaism. Liberal rabbinical seminary in Berlin, established in 1872 until 1942.

Holy One (Blessed be He), The. A commonly used name for God, especially in rabbinic literature.

I and Thou. The phrase associated with MARTIN BUBER that epitomizes his belief that all experience is based on relationships. Everyday experiences are I–It, but real communication between people is on a higher level (reflected by a relationship between the individual and God, the ETERNAL THOU).

Immortality of the Soul. Although there is disagreement regarding the nature of the existence of the SOUL after death, this is a widespread belief that the soul has continued existence after death, developing first from SAUL and the witch of Endor, then primarily from the rabbinic period onward.

Ingathering of the Exiles. Primarily found in the prophecies of ISAIAH, JEREMIAH, and EZEKIEL, it is a belief that changes in time and place throughout history but is based on the promise God made, following DEUTERONOMY 30:3–5, in which God promises to bring the Jewish people back to the land of Israel.

Jacobs, Louis. (1920–   ) British RABBI and writer of theology, he accepts some of the methodology of HIGHER CRITICISM and asserts a human element in the compilation of the Bible.

Jakobovits, Imanuel. (1921–   ) Former Chief RABBI of England and spokesman for European ORTHODOX Judaism.

Jewish Catalog, The. Written in the early 1970s, a kind of *Whole Earth Catalog* of/for Judaism that represents a trend toward a contemporary do-it-yourself Judaism.

Judaism as a Civilization. The magnum opus of MORDECAI KAPLAN, in which he articulates the philosophy of RECONSTRUCTIONISM and the foundational principle that Judaism is more than a religion. Rather, it is a civilization that encompasses religion, language, history, a social organization, standard of conduct, and spiritual and ethical ideals.

Kalam. Arabic scholastic theology that influenced, in particular, the Jewish philosophers of the Middle Ages, notably, SAADIA GAON.

Kaplan, Mordecai. (1881–1983) Philosopher, founder of RECONSTRUCTIONISM. He defined Judaism as an evolving religious civilization; his primary work articulating his beliefs is JUDAISM AS A CIVILIZATION. He also founded YOUNG ISRAEL and developed the idea of BAT MITZVAH and the concept of a SYNAGOGUE CENTER.

Karaism/Karaites. Also referred to as *B'nai Mikra,* this is a sect founded by ANAN BEN DAVID that developed in the eighth century and relates solely to the written biblical tradition, as opposed to the ORAL LAW. The Karaites rejected rabbinic traditions of talmudic law and based their religious life on the literal interpretation of the Bible. Since the establishment of the State of Israel, many Karaites from EGYPT have settled in Israel.

Kavod. Referring to both God and humans, this term reflects a respect to either or both. Defined also as divine "glory" in the literature of CHASIDISM, which sees it as the first entity created.

Kelippot. According to the KABBALAH, these "shells" or "husks" are forces of evil that dominate the spiritual lights originally emanating from creation.

Kingdom of God. A reference to God's sovereignty in which God will be acknowledged as the only God, when all humans will accept God's rule. In Hebrew, *malchut shaddai,* alternatively, *malchut shamayim* (Kingdom of Heaven).

Kiviyakhol. Literally, "as if it were possible." A qualifying term generally used to preface statements about God, particularly when God is described anthropomorphically and anthropathically.

Klatzkin, Jacob. (1882–1948) Author, philosopher, and Zionist who, with Nathan Goldman, initiated the ENCYCLOPAEDIA JUDAICA. He was a student of HERMANN COHEN, whose philosophy focused on culture and art.

Kohler, Kaufmann. (1893–1926) Radical thinker, REFORM RABBI, and president of HEBREW UNION COLLEGE.

Krochmal, Nachman. (1785–1840) Referred to as the ReNaK, Krochmal was a philosopher and historian who is considered one of the founders of WISSENSCHAFT DES JUDENTHUMS. An autodidact, he wrote primarily of pure philosophic speculation influenced by German idealists. Under the influence of Hegel, he defined reality as the absolute spirit, and God as the absolute being. His philosophy of history is based on an assumption that history depends on spiritual content. Krochmal argues that while Jewish history reflects the structure of the history of other people, it is different in that it is eternal.

Kushner, Harold. Twentieth-century CONSERVATIVE RABBI who wrote of a limited God in his 1981 best-seller, WHEN BAD THINGS HAPPEN TO GOOD PEOPLE.

Kushner, Lawrence. (1943–) REFORM RABBI who attempts to breathe the spirit of mysticism into Reform Judaism.

Kuzari, The. Written by JUDAH HALEVI in an attempt to answer questions posed by a particular KARAITE, it is a work against Aristotelianism, as well as Christianity and Islam. It is a philosophical novella that allows Halevi, in the context of Judaism, to respond to the KHAZARS king's interest in conversion to Judaism.

Lehrhaus. Short for *Freies Juedisches Lehrhaus* (Free Jewish House of Germany); established by FRANZ ROSENZWEIG, it was an educational-type institution in which student and teacher studied classic texts.

Levinas, Emanuel. (1905–) French philosopher who focuses on the significance of the other in metaphysics. A latecomer to Jewish philosophy, he emerges as a commentator of TALMUD and rabbinic literature in the late twentieth century.

Liberal Judaism. A general term for nontraditional Judaism that often includes CONSERVATIVE, REFORM, and RECONSTRUCTIONIST. Often it is used as a synonym for Reform Judaism. In England, Liberal Judaism is the movement that parallels Reform Judaism in the United States; Reform Judaism (also called MASORTI) in England parallels American Conservative Judaism.

Liebman, Joshua Loth. (1907–1948) REFORM RABBI who led Temple Israel in Boston, Massachusetts. He gained a national reputation after publishing *Peace of Mind,* a pastoral volume, offering solace to an America which had suffered during World War II.

Logotherapy. A term coined by Viktor Frankl (1905–) from the Greek word *logos,* or the human spirit; a meaning-centered psychotherapy based on a philosophy that focuses on man's orientation to meaning. Frankl believes that the human spirit is the treasure chest for the most unique human resources.

Lord of the World. Generally used to express the belief that the personal God of Israel, ADONAI, is also the universal God of the world.

Lubavitch Chasidism. Lubavitch was a small town in Russia that became the center of CHABAD, when the son of the founder moved them from Lyady in 1813. The group left there in 1915. Few Jews were left after the pogroms of 1926 and the Nazi machine destroyed its remaining Jews during World War II.

Luria, Isaac ben Solomon. (1534–1572) Called Ha-Ari, the (sacred) lion, he was a KABBALIST who made his way to TSFAT in Israel (in 1570). There he schooled his disciples in his unique kabbalistic system, which came to be known as Lurianic Kabbalah. He believed people could attain identification with the Divine spirit through intense concentration. The unity of God and creation is a fundamental assumption of Lurianic thought.

Ma'aseh Bereshit. Literally, "the act of CREATION (of the world)." Refers to a specific school of mystical thought that speculates about the creation of the world. Also refers to physics.

Ma'aseh Merkabah. Literally, "the word of the chariot," also called merkabah mysticism. Refers to apocalyptic visions and a mystical perception of the throne (of God) in its chariot, as described in the first chapter of EZEKIEL. Also refers to metaphysics.

Magaria. Alternatively Maqaria or Maqariba, an early sect of the ninth century that follows mystical speculation that suggests that the world was not created immediately by God. Rather, God created an ANGEL and the angel created the world.

Maimonides, Moses. (1135–1204) Moses ben Maimon, also called the Rambam, perhaps one of the greatest thinkers in all of Jewish history. Trained as a physician, Maimonides was also a commentator and philosopher. Under the influence of Aristotelian thought as articulated by Arabic philosophers of the Middle Ages, he was best known for his GUIDE FOR THE PERPLEXED, which caused a great deal of controversy, and his MISHNEH TORAH, an "easy-to-use" compilation of Jewish law.

Makor Chayim. Literally, "the source of life." The name of several works of literature, including a philosophical treatise by SOLOMON IBN GABIROL. Sometimes used today as a gender-free and impersonal name for God.

Malkhut. Literally, "kingdom." The tenth level of the SEFIROT in KABBALAH.

Masorah. The tradition, that which is handed down from generation to generation.

Masorti. An adjective for traditional; synonym for the HISTORICAL SCHOOL.

Mechaye Metim. The one who resurrects the dead, traditionally attributed to God. The phrase occurs in the liturgy in the AMIDAH, changed by REFORM JUDAISM to read *mechaye hakol* (who gives life to all).

Memra. A statement of the AMORAIM.

Mendelssohn, Moses. (1729–1786) Sometimes referred to by the acronym RaMbeMan, he was the philosopher par excellence of the German ENLIGHTENMENT who actively worked in the struggle for civil rights for the Jews. His best known work was JERUSALEM. He was the first to translate the Bible into German in order to enable a larger number of Jews to read it in their vernacular.

Messiah. Literally, one who is anointed, referring to an eschatological character. The Jews did not refer to someone who would restore Israel to independence and sovereignty, breaking the yoke of the oppressor, until the post-biblical period. Messiah was a title of honor given in the Bible to the king of Israel. The PROPHETS described the Messiah as a divinely appointed ideal ruler (descended from KING DAVID) who would lead the world in righteousness and peace. Messianism is transformed by the REFORM movement into a messianic era that will be led by a large group of people, rather than one individual alone and does not require a return to Israel. In rabbinic thought, the Messiah is one who as the king of Israel will rescue and then rule Israel at the penultimate period of human history and through whom will be established the KINGDOM OF GOD.

Minim. A general term for heretics and sectarians.

Mission of Israel. Because of the unique relationship of the Jewish people and God, the Jewish people have a responsibility to share this relationship with the rest of the world by fulfilling the obligations of the COVENANT. The Jewish people are also to be a light to the nations (Isaiah 42:6, 49:6) in order to bring the world the light of SALVATION.

Mitnaged. Literally, the one who is against, referring to the "intellectual" opponents of CHASIDISM. It originally referred to the bitter strife between the *chasidim* and their opponents, but later became a positive description as evidenced by the GAON of VILNA. Salient elements include a skepticism of charismatic leadership and a critique of authoritarianism.

Mosaic Law. A term used to refer to biblical law as given by God to MOSES.

Musar. Ethical guidance and advice encouraging strict behavior regarding the HALAKHAH. It developed into a full-scale literature, beginning in the nineteenth century, especially prevalent as a movement among the MITNAGEDIM.

Nachmanides. (1194–1270) Moses ben Nachman or the Ramban, a leading Spanish commentator in the Middle Ages, he attempted to establish a road of compromise within the context of the controversy over MAIMONIDES. Most of his work focused on the TALMUD and HALAKHAH, and he was well-known for his commentary on the TORAH. Unlike some commentators (like RASHI) who simply bring the views of tradition to bear on the text under discussion, Nachmanides, like ABRAHAM IBN EZRA, expressed his own view, reflecting on the Torah as the word of God and the source for all knowledge.

Negative Attributes, Doctrine of. As articulated by MAIMONIDES, once one begins to try to list the attributes of God, knowing full well that the list must be concluded without fully expressing all the attributes, we therefore limit God. As a result, we should not try to list any attributes.

Neo-Orthodoxy. Originated as modern faction of German ORTHODOXY, originally used in a derogatory sense; essentially connected to SAMSON RAPHAEL HIRSCH.

Neshamah. A soul, sometimes used to refer to a good person, or a Jewishly conscious person. In the Bible, the soul was not distinguished from the body. Later it came to refer to the divine part of the person that was immortal.

Notaricon. One of the methods of interpreting the Bible, a HERMENEUTIC, it is a system of shorthand, shortened in abbreviated words.

Olam HaBa. The world to come. Although difficult to define in generally accepted terms, it is in contrast to this world and begins at the end of life on earth. On a technical level in theology, the term refers to the period that ushers in the COMING OF THE MESSIAH, which is connected to the RESURRECTION of the dead (in rabbinic theology). It is rejected by REFORM JUDAISM. REWARD AND PUNISHMENT is also promised.

Orthodox Judaism. A synonym for traditional Judaism, which acknowledges DIVINE REVELATION OF TORAH and the binding authority of Jewish law.

Particularism. A focus on Israel's unique relationship with God rather than God's general relationship with the world.

Peoplehood. A variant construct of the philosophy of MORDECAI KAPLAN in describing Judaism as a peoplehood rather than a religion.

Philo (Judaeus) of Alexandria. (ca. 20 B.C.E.–50 C.E.) Philosopher whose Greek writings primarily focused on the TORAH. One of his works serves as a legal code, one as an explanation of the Torah as a philosophical treatise, and one as commenting in the form of EXEGESIS.

Plaskow, Judith. Feminist theologian, best known for her 1979 landmark book on feminist spirituality *Womanspirit Rising* and its 1989 sequel *Weaving the Visions.* Her recent book is called *Standing Again at Sinai:*

Judaism from a Feminist Perspective. She has been on the forefront of the Jewish feminist movement for the last twenty years.

Polydoxy. According to ALVIN REINES, REFORM JUDAISM is a polydoxy, a combination of several approaches rather than a monolithic approach, whose parameters are set by what Reines calls the freedom COVENANT, "my freedom ends where yours begins."

Progressive Judaism. A synonym for REFORM JUDAISM, the Hebrew translation of *Yahadut Mitkademet,* Reform Judaism in Israel.

Prophecy. Understood within the context of the premise that God makes God's will known to selected individuals in successive generations. The PROPHET receives and imparts God's REVELATION. Thus, prophecy is knowledge from God in regard to God's future actions in history.

Prophetic Judaism. It refers to the approach to Judaism by some of the PROPHETS in which the individual PROPHET, armed with God's REVELATION, confronts wrong in the world and tries to make it right. An understanding of prophecy was championed and institutionalized by REFORM JUDAISM in its platform of social action.

Radical Amazement. A phrase coined by ABRAHAM JOSHUA HESCHEL, it refers to individual experiences of the divine in this world. Heschel argues for an extraordinary sensitivity to the hidden reality inherent in the seemingly ordinary.

Rational Commandments. According to SAADIA GAON, commandments that have their basis in reason as opposed to traditional commandments, which do not have their basis in reason (such as dietary restrictions and rituals).

Razei Torah. A term used in the TALMUD, secrets of the TORAH, which the mystics used to establish a precedent for KABBALAH in Jewish tradition.

Reconstructionist Judaism. The institutionalized movement whose foundation and infrastructure emanate from the philosophy of MORDECAI KAPLAN, its founder and guide for much of the twentieth century. Kaplan argued that Jewish beliefs have broken down, and Jewish identity, therefore, needs to be nurtured so that the Jewish historical belief in SALVATION in the world to come, which has kept him alive, can be transformed into a belief in salvation in this world. Kaplan further defined Judaism as an evolving civilization whose common denominator is the continuous life of the Jewish people.

Redemption. In Hebrew, *geula.* A religious concept which expressed one's desire for personal and social improvement; generally refers to deliverance by God. Modern philosophers argue that redemption is the triumph of good over evil, which is defined in various ways. Many religions place redemption at the end of history. The most famous Jewish example of redemption is the EXODUS from EGYPT.

Reform Judaism. The first modern movement to develop as a result of the changes in Europe brought about as a result of EMANCIPATION. While there is a variance of agreement of Reform Jews regarding individual customs and practices, there is agreement concerning the legitimacy of change and the fact that no formulation has eternal validity.

Reines, Alvin. (1926–) Twentieth-century philosopher/theologian who argues that REFORM JUDAISM is a POLYDOXY. He has applied this approach to ceremonial practices, arguing, for example, that since CHANUKAH has its origins in the pagan solstice festival, as does Christmas, both festivals should be celebrated on December 25th. Rejecting divine REVELATION and MITZVAH, he has transformed BAR MITZVAH, the son of the COMMANDMENT, into *Baal Mitzvah,* the master of the commandment.

Religion of Reason. MOSES MENDELSSOHN argued that Judaism is a universal religion of reason; eternal truths, which are self-evident to reason, opposed to temporal truths, which are subject to experiences of sensation. HERMANN COHEN also uses this term in a similar fashion.

Religious Consciousness. According to LEO BAECK, the individual must move beyond assigning only ETHICAL MONOTHEISM to Judaism. For Baeck, rationalism alone could not adequately explain Judaism. Thus, consciousness points to a realm beyond the scientific–ethical rationalism. Baeck therefore speaks to the consciousness of mystery as the deepest root of our religiosity.

Renews the Work of Creation Every Day. From the liturgy, a reference to God who, as creator of the world, continues this process in the imitation of immortality through procreation, as well as rebirth and renewal of nature.

Restoration. The returning of the Jewish people to the land of Israel; also the name of a Christian movement beginning in sixteenth-century England that sought to restore the Jews to Israel in order to usher in the MESSIANIC ERA.

Resurrection. A notion of rabbinic Judaism, influenced by the Persian religion of Zoroastrianism (and rejected by REFORM JUDAISM) that at the end of days, the body will arise and be joined with the soul. This notion was rejected by the SADDUCEES.

Revelation at Sinai. Refers to the experience at Sinai when God gave the TORAH to the Jewish people through MOSES. Even for those Jews who may reject the divine origin of Torah, many acknowledge the unspecified revelation of God at Sinai or one that was interpreted by those present and given written form in the Torah.

Reward and Punishment. A concept from rabbinic Judaism that suggests that God rewards good acts and punishes those who do evil—to take place in the world to come.

Rosenzweig, Franz. (1886–1929) Philosopher and theologian whose magnum opus was THE STAR OF REDEMPTION. An exponent of existentialism, he rejected the notion of traditional philosophy that the three elements we encounter in experience—God, man, and the world—all share the same essence. He argued that they are separate entities with independent existence and essence and cannot be reduced one to another. Rosenzweig's system validates the Jewish view of God and the world but is not an exposition of Jewish philosophy; rather he validates it on the basis of his own personal experience.

Ruach Elohim. Literally, "the spirit of God" (as quoted in the creation story in the first chapter of GENESIS); may also be translated in philosophical terms as the essence of God.

Rubenstein, Richard L. (1924–   ) Theologian who is primarily associated with the post-HOLOCAUST "God is Dead" movement, particularly focused in the 1960s and beyond. He argues that we should reject the notion of a CHOSEN PEOPLE since following the Holocaust it means that we are the suffering servant of God. For Rubenstein, none of the theodicies are tenable in Judaism following AUSCHWITZ.

Sa'adia Gaon. (882–942) From Fayyum in EGYPT, he is considered the father of medieval Jewish philosophy. As GAON of SURA, his work is important for the information he provides about other Jewish thinkers, as well as his own. He pioneered in philosophy and in other areas of medieval Jewish science. Considered to be one of the fathers of Hebrew philology, his Arabic translation of the Bible and his commentaries on it laid the foundation of scientific biblical EXEGESIS among RABBINATE Jews. Even in his talmudic studies, he opened up new paths of exploration because of the systematic presentation of his subjects. Most of his works are colored by a polemic against KARAISM. His major work combines an exposition of his own thinking with a criticism of opposing viewpoints.

Sabbateanism. The messianic movement named for SHABBATAI ZEVI.

Salvation. The saving of the individual or the world through the arrival of the MESSIAH.

Satmar Chasidism. A CHASIDIC dynasty whose nineteenth-century leader, Joel Teitelbaum, led the community in Sato-mare, Rumania, from where the movement took its name. Allied with the NETUREI KARTA community in JERUSALEM, it is fiercely anti-ZIONIST, regarding the modern state of Israel as blasphemous; it also argues against the use of HEBREW as a spoken language because it is a holy tongue.

Scholem, Gershom. (1897–1982) Scholar who was considered the foremost modern authority on KABBALAH. His most famous work is *Major Trends in Jewish Mysticism.*

Science, Jewish. Founded by Morris (1889–1938) and Tehilla (1893–1973) Lichenstein, this is the Jewish parallel of Christian Science.

Sefer HaIkkarim. The book of basic ideas, prepared by JOSEPH ALBO, it is devoted to a discussion of Jewish DOGMAS. It is a well-circulated volume due to its fluent style and spirited exposition. Drawn from other philosophies, it is a clever exposition, but not very profound.

Sefer Yetzirah. Probably composed around the eighth century, a brief work of 1600 words, it is the first Hebrew work of speculative thought whose central theme is a cosmology and cosmogony.

Sefirot, Ten. A fundamental aspect of the KABBALAH, a term coined by the author of SEFER YETZIRAH, it denotes the ten stages that emanate from the EIN SOF (God) and form God's manifestation in each of God's ten attributes. Each sefirah (sing.) relates to God's work in creation.

Shekhinah. A mystical concept, the in-dwelling presence of God on earth, also considered to be those feminine aspects of God; sometimes referred to as the holy spirit.

Shelilat HaGalut. The negation of Jewish life is the EXILE, a theory proposed by some ZIONISTS who believe that there is nothing positive about Jewish experience outside of Israel.

Shemittot, the Doctrine of. From the notion of a JUBILEE YEAR, a mystical concept that suggests that the world to come will be the creation of another link in a chain of creation of shemittot, sabbaticals.

Sitrei Torah. Literally, "secrets of the Torah"; it is a term the TALMUD and also philosophers use to refer to adherents of the KABBALAH.

Soloveitchik, Joseph B. (1903–   ) ORTHODOX RABBI, foremost proponent of modern orthodoxy, the fusion of classic halachic Judaism and American culture, epitomized by graduates of YESHIVA UNIVERSITY. He has been a leading spirit of the RABBI ISAAC ELCHANAN THEOLOGICAL SEMINARY and chairman of the HALACHAH Commission of the RABBINICAL COUNCIL OF AMERICA. Since much of his work has not been published, it is hard to come to a systematic understanding of his thinking. His published papers do focus on the human condition—what it means to be an individual in relation to God in the context of Jewish tradition.

Spinoza, Baruch (Benedict) de. (1632–1677) Dutch philosopher. Unlike previous Jewish philosophers, who sought to understand Judaism from the perspective of philosophy, he recognized from the outset that his thinking was not in accord with Jewish thought and therefore did not attempt to harmonize it. As a result, he was excommunicated by the Jews; he directed his work to the community of European thinkers. Thus, he could be better considered in the history of modern philosophy than in Jewish philosophy. Best considered a pantheist, he advanced a polemic point of view against the Bible.

Spiritual Center. In Hebrew, *merkaz ruchani*. According to AHAD HA'AM, the revived Jewish state he sought in Israel was to be the spiritual center of the Jewish people. For Ahad Ha'Am, the word spiritual is totally secular, not religious, and is equated with the Jewish ethos.

Spirituality. A buzz word of the 1980s, it is an undefined term in Judaism (borrowed from Christianity) that reflects some sort of a sense of a relationship of the individual with the Divine.

Star of Redemption, The. The primary work of FRANZ ROSENZWEIG, divided into the classic sections of CREATION, REVELATION, and REDEMPTION, in which he seeks to demonstrate what existence says about God, the world, and the human species, as well as how the relationships are drawn among them. In the second section of the book Rosenzweig moves from CREATION to REVELATION, understanding existence as temporal. In the third section, he shows how the previously defined temporal existence can take on aspects of eternity, concluding that the ultimate goal of the evolution of the world is the unification of the world and man with God.

Steinheim, Solomon. (1789–1866) Philosopher whose work *Revelation According to the Doctrine of the Synagogue* was opposed to all philosophic rationalism. In its stead, he developed a doctrine that stated that religious truth was given exclusively in REVELATION. He further said that reason must abandon itself in order to find the truth in revelation.

Steinsaltz, Adin. (1937–   ) Contemporary Israeli talmudist who has prepared a modern English translation and commentary on the TALMUD.

Tanya. A CHASIDIC work, authored by SHNEUR ZALMAN OF LYADY (1747–1813) which was written to clarify the complexity of chasidic teaching.

Tendler, Moses. (1926–   ) Rabbi and scientist who teaches both TALMUD and science at YESHIVA UNIVERSITY; he is also a congregational rabbi in Monsey, New York.

Tikkun. Literally, "repair." According to the KABBALAH, it is essential to bring about world order (to repair the world) in order to bring about the END OF DAYS and REDEMPTION. To return the world to its original state, one must repair the vessels that were broken by God at creation.

Torah and Derekh Eretz. A quotation from Pirke AVOT, used by SAMSON RAPHAEL HIRSCH to mean that the modern Jew needs a traditional education as well as a high-level secular education.

Torah-true Judaism. A self-proclaimed description of ORTHODOX Judaism, which argues only that it is true or faithful to the TORAH.

Tzimtzum. Literally, "constriction." In KABBALAH, it refers to God's self-concentration; in order to create the world God entered Godself, making it possible for something besides EIN SOF to exist.

Ultra-Orthodox. Often referring to fundamentalists among ORTHODOX Jewry, especially in terms of a political reference to settlers on the WEST BANK in Israel, as well as those who live in MEA SHEARIM.

Universalism. In opposition to PARTICULARISM, this refers to a Jewish posture that rejects the ELECTION OF ISRAEL as a CHOSEN PEOPLE. Instead, in the spirit of the Hebrew PROPHETS, it sees the MISSION OF ISRAEL as a light unto the nations, beyond the confines and needs of only the Jewish people.

Waldenberg, Eliezer. Twentieth-century POSEK who, as RABBI and DAYAN in JERUSALEM, wrote *Tzitz Eliezer,* ten volumes of RESPONSA that include answers to questions about various issues such as departure on an airplane on SHABBAT and the use of a hearing aid on Shabbat.

When Bad Things Happen to Good People. A best-selling book by HAROLD KUSHNER that basically describes a limited God who does not directly impact on what happens to people in the world.

Wiesel, Elie. (1928–) Writer, primarily of fiction, who is the pivotal figure in intellectual culture related to the HOLOCAUST. His writings are reflective explorations of a range of responses to the Holocaust. Often characterized as a witness, he sees his responsibility as offering truthful testimony—a measurement for all who discuss this topic.

Wine, Sherwin. (1928–) REFORM RABBI, a humanist, who has rejected the existence of God. He founded the Society for Humanistic Judaism.

Wissenschaft des Judenthums. Literally, "the science of Judaism"; refers to the scientific, critical study of Judaism using modern methods of research, historically allied with German REFORM JUDAISM.

Written Law. A synonym for the TORAH because it is traditionally understood as revealed by God and written down by MOSES, as opposed to the ORAL LAW.

Yigdal. Medieval hymn that poetically described MAIMONIDES' Thirteen Principles, written by Daniel ben Judah, a DAYAN in Rome in the first half of the fourteenth century.

Yoke of the Kingdom. Reflecting one's acceptance/obedience to MITZVOT; acknowledging God as sovereign in the world.

Young Israel. Formed in 1912 in the United States by young ORTHODOX Jews in New York's LOWER EAST SIDE, who considered themselves AMERICANIZED and rejected the folkways of their immigrant parents.

Zangwill, Israel. (1864–1926) English author whose well-known works include *Children of the Ghetto, The King of the Schnorrers,* and the play *The Melting Pot.* He was also active in women's suffrage and pacifism. He was a follower of THEODOR HERZL. He founded the Jewish Territorial Organization, when the Seventh Zionist Congress rejected the UGANDA offer in 1905, arguing that the Jewish homeland need not be in PALESTINE.

Zunz, Leopold. (1794–1886) Hebrew name Yom Tov Lippmann. He was among the founders of WISSENSCHAFT DES JUDENTHUMS in Germany. His chief interest was research in Hebrew liturgy.

CHAPTER 8

Daily Jewish Living

In order for the individual to interact with others in the community, that person needs a vocabulary of common discourse to express the folk values integral to Jewish life. While emphasizing the value concepts of the common folk and not the grandiose ideas of history, this chapter provides the reader with word concepts from daily Jewish life, a kind of "Jewish culture code."

The Jewish community is not a monolithic community with one set of peculiar folkways, as anti-Semites might have it. Instead, it is an amalgamation of ideas expressed in the modest forms of the everyday routine of the individual. Many of the ideas that these words represent emanate from the ethnic identity of the Jew, formed through the give-and-take with secular culture, as found in the Jewish home, in the midst of family. Others are found in social discourse in the community. They have all been selected from the folk culture of the Jew, as they are used, regardless of their community of origin.

Together, all of these terms, when coursing through the blood of the individual, help determine when the home is Jewish and the individual a Jew.

Adar. The last month of the year (approximately February-March). Occurs twice in a leap year (as Adar I, Adar II). Unlike the Gregorian calendar, the Hebrew soli-lunar calendar adjusts itself in nineteen-year cycles: the third, sixth, eighth, eleventh, fourteenth, seventeenth, and nineteenth years are leap years. Because PURIM occurs in Adar, the month takes on a happy face.

Alav HaShalom/Aleha HaShalom. Used when speaking of the deceased. Literally, may peace upon him/her—synonymous with "may he/she rest in peace."

Alef-Beis. The ASHKENAZI HEBREW reference to the Hebrew alphabet or alef-bet, reflecting the first two letters of the Hebrew alphabet. Used also as a general reference to one's basic Jewish knowledge ("He does not even know his alef-bais") or basic Jewish education for a Jewish child.

Am Berit. Literally, "people of the COVENANT," a reference to the Jewish people.

Am HaSefer. Literally, "people of the book," referring to the TORAH; a reference to the Jewish people. The term has been expanded as a reference to the relationship of the Jewish people to sacred text in general.

Amkha. The unfettered masses, the populace in general.

American Nusach. A recently coined term that refers to contemporary popular Jewish music, which usually combines Jewish musical modality with contemporary musical idioms such as folk, rock, or country.

Av. The fifth month in the Hebrew calendar, approximately July-August. Takes on a somber tone because of its ninth day, TISHA B'AV, which commemorates the destruction of the TEMPLES in 586 B.C.E. and 70 C.E. (Av is also the short form for the Hebrew word father.)

Averah. Literally, "a transgression." Technically referring to the transgression of God's law, it has taken on a more general meaning.

Bar Minan. Within the Sefardi community, an expression that reflects the sense of "God forbid."

Barukh HaShem. Literally, "May God's name be blessed." A loose translation for the expression "Thank God" in response to various situations or polite inquiries such as "How are you?"

Barukh Tihiye. Literally "May it be blessed." A response to YASHER KOACH when expressed to the individual after offering a DEVAR TORAH or when completing an ALIYAH to the TORAH.

Be Fruitful and Multiply. The first of the commandments, as articulated in the first chapter of GENESIS.

Be Happy, It's Adar. Because ADAR is a happy month due to PURIM's presence in it, the phrase expresses this sentiment.

Beadle. In traditional synagogues of prior generations, this refers to the jack-of-all-trades who oversees the SYNAGOGUE; a sort of forerunner of the modern administrator.

Ben/Bat Avraham (v'Sarah). When a person converts to Judaism he/she is given the father of the Jewish people as his/her father, especially when Hebrew names are used (such as during aliyah to the TORAH). Egalitarians have added SARAH's name to this formula.

Ben Bayit. A native son.

Ben Brit. A reference to a Jew; literally, "a son of the COVENANT."

Bet Chaim. According to Rabbinic tradition, opposite terms are often given to describe people, places, and things. For example, a blind person is "the one who is full of light." This term is literally "House of Life" and refers to the cemetery.

Bet Sefer. Literally, "house of (the) book," that is, a school.

B'Ezrat HaShem. With the help of God; an expression that relates reliance on the Almighty for guidance and assistance.

Bitachon. Literally, "security" or "insurance" in modern Hebrew; conceptually refers to the indestructibility of the Jewish people.

B'nai Israel. Literally, the "children of Israel"; a reference to the Jewish people, in general, not age or generation specific.

Chai. Life, related to the number eighteen through GEMATRIA and often referred to in that way.

Chaim Yankel. "So-and-so;" referred to in rabbinic literature as *Plony ben Plony.*

Chakham. Literally, "wise," and in YIDDISH, "a wise guy"; within the Sefardi community, this refers to the community leader or RABBI.

Chamsah. From the Arabic word for five, an amulet that looks like a hand, often containing the evil eye in its center.

Chas VeChalilah. God forfend; alternatively *chas veshalom*.

Chavruta or Chavrusa. A fellowship of friends usually in the context of a learning environment.

Chavurah. A fellowship group akin to a surrogate extended family. In the 1960s groups banded together as alternatives to established SYNAGOGUES in an effort to self-direct worship and study. Later, they became, in most cases, subgroups within synagogues.

Chazak V'Ematz. Be strong and of good courage; taken from the Bible in Joshua 1:6 when JOSHUA is told by God that MOSES is dead.

Chazakah. A type of seniority, incumbency, or "dibs" on something, as a result of having been there or done it previously.

Cheder. Up to and including the early modern era, an elementary religious school in Europe and in America as well.

Chelm. A fictitious European community whose citizens are parodied in various examples of the *maasehbuch* (book of folk tales).

Chesed Ve'Emet. The highest form of a MITZVAH, one done out of unselfish motivation. *Chesed ve'emet* cemeteries or graves are those reserved for the indigent or itinerant.

Cheshvan. The eighth month of the Hebrew calendar, also called *Marcheshvan, mar* meaning bitter or mister. One tradition suggests that the month is called bitter because there are no holidays or special observances in it. Another suggests that adding the honorific title of Mr. to it would give it special honor since it had none of its own as a result of its being without holidays or special observances.

Chevrah. Similar to CHEVRUTA, a fellowship or group of friends.

Chidush(im). An insight, a novel or new approach to something.

Chokhmah. Sage advice, wisdom, a term often used in a facetious manner.

Chutzpah. Moxy, unmitigated presumption, gall.

Davka. Lends itself more to a description of a pattern of speech rather than a definition; can best be defined as "on purpose."

"Ein Breira." An idiomatic expression meaning "there is no alternative." May be colloquially translated as "I have no choice."

Eishes Chayil. Also *eishet chayil,* usually translated as "a woman of valor"; refers specifically to Proverbs 31 which begins, "A Woman of

Valor, who can find?" From that context, the phrase takes on the meaning of a righteous woman in general.

Elokim. Out of fear of taking God's name in vain, the custom arose not to pronounce God's name properly or even use the euphemism of God's name (cf. ADONAI), except in prayer. Thus, *elohim* becomes *elokim;* ADONAI becomes *Adoshem.*

Elul. The sixth month of the Hebrew calendar, usually in August; takes on the character of REPENTANCE because it precedes the HIGH HOLIDAY period.

Emes. Alternatively, EMET, truth.

Frum. A referent in YIDDISH for a traditionally observant individual.

Galitzianer. One whose ancestors hail from Galicia.

Ganef. Thief.

Gastronomical Judaism. A reference to those whose Jewish identity is solely described by what has come to be known as Jewish ethnic foods such as bagels and lox; sometimes also called "bagels and lox Judaism." This term is sometimes used to describe the foods that go along with holiday celebrations and the like in a nonpositive way.

Gefilte Fish. A Russian peasant food of primarily ground up carp or pike that has become associated as an ASHKENAZI Jewish food.

Ger Tzedek. While originally used to make a technical distinction between various kinds of nonresidents in a community, the term has come to be used to refer to a righteous Gentile, especially used for those non-Jews who helped to hide and save Jews during World War II.

Golem. From eastern European Jewish folktales, a monster-like creature created by a Rabbi Loew in Prague, to save the Jewish people or Jewish individuals from the dangers of ANTI-SEMITES. The word *emet* was written on his forehead. He was deactivated when the "e" was removed from *emet* to spell *met* or dead.

Hakhnasat Orchim. Welcoming the stranger, hospitality; takes its lead from ABRAHAM, who is said to have opened all four flaps on his tent so that he would be ready to provide hospitality as he saw strangers approach from any direction.

HaKadosh Barukh Hu. Literally, "the Holy One, May He be Blessed." Also translated as the Holy One of Blessing, a euphemism for God often found in rabbinic literature.

HaShem. Literally, "the name (of God)." A euphemism for God as a referent so one does not say God's name except in prayer (cf. ELOKIM).

Henna Ceremony. A ceremony among some SEFARDI communities prior to the wedding, when the young woman applies henna to her hair.

Im Yirtzeh HaShem. Literally, "if it is the will of God." An expression that qualifies some activity, "I will see you next week, *im yirtzeh hashem*."

Ivrit B'Ivrit. An educational methodology in which the Hebrew language is taught using only HEBREW in the classroom; eventually evolves into the ULPAN method.

Iyar. The second month of the Hebrew calendar, April-May, includes the modern observances of YOM HAZIKARON, YOM HASHOAH, YOM HAATZMA'UT, as well as LAG B'OMER.

J.A.P. A derogatory description of "Jewish American Prince/ss," used to refer to wealthy spoiled children of American Jews who inherited the legacy of the hardworking immigrants without any of their values.

Kasha. Literally, "groats." An ethnic food brought over from Eastern Europe.

Ken Yehi Ratzon. May it be according to God's will; often used to end a presentation, a SERMON and the like; an expression and affirmation of faith.

Ken Yirbu. May they increase; an expression usually said in response to a birth announcement or an announcement made regarding students and the like.

Keren Ami. Literally, "the fund of my people." A generalized term for TZEDAKAH, especially in the religious school, referring to collections made for funds to be sent to Israel.

Kibud Av Va'em. Honor/respect shown to parents, derived directly from the TEN COMMANDMENTS.

Kislev. Ninth month of the Hebrew calendar, usually in December; includes CHANUKAH.

Klal Yisrael. A term referring to the entire Jewish people or country of Israel. Often used to express the sense of unity or value of unity among the Jewish people.

Klei Kodesh. Holy vessels, usually referring to those who lead the Jewish people, such as RABBIS.

Klezmer. Eastern European instrumental music.

Kol B'seder. Everything is A-OK, often corrupted in English to *Kol b'sedek*.

Kol Yisrael Arevim Ze Lezeh. Literally, "all Israel is responsible one for the other." It suggests that Jews are responsible for one another. Hence, the tradition of Jews taking care of their own throughout the world, whatever the need.

Kolel. A post-YESHIVAH study environment, usually residential and usually among traditional Jews.

Koved. Honor, respect, recognition; alternatively *kavod*.

Kreplach. A pastry shell filled with meat, similar to ravioli, usually served in soup.

Kugel. A noodle pudding.

Lamdan. A learned individual.

Lamed Vavnik. Righteous person. According to tradition, in each generation there are thirty-six righteous people on whose behalf the world is not destroyed.

L'Chayim. Used as a toast, usually translated as "to life." Literally, "for life."

L'Havdil. Term used when speaking of several things, usually good and bad, to separate one from the other; literally means "to distinguish or separate."

Lishma. For its own sake, as in study.

Litvak. One who hails from Lithuania.

Lox/Laks. Salted fillet of salmon.

Ma'asim Tovim. Good deeds or acts of goodness.

Machetonim. Generally used to refer to parents-in-law, the term really refers to the relationship between the two sets of parents.

Magid. An itinerant storyteller, usually among the early CHASIDIC communities in Europe.

Mame-loshen. Literally, "mother tongue"; generally refers to YIDDISH among Eastern European Jews.

Mamon. Material goods or money, as opposed to spiritual rewards.

Marit Ayin. Alternatively, *maris ayin,* what is seen in the public eye.

Matan Torah. The giving of TORAH at MOUNT SINAI.

Mazel. Luck.

Mazel Tov. Good luck.

Mechayeh. Something refreshing and invigorating; literally, resurrecting.

Mechulah. Bankruptcy.

Meivin. Alternatively, *maaven;* one who knows it all, sometimes used in a derogatory sense.

Melamed. A teacher, often untrained and itinerant; usually referring to teachers in Europe and in America up to the early twentieth century.

Mentsch. A good person, one whose behavior reflects a high standard of values.

Meshuge. Crazy.

Midat HaDin. In reference to God, God's attribute of justice or judgment, used in contradistinction and to balance God's MIDAT HARACHAMIN.

Midat HaRachamin. In reference to God, God's attribute of mercy, used in contradistinction and to balance God's MIDAT HADIN.

Milk and Honey. Said to flow in the land of Israel, a metaphoric description of its natural resources and the beauty of the land.

Mishpocheh. Alternatively, *mishpachah*; family, used to refer generally to relatives in addition to the immediate and/or extended family.

Mitzveh. A good deed, in contradistinction to MITZVAH, a commandment.

Mitzvah Mobile/Mitzvah Tank. A portable recruitment vehicle used by CHABAD CHASIDIM to encourage people to put on TEFILLIN or shake the LULAV during SUKKOT, or to give out candles for SHABBAT.

Mitzvot Bein Adam La'Atzmo. One of the three major classifications of MITZVOT, referring to those commandments that direct the behavior of an individual toward himself.

Mitzvot Bein Adam LaChavero. One of the three major classifications of MITZVOT, referring to those commandments that direct the behavior of an individual toward one's neighbors.

Mitzvot Bein Adam LaMakom. One of the three major classifications of MITZVOT, referring to those commandments that direct the behavior of an individual toward God.

Mizrach. A plaque placed on the Eastern wall of one's home to direct one's heart and prayers toward JERUSALEM. Shivitti plaques serve a similar purpose in the SYNAGOGUE itself.

Moshav Zekeinim. An old-age home.

Moshe Rabbenu. Our teacher MOSES.

Na'aseh Venishma. From EXODUS 24:7, in response to God's directive the Jewish people responded, "We will act and we will hearken," or our action is our response.

Nachas. Good tidings, joy, often from children and grandchildren.

Nar. A fool.

Nechemta. A word of consolation, often found in rabbinic literature or in biblical literature after Israel has been castigated.

Nisan. The first month of the Hebrew calendar, April-May, which includes PESACH.

Ohev Yisrael. One who loves Jewish people, often used to refer to non-Jews who help the Jewish people or individual Jews.

Parnasah. One's living, or worldly occupation.

Pilpul. Literally, "pepper," a reference to a talmudic form of argument or discussion of minutiae.

Protekziah. Influence or pull.

Pushke. A TZEDAKAH tin or can.

Rachmonis. Pity.

Raisins and Almonds. *Rozhinkes mit mandlen,* a reference to YIDDISH culture similar to baseball, mom, and apple pie in American culture.

Rebbetzin. The rabbi's wife.

Ribbi. A SEFARDI alternative for RABBI.

Ribbono Shel Olam. Alternatively, *riboyne shel olam,* master of the world, a euphemism (and description) of God, usually a reference used in a plaintive mood.

Shadkhen. Matchmaker.

Shalom. Usually translated as peace, hello, and goodbye, it really refers to wholeness or completeness. The world is not whole or complete without peace and tranquility; hence the transfer of terms. The sense of hello and goodbye developed as abbreviated forms of the greeting or inquiry, "Is your clan at peace?"

Shalom Bayit. Literally, "peace in the home." Family union or harmony.

Shavua Tov. Literally, "(have) a good week," spoken in particular after HAVDALAH. Alternatively, in YIDDISH, *a guteh voch.*

Shidakh. Originally a match referring to the potential husband and wife, but used generally to refer to bringing any two people together.

Shiur(im). Lesson or study session(s).

Shnudering. YIDDISH for HEBREW, "because he vowed." To make an offering in the SYNAGOGUE, drived from the *Mi sheberach* prayer; the practices in traditional synagogues of requesting funds for blessings.

Simchah(s). A happy, joyful occasion, usually a family life-cycle event, such as a BAR/BAT MITZVAH or a wedding.

Sivan. The third month of the Hebrew calendar, May-June, includes the observance of SHAVUOT.

Smikhah. Ordination certificate.

Takhlis. The bottom line, the essential element.

Talmid Chakham. Wise student; the person in the classroom with high potential; the teacher's disciple.

Tammuz. The fourth month in the Hebrew calendar, usually in July; on the seventeenth of the month (Shivah Asar B'Tammuz) is a fast that commemorates the penetration of the walls of the Temple, just prior to its destruction.

Taryag Mitzvot. An acronym for the 613 commandments said to be included in the revelation of Torah.

Tevet. The tenth month in the Hebrew calendar, usually around January.

Therefore Choose Life. A reference to the text in Deuteronomy 30:19: "I call heaven and earth to witness for you this day, that I have set before you life and death, the blessing and the curse; therefore choose life, so that you and your seed may live." Later taken as a slogan for the United Jewish Appeal, has become a sort of practical philosophy of the Jewish people.

Tishrei. The seventh month of the Hebrew calendar, takes on the character of reflection and repentance because this month includes the observance of Rosh Hashanah and Yom Kippur.

Tokhachah. Rebuke, traditionally articulated by the prophets on behalf of God.

Tzaar Ba'alei Chayim. Preventing and alleviating the unnecessary suffering of living creatures; expressed as a compassion and concern for animals in particular.

Tzaddik. A righteous individual, also used to refer to leaders of the Chasidic dynasties.

Tzedakah. From the root for justice, righteous giving through charity.

Tzuris. Alternatively, *tzarot,* troubles or misfortune.

Women's Section. In the traditional synagogue, men and women do not sit together in prayer. The women are separated by a *mechitzah* into a special area called a women's section or gallery.

Yasher Koach. When one offers a devar Torah or makes aliyah to the Torah, for example, others say to that person, *"Yasher koach,"* literally, "may your strength be increased." The person responds, "Baruch Tihiye."

Yeshivah. A traditional educational institution whose focus is on primary text and sacred literature. The yeshivah is a continuation of the academies that flourished in Babylon and Palestine in the talmudic period. Today, the yeshivot in America and in Israel also maintain a secular program of study in addition to the Judaic studies.

Yeshivah Bocher. A student who attends yeshiva; used generally to refer to younger traditional students.

Yetzer HaRa. The evil inclination, that part of one's psyche that drives the individual for food, shelter, and so on. This is not intended entirely in the negative, for as it drives the male to want to take a wife, it also drives him to procreate, as well. Sometimes it is translated as the libido; together with the YETZER HATOV, they make up the id.

Yetzer HaTov. The good inclination, keeps the YETZER HARA in check; sometimes translated as one's conscience or superego.

Yichus. A family relationship that offers influence or credentials; one's roots or heredity.

Yid. A Jew, sometimes used pejoratively. When spelled or pronounced *Dzhid* in Russian, it is an approbation.

Yiddish. High German with a mix of words borrowed from other languages, depending on where the Yiddish is spoken. A folk language associated with Eastern European Jews.

Yiddishkeit. Ethnic Jewish identity, expression, and life-style.

Yordim. Literally, "going down," opposite of ALIYAH; refers to Israelis who have left Israel. An individual is a *yored/et*.

Zekhut Avot. The merit of one's ancestors which individually credits the offspring, especially if he has done wrong.

Index